incompleteness

BOOKS BY AMIT CHAUDHURI
PUBLISHED BY NEW YORK REVIEW BOOKS

Afternoon Raag
Introduction by James Wood

Calcutta (forthcoming)

Château Rouge (forthcoming)

Finding the Raga: An Improvisation on Indian Music

Freedom Song
Introduction by Wendy Doniger

Friend of My Youth

The Immortals
Introduction by Pankaj Mishra

Incompleteness: New and Selected Essays, 1999–2023

A New World
Introduction by Edwin Frank

Odysseus Abroad (forthcoming)

Sojourn

A Strange and Sublime Address
Foreword by Colm Tóibín

Sweet Shop: New and Selected Poems, 1985–2023

Incompleteness

New and Selected Essays 1999–2023

AMIT CHAUDHURI

nyrb New York Review Books New York

This is a New York Review Book

published by The New York Review of Books

207 East 32nd Street, New York, NY 10016

www.nyrb.com

Library of Congress Cataloging-in-Publication Data
Names: Chaudhuri, Amit, 1962– author
Title: Incompleteness: selected essays (1999–2023) / Amit Chaudhuri.
Description: New York: New York Review Books, [2025] | Identifiers: LCCN 2025024442 (print) | LCCN 2025024443 (ebook) | ISBN 9781681379654 paperback | ISBN 9781681379661 ebook
Subjects: LCGFT: Essays
Classification: LCC PR9499.3.C4678 I67 2025 (print) | LCC PR9499.3.C4678 (ebook)
LC record available at https://lccn.loc.gov/2025024442
LC ebook record available at https://lccn.loc.gov/202

ISBN 978-1-68137-965-4
Available as an electronic book; ISBN 978-1-68137-966-1

The authorized representative in the EU for product safety and compliance is eucomply OÜ, Pärnu mnt 139b-14, 11317 Tallinn, Estonia, hello@eucompliancepartner.com, +33 757690241.

Printed in the United States of America on acid-free paper.

10 9 8 7 6 5 4 3 2 1

Contents

Preface

THE NINETEEN ESSAYS in this volume are mainly selected from two previous collections: *Clearing a Space* (2008) and *The Origins of Dislike* (2018). For reasons of space and the way the selection focusses on certain preoccupations, there's nothing here either from *Telling Tales* (2013), with its brief meditations on the everyday, or of my political writings. Four essays here are previously uncollected: two of them on musicians, Joni Mitchell and Neil Diamond; a third bearing the self-explanatory title "Why I Write Novels"; and the fourth being "Storytelling and Forgetfulness." I have left the essays in this book mostly unchanged—in this, they're also a record of the time in which they were written.

I notice that many of them are quite long: some (not included here) almost approach the length of my shortest novel, *Sojourn* (2022). At least some of these long essays argue for the significance of brevity in the novel and, sometimes, of its marginalisation in Anglophone writing. This sounds ironic, but it's related to my ongoing relationship with the non- or imperfectly representational. Length, conventionally (though not in a writer like Joyce or Bibhutibhushan Banerjee), lends itself to completeness, and completeness to the idea of perfectibility and thoroughness of representation. There are forms that might pursue the incomplete on a large scale, such as Joyce's and Banerjee's novels; the musical form called the *khayal* is another example. I guess I too want to trace a bits-and-pieces but large-scale engagement with incompleteness through an idea like a Selected Essays. This bits-and-pieces project has been important to me, and this method has been the only way by which I have been able to arrive at an argument. People (including my wife) have sometimes told me: "You write in a sentence what others would spend a PhD on." The remark is not an unqualified compliment; it expresses a concern that readers, including those who are part of the current academic dispensation, might miss, or not engage with, some of these interventions because they haven't taken a monograph-like shape. But, for me, the monograph as a form would make it impossible to arrive at the kind of observations I try to arrive at here. They need, in order to exist, to be contained in a sentence or half a sentence, and be slightly in danger of being barely noticeable.

I don't know if it's possible for me to make a clear demarcation between the so-called "personal" or memoiristic essays and the critical ones in this volume. Many of the essays here are certainly directed by a critical impulse, and they continue to be involved in "clearing a space." The nonacademic form these essays take is part of that project. I have written very seldom (maybe only a couple of times) for peer-reviewed journals. The DPhil I wrote at Oxford on D. H. Lawrence's poetry was experimental in nature, and the liberties I'd taken as a result (contra Oxford's rules about what constituted "original" scholarly work in doctoral dissertations) made me very nervous until my viva was over. I had a bad dream two weeks before the viva: I was on Holywell Street and the gentle teacher of the bibliography class in my first year, Don McKenzie, was walking some way ahead of me, and, turning at Mansfield Road, he glanced back at me and said: "Culpable." That it was bibliography—the measure of honest research and thorough footnoting—that caused me such disquiet about my errant relationship to the DPhil was not really surprising.

I did, though, decide one thing then, in 1993: that I would avoid writing footnoted criticism as far as possible in the future. I use the idea of the footnote as a perhaps unjust shorthand to denote the air of sociological verifiability and propriety that I wanted to avoid, alongside the selfless, universal critical voice. Maybe I instinctively realised that we were, in the early nineties, at the inception of a professionalisation that has, today, more or less killed off literary studies and the humanities. It has been impossible for around three decades now for a person without a PhD, however brilliant a critic they might be, to get a permanent job in a literature department. If they're writer-critics, they have to work, especially in institutions that model themselves on American universities, on renewable contracts as Professors of Practice. No sooner did this reality begin to come into existence than at least some writers and critics would have realised that the essay, from the late 1990s onwards, constituted, among other things, a countermovement, a form of activism against a professionalisation that has often turned out to be inimical to criticism. I had a doctorate but never taught in an English department (that is, when I did finally start teaching) except for an interlude in Cambridge from 1997 to 1999, when, as a Leverhulme Special Research Fellow, I lectured on "Commonwealth and International Literatures" while otherwise beginning to formulate and put down the thoughts that went into *Clearing a Space*. When I started teaching literature more regularly, it was in creative writing departments (a brief one-off semester at Columbia University in 2002 was followed, after a gap of four years, by the University of East Anglia, my first proper job, and then Ashoka University). The course I most enjoyed teaching (at Columbia's School of the Arts, it was the one course I taught) was on literature and modernism. Such sleight of hand (being a teacher in the wrong department) might be one way of bypassing professionalisation as both a fiction writer and a critic.

I guess that many of these essays make a case—either through argument or through the approach they take to their subject matter—for a practice and sensibility that, for want of another term, I call "modernist." Any term that encompasses a poetics of unfinishedness will do. It's just that I was first conscious of encountering this poetics in modernism. As a teenager, I read it, or misread it, along lines encouraged by commentaries I was exposed to as a student. This misreading saw modernism's preoccupation with unfinishedness as part of a historical narrative: as an allegory of the fragmenting of a Western culture which, until the nineteenth century, had been unitary and whole. Modernism, then, was a dramatic, elegiac, and anguished narrative located in, emerging from and about Europe.

I couldn't subscribe to this account because I, as both a writer and a reader, found (as I think other writers and readers did) modernism's poetics enlivening and liberatory rather than sobering; I found the twentieth century, in particular, poetically alive. I had little time for "beauty" in the Hellenistic sense. I had to figure out why. This has led me to think of what I call "modernism" as a form of thought and absorption that is neither period- nor location-specific but is related to an ongoing means of argumentation and enchantment that surfaces at different points in history and, over periods of time, recedes again. The reason for its most recent resurfacing in Europe in the twentieth century was, it increasingly seems to me, an intercultural upheaval in a world that had been globalising by then for two hundred years, and in which a dominant phenomenon called the Enlightenment encountered—with both wonder and a kind of violence—antirepresentational lineages of thought. For Enlightenment Europe, these lineages engendered intellectual and imaginative possibilities that comprised a challenge to itself. One such challenge—one offshoot of the encounter I mentioned above—is what I refer to as "modernism." The intercultural moment leads, I believe, to a liberation from the representational cul-de-sac of the Enlightenment to a newly resurrected poetics of unfinishedness. The essays in which I have explored this idea of modernism, and the provenance of its emergence, are destined for another book and not this one, but my particular proclivities and biases in this regard are already present in the twenty-five years or so this book covers.

As the critical essays in this volume make clear, my preoccupations are related to the kind of writer I am and to the fact that I happen to be the "kind of writer" who's in a minority among writers, especially in the domains I inhabit: the Anglophone world; the postglobalisation world; the world of postcoloniality. These three categories, I sometimes feel, can be used almost interchangeably to refer to a variety of dominance whose impact we have experienced over the last four decades—a kind of reign under which we have lived. Its rhetoric advocates inclusiveness, but it keeps a great deal out. One of the manifestations of its reign is narrative. I have just said that there are possibly epochs in which the poetics of incompleteness recedes; and this period—the time of globalisation and, more specifically (given where I come from), of Anglophone postcoloniality—is one of them. Whenever such a poetics has again emerged, as it has occasionally in the last decade, it has been gentrified by being turned into a Western European inheritance. The inheritors, as I say in one of the essays here, live in Brooklyn. The poetics of incompleteness in what's often been called "postcolonial cultures" has been subjected to a steady erasure, as have been the languages in which that poetics was to be found from the late nineteenth century onwards; among the instruments of erasure are the novel and the English language. My object is not "decolonisation"; it's always been to understand my own compulsions, and also to understand why the present academic vocabulary—or even "writing back" to the Empire, say—doesn't address these questions, and never has. Many of these essays, then, were written to take issue with a period of, and with forms of, dominance. The fact that they were published at all—and, along with my fiction, and the works of others like myself, read—is a reminder that there must be cracks in the increasingly powerful consensual edifice. They subsist in those cracks and praise the history from which the cracks emerge.

Amit Chaudhuri
6 October 2024

The Flute of Modernity
Tagore and the Middle Class

1999, *The New Republic*

RABINDRANATH TAGORE was born on 7 May 1861, or the 25th day of Baishakh in the Bengali calendar. The 25th of Baishakh is still celebrated in Bengal, especially in Calcutta, with performances of Tagore's songs and dance dramas, and the heat of midsummer is associated in the minds of Bengalis with Tagore's birthday. His name itself conjures up light and heat, for Rabindranath means "lord of the sun." For quite a few years, however, the celebrations have had the slightly exhausted air of ritual, a ritual by which Bengalis not only commemorate an anniversary but also observe the passing away of something more than Tagore, the passing of something that defined themselves and their own Bengaliness; though this is never articulated in so many words.

In 1778, roughly a century before Tagore's birth, an English scholar-administrator named Nathaniel Halhead wrote the first Bengali grammar, probably with the collaboration of Brahmin pandits. Calcutta was then the East India Company's main port of trade, and Bengal, of which Calcutta is the capital, was the province upon which the commercial and cultural exchange of the colonial world would leave its most profound impress. Halhead wrote the grammar for the instruction of English officials and administrators. Though the machinery of colonialism had already begun to whir after Mughal rule was deposed in Bengal in 1757, officials of the Company still behaved like traders in a foreign land, taking the trouble, for their own purposes, to comprehend the local language and customs.

William Jones arrived at Calcutta from Oxford in 1783. He had been an Arabist before, but now in Calcutta he unofficially inaugurated Orientalist scholarship *within* India, translating Sanskrit texts into English, most famously the works of Kalidasa, whom he touchingly and misleadingly called the "Shakespeare of the East." Kalidasa was the court poet in King Vikramaditya's court in the fifth century CE, and he became famous in nineteenth-century Europe, especially for his play *Sakuntala*, which Jones translated and Goethe admired. Kalidasa was also to become Tagore's favourite poet, and this, too, must surely owe something to the renewed attention directed to the long-dead poet by the Welshman in one of the earliest in a series of cultural collaborations that characterised the formation of modern Indian culture.

•

An overarching, to all outward purposes secular, narrative about the historical past, in the crude sense in which we understand it now, was absent from the consciousness of Indians at the time; and the spiritual and political history of India reconstructed by Orientalist scholars in the late eighteenth and early nineteenth centuries supplied, substantially, that narrative as we—whatever our politics—recognise, or argue with, it today. By the 1830s, the young Anglo-Portuguese poet and teacher Henry Louis Vivian Derozio, who was born in Calcutta and identified himself as "Indian," had taken the presence of that golden past sufficiently as a given to mourn its passing in sonnets such as "To India—My Native Land," which is studied and recited in schools even today. That sonnet was one of the first utterances of an incipient nationalism, a collective identity that had crossed over into the domain of the aesthetic; and Derozio's students at the Hindu College, Calcutta, members of newly formed middle class, who would read Thomas Paine and have their heads full of radical notions, were among the first to articulate nationalist ideas.

•

Yet the recovery of history, for the Indian, was also fraught with ambiguity; this becomes clearer with the passage of time in the nineteenth century. History was akin to an idea of the subconscious; it had been buried, and now, in an act of translation, it was being recovered. It was as if Indians, in invoking history, were recalling a past that they did not remember having forgotten. While Derozio, in the early nineteenth century, is proprietary about the past, declaiming on "our days of glory past," Tagore, eighty years later, is ambivalent and full of doubt: like the subconscious, history, for the Indian, is both one's own and the Other. The awareness of it is accompanied not only by the vantage point of modernity and identity, but also by a sense of loss and imprisonment.

These paradoxes are played out in Tagore's poem "Meghdut," or "The Cloud Messenger," which is about Kalidasa's long Sanskrit poem of the same name, set in the rainy season beloved of Tagore; Kalidasa's poem is a homage to the specificities of the natural world and a record of romantic, metaphysical separation (*biraha*). The speaker in the poem asks the rain-carrying clouds to carry a message from him to his beloved in the faraway city of Alaka. And Tagore's poem about this poem is not only a characteristic celebration of the rains, but of the intellectual ambience of early colonial India.

Kalidasa had become world-famous in the early nineteenth century, well before Tagore's birth, with Jones's translation; and the scholar H. H. Wilson had translated the *Meghadutam* in 1813, a translation that was well known in educated middle-class Bengali circles. By the time of Tagore's birth, Calcutta was not only a site of scholarship, it had printing presses proliferating in Bengali and English, and was producing more books than almost anywhere else in the world except London.

William Dune, the editor of a journal published from Calcutta called *The World* (a telling and ambitious name for a colonial journal, but indicative of the city's by-then self-consciously internationalist temperament and of the construction of a certain self-image), had observed in 1791 that "in splendour London now eclipses Rome . . . and in similar respects, Calcutta rivals the head of the empire. But in no respect can she appear so eminently so, as in her publications . . . we may place Calcutta in rank above Vienna, Copenhagen, Petersburg, Madrid, Venice, Turin, Naples or even Rome." It was almost inevitable that Kalidasa would be present in the library of a family such as the Tagores—benefitting in all kinds of ways from the articulations of "world literature"—which was itself instrumental in reshaping cosmopolitanism.

Tagore's poem is an implicit tribute to an intellectual ambience and the possibilities it created; and it is also a tribute to the secular, silent act of reading, which, in that culture, had become a significant activity whereby old texts, and the printed page, were being placed in new contexts, and reassessed and reimagined. Tagore's poem is pervaded both by the sound of thunder (it is raining outside as he reads) and the silence of perusal:

> Today is a dark day, the rain is incessant . . .
>
> In a gloomy closed room I sit alone
> And read the *Meghadūta*. My mind leaves the room,
> Travels on a free-moving cloud, flies far and wide.
> There is the Āmrakūṭa Mountain,
> There is the clear and slender Revā river,
> Tumbling over stones in the Vindhya foothills . . .
>
> (translated by William Radice)

Yet recalling the past meant, for the Indian, confronting the question: why, and at what point, had he ceased to have recourse to it, as an entity uncomplicatedly available to rational apprehension? As Tagore wrote, in an essay on Kalidasa: "Not merely a temporal but an eternal gulf seems to separate us from the great slice of ancient India—stretching from the Ramgiri to the Himalayas—through which life's stream flowed in the form of the *mandakranta* metre of the *Meghadutam*." In his poem, Tagore brilliantly reworks Kalidasa's tale of separation from the loved one into a narrative of the separation of the self from history; the beloved pining in the city of Alaka becomes a figure of the past, intimate but distant, beautiful, but not quite recoverable. From the English Romantics Tagore had learned of the Imagination, and here he uses Kalidasa's cloud in a Wordsworthian way, making it a symbol for the modern Indian's desire to be one, through the Imagination, with identity and history:

My heart travels thus, like a cloud, from land to land
Until it floats at last into Alakā—
Heavenly, longed for city
Where pines that most loved of loves,
That paragon of beauty. Who but you, O poet,
Revealer of eternal worlds fit for Lakşmī to dally in,
Could take me there? To the woods of undying spring flowers
Forever moonlit, to the golden-lotus-lake . . .
Through the open window she can be seen—
Wasted in body, lying on her bed like a sliver of moon
Sunk low in the eastern sky.
Poet, your spell has released
Tight bonds of pain in this heart of mine.
I too have entered that heaven of yearning
Where, amidst limitless beauties,
Alone and awake, that adored one spends her unending night.

The vision goes . . . I watch the rain again
Pouring steadily all around. (translated by William Radice)

While Tagore wrote patriotic verses, often for children, about the heroes and heroines of precolonial India (there was a renewed focus on these figures among the Bengali intelligentsia, owing to influential Orientalist histories such as James Tod's *Annals and Antiquities of Rajasthan*), he was also the first poet to articulate the educated Indian's anxiety about the loss and the recovery of the past. In another poem, "Dream," Tagore invokes his sense of his historical past not in the aestheticised language of the new nationalism (as, say, Derozio might have), but in terms of fantasy, loss, and incommunicability:

> A long, long way away
> in a dream-world, in the city of Ujjain,
> by River Shipra I once went to find my first love
> from a previous life of mine.
>
> (translated by Ketaki Kushari Dyson)

And ten stanzas later:

> I looked at her face,
> tried to speak,
> but found no words.
> That language was lost to me....

"That language": the nineteenth century in India, and especially in Bengal, was a time of radical crossings-over in language, when languages were both lost and regained. Derozio and his circle of contemporaries and students at the Hindu College wrote in English, the language that was present at the inception of the Indian middle class and that would always, in one way or another, define its existence. Michael Madhushudan Datta, one of those who studied there after Derozio died, began his career as a poet who wrote in English, and who aspired to be a canonical "English" poet. (He even converted to Christianity, possibly to expedite this process.) But later in 1861, faced with failure, he wrote the first modern poem in Bengali, which was also, in a sense, a translation and a revision: *Meghnadabadha Kabya*, an epic poem based on an episode and a character from the ancient Indian epic the *Ramayana*, written in Dutt's singular Bengali approximation of blank verse as a gesture towards Milton, and using Milton's sympathy "for the Devil's party" to invert the epic.

A few years later, Bankim Chandra Chatterjee, a Bengali magistrate who worked for the British, wrote the first Indian novel in English, *Rajmohan's Wife*, an economical exploration of the Bengali family and domesticity. Partly from a feeling of nationalism, Chatterjee crossed over to Bengali, and embarked on the project of creating the first modern corpus of Bengali, indeed Indian, fiction. Once, Sanskrit and Persian had been the official and "high" languages, Brajbhasha a Northern and Eastern Indian literary language; more recently, English, among the Bengali bourgeoisie, had briefly played its part in this configuration.

With the adoption of English and the formation of the middle class, there came, in the shape of a well-known paradox, the idea of writing in the mother tongue. Bengali, whose grammar had been written approximately a hundred years ago by Halhead, became a respectable language of self-expression for the Bengali bourgeoisie and its intellectuals. So began what's been often, and for a long time debatably, called the Bengal Renaissance, one of the greatest (despite anxieties to do with categorising it) cultural efflorescences of the modern age, its critical demands all the more intriguing because of its disputable nature. Tagore was at once its product, its spokesman, its inquisitor.

•

Krishna Dutta and Andrew Robinson have produced a very readable and generally sympathetic biography of Tagore. Dutta and Robinson wish to give us Tagore in his time, his public persona, and so they tend to put him in the company of other world figures of his day, such as

Gandhi and Einstein; though it must be said that they do a good job of rendering also the inward complexity, the self-contradictoriness, and the insecurity of the man. What is most missing from this life of the poet is the poetry. This is partly because the authors have set out to avoid the reverential literary effusions of earlier biographers. And yet a biography that takes the poetry into account with knowledge and sensitivity is essential. (Almost the only thing of this sort in English is Buddhadeva Bose's elegant monograph on the poet, now available only on a few dusty library shelves.)

Dutta and Robinson do provide an interesting, and sometimes penetrating, account on Tagore's ancestry and his family. The Tagores were Brahmins; they apparently moved to Bengal around 1000 CE. Yet they came to exist at one remove from their caste, for members of a section of the family converted to Islam in the seventeenth century, and they were ostracised for it. Ostracism probably pushed the Tagores away from a more conventional Brahminical lifestyle towards entrepreneurship. They became successful middlemen, and were among the first to benefit substantially from trade with the British.

In the eighteenth century there was a rift within the family, and this led to the departure of Nilmoni Tagore, Tagore's great-great-grandfather, from the family home at Pathuriaghata in North Calcutta and to his arrival in neighbouring Jorasanko, to the mansion in which Tagore would be born three quarters of a century later. "From then on," Dutta and Robinson write, "especially during the high noon of Empire in India after 1857, the two branches of the Tagores at Pathuriaghata and Jorasanko would have little to do with each other." This small history of migration, ostracism, and fracture is important, for it allegorises the split, gradual but irrevocable, between the old Bengal, and the old India, and the new; and it helps us to comprehend the independent-mindedness of Tagore's immediate family, and in what way it had been prepared, by the time of Tagore's birth, to contribute to an emergent India.

The contrast between Tagore's father and his grandfather is obvious.

The latter, "Prince" Dwarkanath Tagore, was one of the first great Bengali entrepreneurs (a gradually disappearing breed, since business acumen came to be looked down upon in bourgeois Bengal). He was famous for his dinner parties in London: Dickens wrote about him. When he died he left his son Debendranath his lands and his debts. Debendranath was a Platonic figure, and could have been one of the philosopher-aristocrats of the *Republic*: a man both this-worldly and other-worldly. Probably sometimes in 1838, he experienced an epiphany after reading, by chance, a page of the *Upanishads*. He became a member of the Brahmo Samaj in 1843, a Hindu reform movement that owed something to Protestant Christianity: it was seen to turn away from what it perceived to be the polytheism of middle and late Hinduism to what it interpreted as the philosophical monotheism of the early Hindu texts, the *Vedas* and the *Upanishads*. The gods and the goddesses, according to this account, were replaced by a *nirakaar* force, a spiritual meaning without form or name.

The Brahmo Samaj went on to become one of the most powerful intellectual movements to shape modern, secular India. Indeed, an important dimension of secular India was prefigured by its tenets. In place of a varied, polyphonic, amorphous heterogeneity, there was now a unifying, all-encompassing meaning that was capable of accommodating and subsuming what it had replaced; and if this was the Brahmo Samaj's reworking of the Hindu religion, it was also Nehru's concept of what India as a nation-state should be. It's no wonder that, with hindsight, the bases of the Brahmo Samaj seem to lead so logically to those of secular, Nehruvian India.

•

Debendranath's Brahmoism was a great influence on his son, though Tagore was never entirely comfortable with it. Tagore's poetry, especially his songs, are among the first and the most profound utterances of a secular Indian sensibility; they speak of an old world that is lost but is being transformed into something new. Here are the first two lines of a song:

> I haven't seen him with my eyes as yet,
> I have only heard a flute playing.

A couple of clarifications need to be made about the translation of those lines, which is my own. First, my line has the pronoun "him" in place of intermediate Bengali *taare*; the Bengali pronoun never specifies gender, but derives it through context. Second, I have deliberately translated the second line literally. The Bengali reader or listener would automatically interpret Tagore to be saying "his flute"; yet the exact literal meaning suggests only "a flute" or "the flute." And both these points, small as they are, are pertinent to our understanding of the Brahmo-influenced, secular spirituality of Tagore's poetry, the leap he is making, very subtly, from the old world to the new.

In a traditional devotional song, the flute would be played by Krishna, the cowherd-god. In Tagore's song, the player is not named, and the indeterminate Bengali pronoun is apposite to the nameless, secular meanings of modern India that have replaced the familiar names and significances. The old world has become invisible and cannot be seen "with my eyes"; what remains is the auditory signal that the flute sends forth. And by not using a possessive pronoun, by saying "flute" instead of "his flute," Tagore causes another fracture, a small disjunction, to occur. The sound of the flute represents the appeal of Hindu divinity; it represents the known and the yearned for. But the flute cut off from its original context becomes a more ambiguous sign; it represents what is unknown, new, transformed. The listeners of the song traverse a distance as they hear these two lines, and it is the distance between old devotional contexts and the psychological terrain of modern India.

•

Growing up in the great house in Jorasanko, Tagore would have experienced the stirrings of a new Bengali cosmopolitanism around him, and sensed them, indeed, in the presence of his own family. Here Dutta and Robinson's biography is useful and involving. There was Tagore's father, of course; but there was also his older brother Dwijendranath, who, according to the biographers, "was the most intellectual and the least worldly of the siblings. Deeply immersed in the study of Indian philosophy, mathematics, and geometry, he also revelled in folding complex paper boxes and was responsible for inventing the first Bengali shorthand and musical notations." Another brother, Satyendranath, was the first Indian to enter the Indian Civil Service. And the most remarkable of Tagore's elder brothers was probably Jyotirindranath, who, among other things, composed his own songs on the piano.

Tagore was the youngest of thirteen children, and he grew up in that house with something of the solitariness and the freedom of an only child. There are whole pages in his memoirs, *Jiban Smriti*, or *My Reminiscences*, which appeared in 1911, devoted to meticulous descriptions of the hours that he spent daydreaming as a boy. He was a recalcitrant pupil, he hated school, and much of his education took place at home. The English language was especially hated, but it was compulsory; Tagore's account of himself as a boy hoping, on a rainy day, that his English tutor would fail to turn up, and his deep unhappiness, a few minutes later, upon seeing the tutor's black umbrella approaching stubbornly through the rain, is a classic of Bengali children's literature.

Meanwhile, Tagore's father would be away for long spells, either overseeing his lands, or doing the opposite, withdrawing from his duties to some Himalayan resort in the North for a period of meditation. His often-unannounced returns home created consternation, joy, and a tumult in the household; and these seemingly far-off tremors were also felt by the family's youngest member. Tagore's relations with his parents are more mysterious than they at first might appear to be.

His mother is a figure largely in the background; she enters his poetry as a generalised maternal presence. The father's incarnation in his son's imaginative writings is more intriguing. Debendranath's mixture of aristocratic power and renunciatory spirituality and his relative inaccessibility seem to have made him, in Tagore's poems, a natural emblem for a certain kind of divinity that was spiritual and nonmaterialistic, masculine and powerful. Both the power of the old landowning aristocracy and the reformist spiritualism of the Brahmo Samaj—contraries that were brought together in Debendranath—are integral to Tagore's idea of divinity in many of his poems. It is no accident that the divine being is called "Raja," or "king" in the poetry. A poem called "Arrival" seems to recall those sudden returns home by Debendranath:

> Our work was over for the day, and now the light was fading;
> We did not think that anyone would come before the morning.
>   All the houses round about
>   Dark and shuttered for the night—
> One or two amongst us said, "The King of Night is coming."
> We just laughed at them and said, "No one will come till morning."
>   (translated by William Radice)

But later:

> O where are the lights, the garlands, where are the signs of celebrations?
> Where is the throne? The King has come, we made no preparation!
>   Alas what shame, what destiny?
>   No court, no robes, no finery—
> Somebody cried in our ears, "O vain, O vain this lamentation":
> With empty hands, in barren rooms, offer your celebration.

These stanzas, in, Bengali, not only convey the physical upheaval Debendranath's return caused in the household of Jorasanko; they imply, too, the complex, dazzling paradox that the appearance of a figure such as Debendranath—aristocratic but unworldly, a "King" but of "Night"—signified on the horizon of Bengali culture. His appearance caused not only a tumult, but also a reordering of values and an anxiety, in the household. It provoked questions.

Tagore's first memorable literary endeavour was accomplished when he was probably sixteen, in the shape of a literary fraud. Pessoa-like, the young Tagore created a "heteronym," Bhanusingha, a medieval poet who wrote in Brajabali, one of the older literary languages; Bhanusingha's oeuvre of songs is sung today as part of the Tagore repertoire. Years later, in his memoirs, Tagore was still gleeful that these songs had deceived an authority on Bengali literature who would later mention Bhanusingha in a thesis on medieval Bengali poetry.

The literary models and inspirations behind Tagore's imaginative leap are interesting in themselves, and they remind us of the hybrid context of Tagore's work and, indeed, of that Bengal Renaissance. This is worth pointing out, because cultural commentators today lazily identify postcolonial uses of English with hybridity and the indigenous languages of once-colonised countries with some sort of authenticity. Yet more than one language is written into Tagore's poetry.

Around the time that Tagore composed the *Bhanusingher Padabali*, Bengal was in the midst of unprecedented intellectual activity. Bengali scholars had recently collated the works of the great medieval Bengali poets, Chandidas and Vidyapati, and compiled the *Vaishnav Padavali*. It was the music of these poets with which the young Tagore fell in love, and was moved to produce a comparable music through the persona of Bhanusingha. Yet the idea for the pastiche (if that is what it was) came from Chatterton, whose work Tagore also loved. Tagore's heteronym leads us to a moment of transition in the development of an artist and a culture. It is evidence of the pressure exerted upon him by what one might tentatively call a polyphonic, multilingual reality, but in a way seemingly different from the way we understand such transactions today; the notion of "pressure" itself, and secrecy, and the idea that polyphony is not necessarily extroverted display, but might involve a long history of ellipses and concealment, are somewhat alien to us. Here, again, Pessoa reminds us it might be otherwise.

Tagore began his career in print as a lyric poet in the strictest sense: he was a writer of songs. His first book of poems, *Kabi-Kahini* (*The Tale of a Poet*), was published in 1878, when he was still sixteen. The core of his achievement may lie in his songs; and for these he was both admired and, at first, reviled by his contemporaries. It was for his own inexact prose version of another book of songs, the *Gitanjali* (a compilation, in the English version, of songs from the original collection and several others), that Tagore was awarded the Nobel Prize many years later.

•

The story of his rise to international celebrity and the Nobel Prize is well known: Tagore completing his English "translation" (they were really reworkings) on board a ship to England in 1912; the painter Rothenstein reading the handwritten "translations" and, stunned, passing them on to Yeats; the excitement that followed; Yeats introducing Tagore to an elite circle of friends in London, including Pound, who would confess to feeling like a "painted pict with a stone war-club" when he met Tagore; publication of some of the prose poems in Harriet Monroe's *Poetry* on Pound's recommendation; the Nobel Prize in 1913; Pound's and Yeats's swift and shocking disenchantment with Tagore; Tagore's ascension as a world figure from the "East" coinciding with his banishment from the serious Western literary establishment. A part of this story is given in Dutta and Robinson's anthology of Tagore's writings, in intermittent epistolary form, beginning with Tagore's letter to Yeats in 1912: "It has been such a great joy to me to think that things that I wrote in a tongue not known to you should at last fall in your hands and that you should accept them with so much enjoyment and love."

Few poets have led, in the modern age, so public a life, have lectured and spoken on so many subjects, occasionally badly and verbosely. And few poets in the modern age have mastered and left their mark on so many other genres: on musical composition, on the novella, and on the short story (the writer Buddhadeva Bose pointed out that Tagore brought the modern short story to Bengal at a time when it had hardly any practitioners—Kipling is the obvious exception—in England), not to speak of the novel, the theatre, and even painting.

In their anthology, Dutta and Robinson have attempted to give the reader a sense of this range, though it doesn't seem that the quality of the translations of much of the poetry (I have in mind especially Tagore's own problematic "reworkings") will do much to alter Tagore's reputation outside Bengal, or to extend his readership beyond what has long been his constituency in the West: Indophiles, amateur religious enthusiasts, and admirers of Kahlil Gibran. I say this despite the fact that Dutta and Robinson have bravely tried to make to Tagore real, and historical, by including some of his letters, his lesser-known essays, and some of the marvellous early letters written in Shelidah, when Tagore was looking after his father's estates and was still, in his own eyes (and words), "young and obscure." In those letters he recorded, in casual but heightened prose, the life of the estates, the local people who worked on or around them, the weather, and the faint traces of the colonial world: from these experiences would come the first short stories, full of air and light, bringing the ordinary Indian citizen of the colonial world—a postmaster, a servant girl—into Indian fiction for the first time. For all this, one still feels that it is time that Tagore's most recent translators settle their differences, and bring out a volume of their own best translations of Tagore's poems and stories; for there have good translations by each of them, a fact that tends to get lost with each new attempt, as well each translator's implicit assumption that his or her Tagore is the "true" one.

•

Few poets, then, have been so prolific and in so many ways, and, also, in their lifetime, have been so written and spoken about. Yet it is crucial to note that few poets in their work—in the output on which both their popular and critical reputations rest—have devoted so much of their gift to describing what is half understood, partially grasped, unclear, or ambiguous—but that is the temperament of Tagore's songs and his lyricism. This is ironic, of course. In the West, and sometimes in India, Tagore has traditionally been seen as a purveyor of Eastern wisdom, a man who tended to make timeless utterances. He himself, when not composing poetry, wrote repeatedly of "creative unity" and "universalism." Yet his Bengali lyrics have everything to do with uncertainty, with hesitation, with the momentary, and the beauty that resides in the moment of incomplete perception.

How did a lyric, rather than an epic, poet come to be Bengal's national poet? And a poet of uncertainties and absences, which make him an unusual national poet, to say the least. The reason for this is probably that Bengal was the site of India's first modern middle-class culture, a culture neither defined by pre-Enlightenment ways of being nor whole-heartedly entrepreneurial. Unlike various Indian cultures with powerful pre-Enlightenment and religious traditions, Bengal—though it possessed its own rich stream of precolonial culture—found its most characteristic voice in the late nineteenth century, in its bourgeoisie. Modern Bengal began, no doubt, with an entrepreneurial flourish, with the life of Tagore's grandfather Dwarkanath Tagore; but in Tagore's family itself, the gradual distancing, over the next two generations, of the world of business activity from the world of "cultured" or *bhadra* society becomes apparent. More and more, ambitions related to commerce would come to be disdained.

Both pre-Enlightenment societies, with their internalised religious and mythic landscapes, and new capitalistic entrepreneurial ones, with their external upheavals, need epic poets. Thus the ancient poetry of the *Mahabharata* and the *Ramayana* sustained the Indian consciousness until the nineteenth century, and has done so in quite a different way in our time, an age that segued into globalised capitalism. Yet the Bengali middle class—the *bhadralok*, literally, the "civil person" or "civilised person"—chose for its national poet one who sang of the small incommunicabilities of human language. Occupying a perpetual in-between space in history, that middle class, which, by the late nineteenth century, no longer possessed the language to speak to the past that had vanished or of the world that had opened up before it, found in this poet's metaphors a vocabulary of self-definition. Thus, both *diganta*, or "horizon," which suggests that opening-up, and *katha*, or "word," "language," or "story," suggesting self-expression and history, recur in Tagore's songs.

The Bengali middle class consisted of barristers, advocates, schoolteachers, lecturers, doctors, civil servants, people who were both partaking of colonial power and revising its meaning. They constituted the first indigenous governing class in India who experienced power while being cut off from its source. Theirs was a jealously protected world, composed of known and concrete social and secular values: the family; the child; education; respectability; marriage; entry (for males and, gradually and less commonly, for women) into one of the professions. The unknown, for them, was the glimmer of the past, all that their small but all-encompassing world had replaced; the past, and their avowedly buried selves.

Tagore's poetry, especially in his songs, captures this psychological dichotomy with precision. The Bengali bourgeois world of the social, the worldly, the known, becomes in his songs the concrete and physical world of sensation and appearance, of detail; the buried self becomes a passerby or traveller—a *pathik*, seldom met or seen—or a guest—*atithi*—awaited by someone who stands at a window. These are Tagore's recurring motifs.

One can see this duality inform the opening lines of a song chosen at random, though it is a famous song (the translation is mine):

> O moment's guest,
> Whom did you come looking for at dawn
> Climbing a path of shefali blossoms?

The acts of noticing and compression are enshrined in the third line. A Bengali would know that the white, star-shaped *shefali* flowers, redolent with perfume in the evening, fall from their branches in the course of the night, so that the feet of a person trampling them at dawn would be the first things to disturb them from their repose, the first human influence of the day to agitate nature; and the unseen traveller, ghostlike, would leave no sign of his passing except the disturbance of the dead shefali blossoms. The line is as abbreviated a statement as a line in a haiku; the detail is as oblique as the one in Edward Thomas's "In Memoriam (Easter 1915)," where the presence of the war is suggested in terms of the bushes heavy with flowers, because the men who would pick those flowers for their sweethearts are all away.

The physical world, then, is evoked concretely; but the traveller, the stranger, is blurred and indefinite. And he, being a guest, reminds us of both what is ours and not ours. It is as if the poem's speaker at once longs to be hospitable to, and is distanced from, his most intimate self. This—the tensions between the physical, the familiar, the minute, and the unclear and potentially distant—perfectly captures and dramatises the psychological dichotomy of the Bengali bourgeoisie, the dichotomy, in the middle-class psyche, between the social-secular-rational-colonial world and the world of the subconscious and the precolonial.

Again and again in Tagore's songs, the secular world perceives the glimmer of the known or the partially known—the complex religious and feudal world that has vanished, with the self that belonged there—either through a window or while confronting the horizon (which transforms the landscape into a great window). The word *kichhu*, which as an adjective means "a little," and as a noun "something" or "anything," is a common enough word in the language. Tagore makes it a keyword in his songs, using it repeatedly to define the half-understood "something" that exist on the edges of the secular world. It is a euphemism for history and the subconscious. Tagore also uses it to mean "something unsaid": and here, too, a complex emotional register is created, for it evokes the poignancy of the trajectory of Bengali middle-class life, with its *bhadralok* propriety, gentility, rationality, and its ironic lack of fulfilment. Here are the first lines of another song; I have italicised the words that are translations of *kichhu*:

> You may as well sit by me for a *little* while more;
> If you have *anything* more to say, say it, whatever it is,
> See the autumn sky pales.
> The vaporous air makes the horizon shine.

The imperfectly perceived, partially known, unnamed presence—whether it represents the spiritual source of the precolonial world now made semi-visible and nameless, or the regeneration of the new one—is always associated, in Tagore's songs, with conflicting emotions of resignation and joy: resignation, because that spirituality is inaccessible now except through these spots of time; and joy, because these spots of time open up new possibilities, new ways of deriving sustenance from the old. Consequently, songs such as "From time to time I catch glimpses of you" and "Because I wish to find you anew / I lose you moment to moment" are accompanied by conflicting impulses of acceptance and excitement in the interpreter of the song and its listener; they capture the sense of incomplete but revivifying spiritual possibility in the interstitial world of the Bengali, and the Indian, middle class.

Indirectness, in these songs, is both Tagore's literary mode and his subject matter. This indirectness, this articulate evasiveness, was also reflected in the life of the Bengali middle class before, and to a certain degree after, independence. It has been connected in the popular imagination—in laudatory and denigratory ways—to much that is modern about modern India; but it has also been traditionally cut off, and sometimes it has cut itself off, from central political power. It is at least partly for this reason—Bengal's distance from direct political control in the colonial and even the postcolonial age—that epic sweep and candour, in the poetry of Bengal's national poet, have been replaced by lyric suggestion and reticence. At crucial junctures of nationhood, poets narrate and recreate their nation's history in the form of epic; but Bengal was both a nation and not a nation, a region with its own community and history but also a part of the larger nation-state that had been conceptualised, early on, in some measure by some of its own intellectuals. Thus Tagore's most enduring creative legacy to the Bengali bourgeoisie was both epic-like and yet not an epic, a gift of songs in which the consciousness of Bengali modernity first found utterance and in which the impress of its creation and its history was subliminally contained, while relinquishing the overarching narrative of the epic for lyric moments of implication and enquiry

The problem with reading and judging Tagore is not only a problem of translation, or of understanding a seemingly untranslatable and exotic culture. Tagore needs to be placed in the context of modern Indian history, and more specifically in the context of Bengali middle-class culture, before his work can be understood, and the same holds true the other way round. But alas, India is commonly perceived as either possessing no history at all, as being an enchanted place of myths and verities (the jacket of Dutta and Robinson's anthology of Tagore's writings promises that it an "essential guide for readers seeking . . . wisdom"); or else its history is seen in an entirely reactive way, as a parable of postcoloniality, of the confrontation of the colonised with the coloniser. But Tagore does not fit into either formulation, and neither does most of modern India. Tagore is one of the figures who stands at the forefront of India's extraordinary and often traumatic reinterpretation of itself in this century. And his most profound engagement with history lay not in his asides to Gandhi or his opinions on Mussolini, but in the reticent, self-repeating, half-lit world of his poems and his songs.

A Small Bengal, NW3

1999, *Granta*

ABOUT FIVE OR SIX YEARS after the war ended, and soon after India's independence and the beginning of the end of the British Empire, Belsize Park in the borough of Camden became home to a number of Indian, mainly Bengali, students. They lived in neighbouring houses, and were often neighbours in the same house; they talked with, and jostled, and cooked for, each other, and had small rivalries and sympathies between themselves; but they knew they were a transient lot, because they were here to pass exams, and very few intended to stay, to get swallowed by the London that had become their temporary home. Time went by quickly, although, in retrospect, the procession of years would sometimes seem long.

Strangely enough, while Kilburn came to be known as a black and Irish area, and Golders Green a Jewish one, Belsize Park was never identified with its Bengali student population. Perhaps this was so because it was made up of itinerants rather than emigrants; most had left by the mid-sixties—if not England, then at least Belsize Park. They were mainly young men and, now and again, women, in their late twenties or their thirties, diligent and intelligent on the whole, who had come to study for professional examinations whose names seemed to have been invented to enhance their job prospects: Chartered Accountancy, Cost Accountancy, MRCP, FRCP, FRCS. For these Bengalis, at least, there was a romance about degrees that had the words "Chartered" or "Royal" in them which will now probably seem absurd. The few who stayed on in England were often the ones who hadn't been able to get the degree they'd come here to acquire; they couldn't face their mothers and fathers without it; thus they drifted into the civic life of London, became railway clerks or council officials, or moved elsewhere, and eventually bought a house in Wimbledon or Sussex or Hampshire; at any rate, they left Belsize Park. Those who stayed on had their reasons—"staying on": those words had possibly as much resonance for them, though for entirely different reasons, as they did for the last Anglo-Indians—and none of those reasons, it is safe to suppose, had anything to do with an overwhelming attachment to England.

But most studied, and left; and, in Belsize Park, the emphasis was on exams and recreation. They'd brought Bengal with them though Bengal itself had become a state of mind, partitioned into two, half of it in India and half of it East Pakistan. They fell into a routine of buying "wet fish," shopping at Finchley Road, going to work, listening to Tagore songs, in between bouts of memorising the pulmonary functions of the heart or the intricacies of taxation law.

Some of the students had wives, and were newly married. The wife, like Draupadi in the *Mahabharat*, who married five brothers at once, not only played wife to her husband but often to all her husband's friends, making food for them, being indulgent to them when they were depressed, exhorting them to study hard, and generally lightening the air with her feminine presence. Later, the men would always remember these surrogate wives, the Mrs. Mukherjis and Mrs. Basus and Mrs. Senguptas. In India, the new wife comes to her new home and is greeted by her husband's family and a way of life both prearranged and untested; every couple must, in the end, make what they will of their own lives. Here, in Belsize Park, the making of that life was both more naked and more secret; the new bride would be received not by her in-laws, but Cost Accountants-to-be and would-be surgeons and physicians. She would come not to her husband's house but to a bedsit with wallpaper and cooking hobs which was now to be her own, and which cost three pounds and ten shillings a week.

Among the tenants was a young man who was supposed to be studying Chartered Accountancy but was actually doing everything but study. He was thinner than normal; his mother had died when he was seven years old. When he had left India in 1949, he had been twenty-seven years old; he had lost his homeland with Partition; and he had got engaged to his best friend's younger sister. In 1955, she travelled to London with her younger brother to marry the young man. They, my parents, were among the people who lived in Belsize Park in the fifties.

In a photograph taken at the time, my mother leans over my father, who is reading a newspaper; she hides her hands behind her back because she has been kneading dough. In another picture, apparently taken soon after the wedding, my parents have just arrived in Shepherd's Bush and are standing on the steps of a house, seeming slightly unfamiliar with each other though in fact they have known each other from childhood, my father dressed in the bridegroom's white dhoti and kurta, my mother's sari draped over her head. They have recently walked round the holy fire in a town hall near Euston Square. Now they would be reacquainted with each other as husband and wife; my father would rediscover his lost mother's affection in the woman he had married; they would travel in Europe; they would make friends among their neighbours; my mother's singing voice would acquire a new fame in Bengali circles; her reputation as a cook would be established.

Both, in the first years of their marriage, went out to work in the morning, and had their daily meeting-places outside work hours; during break-time, my mother would hurry to Jermyn Street, where my father worked for a few years in the Accounts Office of India House, and they would go for lunch or tea to the Lyons restaurant nearby. Once a week, they would have a Chinese dinner at the Cathay restaurant; watching, through a window, Piccadilly outside. Nearer the exams, my father would study at home while my mother went out to work as a clerk.

Without a harmonium or any other accompanying instrument, my mother would keep practising the Tagore songs that she had learned as a child, in Sylhet, which had become part of East Pakistan. Her singing was full-throated; her voice would carry in the silent afternoons; once, the spinster landlady, Miss Fox, came down to complain.

Then, in 1961, a year before I was born, my parents left for Bombay; my father had, after passing his exams, got a job that paid for his and my mother's fares back; the ship would take two weeks to reach India. As the ship sailed forth, my mother (so she tells me) stared at the cliffs of Dover to imprint them on her memory. In a year, she had conceived, and, at the age of thirty-seven, she gave birth to her first and only child in Calcutta.

This is what they left behind. Haverstock Hill leading on one side to Hampstead, and Belsize Avenue sloping downward to Swiss Cottage and Finchley Road on the other. Other lives begin; other stories; and the human capacity to create is at least as strong as the capacity to forget.

German Sequence

2003, published in the *Telegraph*, Calcutta, and the following year in the *Dublin Review*

1. A Walk Around Schöneberg

Once, in 1973, a Switzerland-bound train I was in with my parents stopped for a few minutes at Bonn. A soldier came into our compartment and sat opposite us, and got off at the next stop: it seems fantastic, but it is true. For many years, this was my only claim to having been in Germany.

It's now more than a month ago that I entered Berlin for the first time. We flew into the Tegel airport; oddly, for a capital city, there is no preeminent international airport in Berlin. This is in keeping with its history; its once lapsed status, its division into two cities, its rehabilitation after reunification. Even its lack of a single international airport seems to be located in its inward, traumatic complexity; its shyness of landmarks and its proliferation of them; its dubious but continuing fascination with its emblems of the past; its being situated in this constant narrative of relocation—mental, ideological, physical, geographic. So, there is the "old" city centre and the "new" city centre, the "old" town hall and the "new" town hall; but these inscriptions of "old" and "new" are themselves fairly recent, and don't predate reunification. The expected movements of history have been compressed unnaturally; it's a little like being in Calcutta during the Pujas, but on a long-term basis, so that one might almost hope to become inured (who knows?) to this intertwining of the fantastic and the factual, this encounter with the banal, the historic, the allegorical, the domestic, and the proximity between them.

It was a brilliant summer. It took me by surprise: this natural affluence of daylight in the midst of such palpable material affluence was difficult to digest. I thought, blinking in the sun, of, at once, those prewar summers when Stephen Spender and company descended on Berlin, to sunbathe with godlike blond boys, and also of the vanishing, in an instant, of sensual innocence, political blindness, devastating pain, into the vacancy of this present-day, new-millennial happiness. Bathed in light, I was there with Spender, in the 1930s, as I could never have been if I had lived then, and I was here, in post-unification, post-Schroeder, post-Iraq Berlin.

We stayed in a lovely flat in Schöneberg ("beautiful hill," apparently, though there was no hill in sight) with large windows and wooden floors, and that most un-English of promontories, a balcony; the flat spacious enough for a dog, let alone humans, to be content in. There was no dog; but my new friend's "children"—a blond sixteen-year-old boy and a dark-haired nineteen-year-old girl—kept coming in, going out. My friend and his wife no longer lived with each other; they spoke to each other on the phone and shared the children; they had become blood relations. His name was Reinhold ("Call me Reini"), and he taught English at the University of Magdeburg in the former East Germany, where, in four days, I was to read my stories.

I went out and stood on the balcony and surveyed the buildings opposite. I looked greedily; more reticent but no less compelling than cathedrals and temples, they wouldn't give up their secrets in a glance. Schöneberg, Reini said, had been a mixture of economic classes and religions before the war; people of varying income groups had lived here, and not a small number of Jews. (I discovered later that the area used to be called the "Jewish Switzerland," and had a sizeable upper-middle-class Jewish population at the turn of the century.) "Tagore might have come here," he beamed. Why? "Einstein lived here. If they met in Berlin, it might have been here!"

The houses I saw from the balcony, like the building I was in, had been erected in the 1920s; they had miraculously survived the bombing. Thus, some of the residential areas of Berlin, which escaped both the bombs and the social levelling of East Berlin, have an extraordinarily ambiguous "inner weather." There are certain cities where the residential districts are even more revelatory to the outsider than their monuments and landmarks. Calcutta, I'd say, is one, for a walk in Mandeville Gardens or a drive through Bhowanipore or Alipore is much more instructive and charged with excitement for the visitor than a pilgrimage to the Victoria Memorial. Berlin, I think, is another.

Next morning (again, glorious), Reini said he'd take us—me, my wife, our daughter—for a walk around Schöneberg. On a plaque at the bottom of the façade of a nearby block of flats, partly hidden by the undergrowth, was the message that Einstein had resided here. We crossed the main road, further rows of buildings, and a bridge. We came to the "old" town hall and the "old" city centre. Before the wall fell, the Schöneberg town hall had been the town hall of West Berlin. Happy, indeed secure, to be at the centre of an American colony, it displayed lapidary words from John F. Kennedy addressed to West Germans. At midday, the stentorian chimes of the "freedom bell" rang out, as it had for fifty years, once a signal to benighted East Berliners that liberty and democracy would one day be theirs. Unlike the Iraqis, the West Germans, till recently, were happy with their liberators (and had chosen to forget their Russian ones); liberated not only from Nazism, but the dreariness of socialism and enforced equality.

On our way back our companion pointed out signs that hung from posts on the pavement, black German words on a white background. I recognised only "*Juden*" as common to them all. These signs were meant to remind you of the exact day when, say, Jews became barred from taking PhDs. Another proclaimed the date when they were deemed ineligible to become professional classical musicians. Another recorded the day when Jews were denied access to well-known areas of recreation. The dates ranged from the late 1920s to the late 1930s: no one (and I mean here, really, the German liberals of the time) could claim that they didn't know what was coming.

Thinking of those signs, I'm reminded of Walter Benjamin and his essay "Theses on the Philosophy of History" for two related reasons. The first is obvious; Benjamin's own history, his destiny and aborted career, are inextricable from the history the signs narrate. Unable to become a professor because of his religion, driven to suicide by fear after the fall of Paris in 1940, it is only after walking around Schöneberg that I understand something of the panic that fuelled his eloquence: "The tradition of the oppressed teaches us that the 'state of emergency' in which we live is not an exception but the rule"; and "The current amazement that the things we are experiencing [that is, fascism] are 'still' possible in the twentieth century is not philosophical."

Part of Benjamin's critique of what he calls the "empty, homogeneous time" of Western history—of the idea that Western history, with its narrative of rationality and progress, stands as a universal paradigm of history itself—surely involves his violently endangered Jewish identity. It was the inability of German liberals and opponents of fascism to imagine outside that paradigm, to imagine in what way fascism might be happening beyond and outside it, that helps bring fascism, in Benjamin's eyes, into existence. The same might be said of many secular individuals and political parties in India—the problem is not just the calculated connivance with fascism, but the inability to imagine it is really present, to acknowledge that it is not an element in our "empty, homogeneous" secular history with which we can quarrel on our own terms.

The other thing that struck me gradually, as I looked at these signs—astonishing, estranging, and puzzling—is the profound, as yet unfathomed importance of the Holocaust to European identity and self-consciousness. This is something I hadn't quite grasped till I travelled to Berlin. Obscene though it might be to say so, it seems that the obsessive righteousness, memorialisation, and remorse surrounding the Holocaust—in Berlin, in Germany, but also everywhere in Europe—suggest that it, too, has become an all-important component of that "empty, homogeneous time" without which history would be unimaginable (although it is imaginable without many other traumas in the twentieth century)—a development that Benjamin, naturally, didn't live to see; nor can we know whether, as a once-divided Zionist, he would have wanted to. The Holocaust cannot be replicated or repeated; it has been universalised, almost aestheticised, with the authority only Europe has, or has had, to universalise and aestheticise. Both Jew and European non-Jew are hurt and outraged if any equivalence is made, say, between what is happening in Israel and Palestine and what happened in Europe. "The 'state of emergency' in which we live is not the exception but the rule," but, ironically, this statement is doomed to be proven true only in retrospect.

2. The Shadow Line

In the afternoon, we slept. We were heavy with jet lag. When we woke, we found Reini was waiting for us. We set out in his car from Schöneberg at about half past four; summer days in Europe are interminable. As the afternoon expanded, it seemed we'd woken up at an untimely hour in the latter half of the day not only to a new time zone, but to the extension of possibility.

Reini drove us to Nollendorfstrasse, where, in a rented room, Isherwood met and became familiar with some of the characters in *Goodbye to Berlin*, and with the "deep, solemn, massive street" itself. His pressing reason for being in Berlin—his search for working-class boys—is, of course, mentioned in neither of the Berlin novels. Is it this story of unspoken desire, this unsaid, that gives the language of these novels, especially *Goodbye to Berlin*, its character, its deceptive transparency, its constant, low-key melody; for what's literary style but a negotiation between the sayable and the unsayable? The unsayable, in the 1930s, was not just a word, or a phrase, but a way of life.

The next day, I'd return here with my wife and daughter, walk down Nollendorfplatz, with its shops and restaurants, eat there, and walk back to Nollendorfstrasse. Not far from Isherwood's abode, a man was arranging things for a jumble sale. Mainly furniture and household objects, which had an exquisiteness that, my wife observed, only European objects once had. We asked him how much a small white porcelain swan, its neck and head bent over the edge of a table as if it were about to drink, would cost us. Its delicacy—the pleated wings, the pale yellow of the beak, its whiteness, which, if it were an illustration in a book, would have made it merge into the page—made it look like something from the 1920s. It would need to placed always at the edge of something, like a basin in a bathroom, because its head and neck were stooped at such an angle that they must necessarily inhabit empty space. We waited for a vast figure. Four euros, came the reply. We decided to buy it. It was wrapped in a polythene bag for travel.

That brief encounter with bric-a-brac dislocated me. Recounting the experience of walking in the Parisian arcades, Walter Benjamin had said, famously, that sometime in the late nineteenth century Paris had become a great interior; the introduction of gas-lit lamps had, in a sense, removed the sky over the city, turning it into a ceiling; to stroll as flaneur or dandy through the arcades was in a way to roam about in your own room; interior and exterior were confused with one another. In Nollendorfstrasse, buying the swan, hovering over the furniture, I felt something of that confusion, and felt, too, that my being there was charged with significance. It was as if I were in someone's house, but the house had been made invisible—by history. On Nollendorfstrasse itself, buildings had been razed in the bombing, then swiftly replaced in postwar reconstruction by what Reini called "prefabricated" houses. These were juxtaposed to the buildings that had survived, with their balconies, their drawing rooms with chandeliers.

The swan might have belonged to one of those houses. In my mind, the history of the bombing had set it free. Certainly, the bombing must have once added to the flaneur's experience of urban rambling, with its interchangeability of inside and outside, a dimension Benjamin couldn't have imagined. This ambiguous extra dimension informs this sentence, about London after the war, from Muriel Sparks's *The Girls of Slender Means*: "Some bomb-ripped buildings looked like the ruins of ancient castles until, at a closer view, the wallpapers of various quite normal rooms would be visible, room above room, exposed, as on a stage, with one wall missing; sometimes a lavatory chain would dangle over nothing from a fourth- or fifth-floor ceiling; most of all the staircases survived, like a new art-form, leading up and up to an unspecified destination . . ." This self-aware aestheticisation, with its comedy of absences and its juxtapositions of castles and wallpaper, takes me back to Benjamin's view of bourgeois Paris. The meandering sentence might not know it, but it is a child of that vision.

That sentence, which I'd read several years ago, prepared me for the Kaiser Wilhelm Memorial Church in the Kurfurstendamm. The latter is a long avenue of shops, cafés and restaurants, Berlin's Champs-Élysées, albeit on a smaller scale; the church, built at the end of the nineteenth century in memory of Wilhelm II, was bombed in the war. The main structure has been largely left as it was; "left as it was" is perhaps a better way of describing it than calling it a "ruin," with its suggestion of slow, timeless attrition; here, although it looks very like a ruin, the sudden impact of devastation, the bruises wrought by a single moment, are permanently on display. It has since been added to, and its interior is open to tourists; before it, like a futuristic offspring, is a new bell tower, modernist in conception, a tall hexagon. The contiguity between the two buildings is astonishing and provocative. The old church, perhaps affectionately, is called the "rotten tooth"; it looked to me uncannily like Brueghel's picture of the Tower of Babel, with its burst centre, except that it, unlike the Tower, overwhelmingly represents silence.

From here, Reini drove us to the Reichstag, which, during the era of the two Berlins, had been disowned by both sides, partly because it stood on the border that separated them; it was now revived as a conference centre and a tourist attraction. We stared at it and walked across the now impalpable dividing line; there was no wall here; it was at this point that the border most approximated the phrase with which Isherwood so movingly evoked it in his account of a postwar visit: the "shadow line."

I have never encountered the past as I did when I was in Berlin. It was not only I who saw the ghost; my wife did too. "It's amazing," she said. If only one of us had seen it, we could say that the person in question had imagined it; but both of us couldn't have had the same dream. Every city gives you a past which is, of course, a construct: London, Paris, Delhi. But, here, the construct is curious. You are meant to confront the past everywhere; but are kept from what is surely the universal human instinct towards it—to mourn it; to commemorate it. Instead, you are dislocated by it in a series of encounters.

We crossed the "shadow line" in Reini's blue car as the sun began to go down; he took us into the former East Berlin and showed us rows of "prefabricated" houses, and old official buildings the government still didn't know what to do with; like some East Bengali refugees, they are still awaiting rehabilitation in some apocryphal narrative of migration. "Don't quote me," said Reini, "but some of the profit-making companies of the East were bought over and discontinued by companies from the West to weed out competition." From there to Checkpoint Charlie, the wall inscribed with artists graffiti, the avenue of resplendent and still-threatening "Stalinist" architecture, the Muscovite buildings looking like a great army without a general.

Can one see a city in a day? Can one absorb it? Certainly, in great modernist texts—*Ulysses*, *Mrs. Dalloway*, *Under the Volcano*—a day is all that is given; and, in that day, a break is made in Benjamin's "empty, homogeneous time of history." Benjamin conceived of that break as a "now": "*Jetztzeit*"; a revolutionary, but also a mystical, moment in the present. The following is from his eighteenth thesis on the "philosophy of history": "'In relation to the history of organic life on earth,' writes a modern biologist, 'the paltry fifty millennia of *Homo sapiens* constitute something like two seconds at the close of a twenty-four-hour day. On this scale, the history of civilised mankind would fill one fifth of the last second of the last hour.' The present, which ... comprises the entire history of mankind in an enormous abridgement, coincides exactly with the stature which the history of mankind has in the universe." This is a bit like the Hindu notion of human history as a blink in the eye of a yuga; it is also a fair definition of the day in a modernist classic. A day is at once infinitesimal and endless.

3. Portrait of Reini

Magdeburg is in what was called vaguely, until fourteen years ago, "East Germany." It is well known for being an important prewar industrial town; for being thoroughly bombed during the war; for a very old cathedral; and for Otto von Guericke, after whom the university is named. This man was a scientist who is renowned for an experiment: he joined two empty hemispheres together and filled them with a vacuum. Then, in an odd tug of war, he had teams of horses try to pull them apart. They failed.

As we stepped out of the railway station into the strong light of six o'clock in the evening, Reini made us turn around and look at the building. It was the most magnificent structure in the area, something that might have been erected at the end of the nineteenth century; one could imagine it as a great terminus for horse-drawn carriages. From it to our hotel was a mere two minutes' walk. The hotel resembled an

American motel, and was just the place for the conference visitor: well equipped, efficient, unlovely, and turn of the century (the twentieth, not the nineteenth). We washed our faces and combed our hair in a brightly lit bathroom before emerging for our walk with Reini.

Our walks give me the illusion of knowing Reini better than I do. His beard, his granny glasses, his long hair, coming down to well below his collar, suggest—and I confirmed this from a black and white picture in his kitchen—that, although he's probably modulated his politics, he's largely left the incarnation he found himself in during the student radicalism of the late 1960s, when he was at Berlin's Free University, untouched.

Naturally, he's put on weight. No sign of his residual left-wing propensities is to be found in his beautiful Berlin flat. Only, in the course of conversation, a professed enthusiasm for Stuart Hall and Raymond Williams betrays not so much an allegiance to a programme as a private romanticism. He has travelled; he lived for years in China; he has been to India; among the pictures in his kitchen is a postcard that shows a place I believed I'd seen before—was it Rome? Only after repeated glances at the brown-stone buildings, the lovely urban arc of traffic around an ancient European statue, did I recognise the Flora Fountain in Bombay I'd pass every day on my way to school.

In the black and white photo, Reini is smoking a cigarette. I think he's given up this habit. Like radicalism, cigarette smoking made an exit from bourgeois European society in the 1980s. The new religion is life; not just the pursuit of happiness, but of health. In this regard, Reini's unfashionable paunch—I could see, from old photographs, that he'd had it for a while—proclaims, more than any political opinion, his anomalousness. I don't know what his relationship to the contemporary world is, but I suspect it isn't an entirely normal one; I suspect that, in spite of his joviality, his apparent satisfaction with his routine of work and leisure, he is secretly bemused by the fallout of the Cold War.

I think that he belonged to a particular subgroup in that generation of Europeans that was defined by the Cold War in profound and contradictory ways; that, while he'd never have given up the pleasures and freedoms of capitalist society, or doubted the veracity of democracy, or doubted the futility of the division of Europe into East or West, or the bane of the Iron Curtain, the flame of some pure, Marxist nostalgia would have been fed, without his being even fully conscious of it, by the existence of the Soviet Union that otherwise, in the daylight of reason, so appalled him. The fall of the wall and the collapse of the Soviet Union must have left him off kilter; ever so slightly, in comparison to his counterpart in the East, but off kilter nevertheless.

That's why, maybe, he likes taking visitors for these walks; why he's such a good guide. I wouldn't mind him as a companion in purgatory. I asked him if he ever found it a nuisance showing people around. He said no, he enjoyed seeing familiar things through others' eyes. I think the walks, punctuated by jokes and gestures of the hand, are a sort of circling round history, a pattern of confirmation and distancing. Because they are an improvised, rather than an actual, form of mapping, they must accrue, rather than lose, significance with repetition.

The walk that sunlit evening too traced a sort of circle. We started from the hotel, went past the station, turned right at Pizza Hut—a signpost of post–Cold War Magdeburg—passed a group of academics who'd come here for the conference on postcolonial literatures, walked down an immense road with tramlines in the middle, then right, into a long featureless avenue that led us to the cathedral—dark, huge, one of Europe's oldest. From there we turned back, past another old and peculiar building, the General Post Office, and, finally, made our way through a path that, by some sleight of hand, returned us to our postmodern hotel.

By our second evening, our last, my wife and I had become well acquainted with this arc. Nowadays, I find it takes me only a day or two to form an emotional link with a place I'm passing through. It's as if I've entered yet another suburb of an indefinite but persistent metropolis

I'll never escape. This suburb is different from the one I was last in, but not wholly strange. I begin to find my way in it; at first, like a blind man; then, with a mixture of circumspection and trepidation, like someone who's never strayed from the route to a particular destination over many years, but who has never found that route boring. All this happens in approximately a day. When I was a child, I recall, I went to Athens, but never felt like seeing the Parthenon. Now, I find that a city such as Magdeburg compels me to discover it.

My reading, on the second day, was at 7 p.m.; we had the rest of the day to ourselves. We visited a pharmacy; chanced upon an open market in a town square; photographed the statue of a man on horseback; and ran, astonishingly, into an Indian selling knickknacks. He told me he'd been a taxi driver in Punjab; he had married a German tourist and come here eleven years ago. They were now divorced; he'd stayed on. My discovery of this man, my compatriot, was, to me, incredible; for I'd begun to imagine I was the only Indian man in Magdeburg. These days, no one stares at you in the West; eye contact is a potential precursor to assault; when it occurs, it's nearly always domesticated by a nod and a smile. In Magdeburg, though, my family and I were stared at intently. During that stare, I became aware not only of my own extraordinariness, but of the extraordinariness of history. These feelings were complicated by a conversation I had had five minutes prior to meeting the Indian vendor.

We were resting, then, on a bench before a fountain; a tramp with a can of lager in one hand sat on the neighbouring bench. "*Indien*?" he said suddenly. Disarmed, I nodded. He then asked me a series of questions in German. "No Deutsch, no Deutsch," I replied. He embarked upon a hoarse, rapid monologue. Finally, he raised his arm in the old Nazi salute. What had this man done and thought, I wondered, during those forty odd years of communism?

Reini tells me that most East Germans, in a fit of collective amnesia, forgot the legacy of socialism overnight. Although an Indian friend says that she found an older generation in Dresden still insisting on speaking Russian as a second language, the second language in question now is not Russian, but English; and, as the Head of the English Department shrugged and sighed, "These Easterners know no English."

It seems a knowledge of English, or the lack of it, has become a metaphor, in certain circles in Germany, for a figurative barrier, a silence that keeps, like Isherwood's "shadow line," one side from the other. Most of the teachers at Magdeburg's English department are, indeed, "Westerners," and, thus, commuters. Just as Reini's life was an intersection in my journey, my journey must have been an intersection in the constant travelling of which his life is composed, the weekly to-ing and fro-ing on the autobahn between West Berlin and what he once laughing called, in a moment of levity, "darkest Europe."

In the Waiting-Room of History

On *Provincializing Europe*

2004, *London Review of Books*

I WENT TO A PROTESTANT SCHOOL in Bombay, but the creation myth we were taught in the classroom didn't have to do with Adam and Eve. I remember a poster on the wall when I was in the Fifth Standard, a pictorial narrative of evolution. On the extreme left, crouching low, its arms hanging near its feet, was an ape; it looked intent, like an athlete waiting for the gun to go off. The next figure rose slightly, and the one after it was more upright: it was like a slow-motion sequence of a runner in the first few seconds of a race. The pistol had been fired; the race had begun. Millisecond after millisecond, that runner—now ape, now Neanderthal—rose a little higher, and its back straightened. By the time it had reached the apogee of its height and straight-backedness, and taken a stride forward, its appearance had improved noticeably; it had become a Homo sapiens, and also, coincidentally, European. The race had been won before it had properly started.

This poster captured and compressed the gradations of Darwin's parable of evolution, both arresting time and focussing on the key moments of a concatenation, in a similar way to what Walter Benjamin thought photographs did in changing our perception of human movement:

> Whereas it is a commonplace that, for example, we have some idea what is involved in the act of walking (if only in general terms), we have no idea

> at all what happens during the fraction of a second when a person actually takes a step. Photography, with its devices of slow motion and enlargement, reveals the secret. It is through photography that we first discover the existence of this optical unconscious; just as we discover the instinctual subconscious through psychoanalysis.

The poster in my classroom, too, revealed a movement impossible for the naked eye to perceive: from lower primate to higher, from Neanderthal to human, and—this last transition was so compressed as to be absent altogether—from the human to the European. These still figures gave us an "optical unconscious" of a political context, the context of progress and European science and humanism. Here, too, Benjamin has something to say. In a late essay, "Theses on the Philosophy of History," he stated: "The concept of the historical progress of mankind cannot be sundered from the concept of its progression through a homogeneous, empty time."

"Homogeneous" and "empty" are curious adjectives for "time": they are more readily associated with space and spatial configuration. Certain landscapes glimpsed from a motorway, or the look of a motorway itself, might be described as dull and "homogeneous"; streets and rooms might be "empty." My mentioning motorways isn't fortuitous. When Benjamin was formulating his thoughts on progress and history, and writing this essay in 1940, the year he killed himself, Hitler, besides carrying out his elaborate plans for the Jews in Germany, was implementing another huge and devastating project: the Autobahn. The project, intended both to connect one part of Germany to another and to colonise the landscape, was begun in the early 1930s; it's clear that Hitler's vision of the Autobahn is based on an idea of progress—"progress" not only in the sense of movement between one place and another, but in the sense of science and civilisation. In India, in other parts of the so-called "developing" world, even in present-day New York, London, or Paris, it's impossible properly to experience "homogeneous, empty time" because of the random, often maddeningly diverse allocation of space, human habitation, and community. It is, however, possible to experience it on Western motorways and highways. Hitler was a literalist of this philosophy of space and movement: he wanted space to be "homogeneous," or blond and European. Benjamin knew this first-hand; he was writing his "Theses on the Philosophy of History" as a Jewish witness to Nazism and one of its potential victims. Hitler's anxiety and consternation at Jesse Owens's victory in the one hundred metres at the Munich Olympics in 1936 came from his literalism of space, his investment in progress and linearity. That idea of space was at once reified and shattered when Owens reached the finishing line before the others.

Benjamin had been thinking of history in terms of space for a while; and, not too long before he wrote about "homogeneous, empty time," he'd posited an alternative version of modernity and space in his descriptions of the flaneur, the Parisian arcades and nineteenth-century street life. The Parisian street constitutes Benjamin's critique of the Autobahn: just as the crowd, according to Benjamin, is "present everywhere" in Baudelaire's work, and present so intrinsically that it's never directly described, the Autobahn is implicitly present, and refuted, in Benjamin's meditations on Paris. The flaneur, indeed, retards and parodies the idea of "progress." "Around 1840 it was briefly fashionable to take turtles for a walk in the arcades," Benjamin writes in a footnote to his 1939 essay on Baudelaire. "The *flâneurs* liked to have the turtles set the pace for them. If they had had their way, progress would have been obliged to accommodate itself to this space. But this attitude did not prevail; Taylor, who popularised the watchword 'Down with dawdling!' carried the day." The flaneur views history subversively; he—and it is usually he—deliberately relocates its meanings, its hierarchies. As far back as 1929, Benjamin had explained why the flaneur *had* to be situated in Paris:

> The *flâneur* is the creation of Paris. The wonder is that it was not Rome. But perhaps in Rome even dreaming is forced to move along streets that

> are too well-paved. And isn't the city too full of temples, enclosed squares and national shrines to be able to enter undivided into the dreams of the passer-by, along with every shop sign, every flight of steps and every gateway? The great reminiscences, the historical *frissons*—these are all so much junk to the *flâneur*, who is happy to leave them to the tourist. And he would be happy to trade all his knowledge of artists' quarters, birthplaces, and princely palaces for the scent of a single weathered threshold or the touch of a single tile—that which any old dog carries away.

There's an implicit critique of the imperial city, and the imperialist aesthetic, in this description of Rome, with its "great reminiscences" and "historical frissons," and in the contrast of "national shrines" and "temples" with the "touch of a single tile." Benjamin is not alone in using these metaphors; both Ruskin and Lawrence (who probably took it from Ruskin) use Rome as a metaphor for the imperial, the finished, the perfected, as against the multifariousness of, say, the Gothic, the "barbaric," the non-Western. Benjamin doesn't quite romanticise the primitive as Lawrence at least appears to: instead, he comes up with a particularly modern form of aleatoriness and decay in the "weathered threshold" of a Parisian street.

Of course, the flaneur was not to be found in Paris alone. There was much wayward loitering in at least two colonial cities, Dublin and Calcutta. This—especially the emergence of the flaneur, or flaneur-like activities, in modern, turn of the century Calcutta—would have probably been difficult for Benjamin to imagine. Benjamin's figure for the flaneur was Baudelaire, and for Baudelaire—and, by extension, for the flaneur—the East was, as it was for Henri Rousseau, part dreamscape, part botanical garden, part menagerie, part paradise. Could the flaneur exist in that dreamscape? Dipesh Chakrabarty, the author of *Provincializing Europe*, whose meditations on the limits of Western notions of modernity and history are impelled by Benjamin but who also has the word "postcolonial" in his subtitle, was born in Calcutta. His inquiry is partly directed by the contingencies of being a South Asian historian in America, and also by being a founder member of the Subaltern Studies project, which attempted to write a South Asian or, specifically, Indian history "from below," by bringing the "subaltern" (Gramsci's word for the peasant or the economically dispossessed) into the territory largely occupied by nationalist history. But the inquiry is also shaped by the Calcutta Chakrabarty was born in, much as Benjamin's work is shaped by the Paris he reimagined and, to a certain extent, invented. From the early nineteenth century, the growing Bengali intelligentsia in Calcutta was increasingly exercised by what "modernity" might mean and what the experience of modernity might represent, specifically, to a subject nation, and, universally, to a human being. Chakrabarty's book is not only an unusually sustained and nuanced argument against European ideas of modernity, but also an elegy for, and subtle critique of, his own intellectual formation and inheritance as a Bengali. The kind of Bengali who was synonymous with modernity and who believed that modernity might be a universal condition—irrespective of whether you're English, Indian, Arab, or African—has now passed into extinction. Chakrabarty's book is in part a discreet inquiry into why that potent Bengali dream didn't quite work—why "modernity" remains so resolutely European.

Chakrabarty's writing is not without irony or humour; the cheeky oxymoron of the title is one example. At least a quarter of Chakrabarty's work was done, and his challenge given an idiom, when he reinvented this terrific phrase, which was probably first used with slightly more literal intent by Hans-Georg Gadamer. According to Ranajit Guha, who is or used to be to subalternist historians roughly what Jesus was to the apostles, the "idea of provincialising Europe" had "been around for some time, but mostly as an insight waiting for elaboration" before Chakrabarty articulated and substantiated it so thoroughly. The "idea" itself is set out and argued for in the introductory chapter. Chakrabarty begins with a disclaimer: "*Provincializing Europe* is not a book about the region of the world we call 'Europe.' That Europe, one could say, has already been provincialized by history itself." The essay has two epigraphs: the first, from Gadamer, seems to speak of Europe as a "region of the world"; the second, more tellingly, from Naoki Sakai, describes the "West" as "a name for a subject which gathers itself in discourse but is also an object constituted discursively." What Chakrabarty wants to do with "Europe," then, is in some ways similar to what Edward Said did with the "Orient": to fashion a subversive genealogy. But instead of Said's relentless polemic, Chakrabarty's book features critique and self-criticism in equal measure. For me, Chakrabarty has the edge here, because for Said the Orient is a Western construct, an instrument of domination: he doesn't—and never went on to—explore the profound ways in which modern Orientals (Tagore, say) both were and were not Orientalists. Chakrabarty's work suggests, I think, that the word "Eurocentric" is more problematic than we thought; that, if Europe is a universal paradigm for modernity, we are all, European and non-European, to a degree inescapably Eurocentric. Europe is at once a means of intellectual dominance, an obfuscatory trope, and a constituent of self-knowledge, in different ways for different peoples and histories.

Said's great study takes its cue from the many-sided and endlessly absorbing Foucault, in its inexhaustible conviction and its curiosity about how a body of knowledge—in this case, Orientalism—can involve the exercise of power. Much postcolonial theory, in turn, has taken its cue from Said and this strain of Foucault. Chakrabarty's book comes along at a time when this line of inquiry, which has had its own considerable rewards and pitfalls, seems one-dimensional and exhausted. In spite of the "postcolonial" in the subtitle, it owes little to the fecund but somewhat simplified Foucauldian paradigm. Instead, its inspiration seems poststructuralist and Derridean, and it rehearses a key moment in Derrida: the idea that it is necessary to dismantle or take on the language of "Western metaphysics" (which for Derrida is almost everything that precedes poststructuralism and, in effect, himself), but that there is no alternative language available with which to dismantle it—so that the language must be turned on itself. For Derrida's "Western metaphysics" Chakrabarty substitutes "European thought" and "social science thought":

> European thought... is both indispensable and inadequate in helping us to think through the various life practices that constitute the political and the historical in India. Exploring—on both theoretical and factual registers—this simultaneous indispensability and inadequacy of social science thought is the task this book has set itself.

This is not very far from Derrida, who writes at an important juncture in *Writing and Difference* of

> conserving all these old concepts within the domain of empirical discovery while here and there denouncing their limits, treating them as tools that can still be used. No longer is any truth value attributed to them: there is a readiness to abandon them, if necessary, should other instruments appear more useful. In the meantime, their relative efficacy is exploited, and they are employed to destroy the old machinery to which they belong and of which they themselves are pieces. This is how the language of the social sciences criticises *itself.*

Derrida is reflecting here on Claude Lévi-Strauss, who when confronted with South American myths finds the tools of his trade obsolete but still indispensable. The idea of Chakrabarty registering a similarly self-reflexive moment about thirty years later, in relation to Europe, modernity, and "life practices... in India," is poignant and ironic: he belongs to the other side of the racial and historical divide; to a part of the world that should have been, at least in Lévi-Strauss's time, and by ordinary European estimation, the object rather than the instigator of the social scientist's discipline. It would have been next to impossible for Lévi-Strauss to foretell that something resembling his anxiety about the social sciences would one day be rehearsed in the work of a man with a name like Dipesh Chakrabarty.

And this, of course, is the crux of Chakrabarty's book. "Historicism—and even the modern, European idea of history—one might say, came to non-European peoples in the nineteenth century as somebody's way of saying 'not yet' to somebody else." To illustrate what he means, he turns to John Stuart Mill's *On Liberty* and *On Representative Government*— "both of which," Chakrabarty says, "proclaimed self-rule as the highest form of government and yet argued against giving Indians or Africans self-rule."

> According to Mill, Indians or Africans were *not yet* civilised enough to rule themselves. Some historical time of development and civilisation (colonial rule and education, to be precise) had to elapse before they could be considered prepared for such a task. Mill's historicist argument thus consigned Indians, Africans and other "rude" nations to an imaginary waiting-room of history.

The "imaginary waiting-room of history" is another of Chakrabarty's compressed, telling images. I don't know if he picked it up from the German playwright Heiner Müller, who uses it of the "Third World" in a 1989 interview; but he employs it to great effect. The phrase has purgatorial resonances: you feel that those who are in the waiting-room are going to be there for some time. For modernity has already had its authentic incarnation in Europe: how then can it happen again, elsewhere? The non-West—the waiting-room—is therefore doomed either never to be quite modern, to be, in Naipaul's phrase, "half-made"; or to possess only a semblance of modernity. This is a view of history and modernity that has, according to Chakrabarty, at once liberated, defined, and shackled us in its discriminatory universalism; it is a view powerfully theological in its determinism, except that the angels, the blessed, and the excluded are real people, real communities.

Chakrabarty's thesis might seem obvious once stated; but the "insight waiting for elaboration," to use Ranajit Guha's words, must find the best and, in the positive sense of the word, most opportunistic expositor. In Chakrabarty, I think it has. (The urge to provincialise Europe has, of course, a very long unofficial history. It's embodied in jokes and throwaway remarks such as the one Gandhi made when asked what he thought of Western civilisation: "I think it would be a good idea." Shashi Tharoor is having a dig at historicism when he says, in *The Great Indian Novel*, "India is not an underdeveloped country. It is a highly developed country in an advanced state of decay.") Chakrabarty has given us a vocabulary with which to speak of matters somewhat outside the realm of the social sciences, and to move discussions on literature, cultural politics, and canon formation away from the exclusively Saidian concerns of power-brokering, without entirely ignoring these concerns.

In the light of Chakrabarty's study, Naipaul's work begins to fall into place. Here is a writer who seems to have subscribed quite deeply to the sort of historicism that Chakrabarty describes. From the middle period onwards, in books such as *The Mimic Men*, *A Bend in the River* and *In a Free State*, Naipaul gives us a vision—unforgettable, eloquent—of the Caribbean and especially Africa as history's waiting-room. Modernity here is ramshackle, self-dismantling: it exists somewhere between the corrugated iron roof and the distant military coup, the newly deposed general. The "not yet" with which Forster's narrator indefinitely deferred, in *A Passage to India*, the possibility of a lasting friendship between Fielding and Aziz are also the words that describe Naipaul's modern Africa. The opening sentence of *A Bend in the River* (which so exasperated Chinua Achebe)—"The world is what it is; men who are nothing, who allow themselves to become nothing, have no place in it"—owes its tone less to religious pronouncements than to a belief in what Benjamin called "the march of progress" in the "homogeneous, empty time of history." Naipaul's theology stems not so much from Hinduism, or the brahminical background he's renowned for, as from Mill. It was Mill, as Chakrabarty points out, who consigned certain nations to a purgatory, in which, in different concentric circles, they've been waiting or "developing" ever since. In fiction, the greatest explorers of this Millian terrain have been Naipaul and Naipaul's master, Conrad.

Chakrabarty's study also helps to clarify the ways in which we discuss and think of the "high" cultures of the so-called developing countries: not only the ancient traditions, but the modern and modernist ones as well. This is an area of self-consciousness, and a field of inquiry, that is potentially vast, important, and problematic; it also happens to be one that "cultural studies" has largely missed out on, being more concerned with popular culture and narratives of resistance to empire. Yet for almost two hundred years, in countries like India, there has been a self-consciousness (and it still exists today) which asks to be judged and understood by "universal" standards. It isn't possible to begin to discuss that self-consciousness, or sense of identity, without discussing in what way that universalism both formed and circumscribed it.

In some regards, then, cultural studies is hostage to the kind of historicism that Chakrabarty talks about: it can't deal with the emergence of high modernism in postcolonial countries except with a degree of suspicion and embarrassment, partly because of the elite contexts of that modernism, but partly, surely, for covertly historicist reasons, such as a belief that no modernism outside Europe can be absolutely genuine. Take the Bengal, or Indian, Renaissance: the emergence of humanism and modernity in nineteenth-century Calcutta. The term "renaissance" was probably first applied to this development by the eminent Brahmo Shibnath Shastri; it was later employed by historians such as Susobhan Sarkar. Marxist and, later, subalternist historians have with some justification raised their eyebrows at the term. They have tried to dismiss it as intellectually meaningless, mainly because they see it as an elite construct, an upper-middle-class invention that raises too many questions, and which, while identifying too closely with British ideas of "progress," was also an instrument of vague but voluble nationalist blarney. All this is true. But it ignores the fact that a construct can be a crucial constituent of an intellectual tradition. The European Renaissance is a case in point: we now know that it is largely a nineteenth-century invention, but that doesn't reduce the role it has played in the drama of European intellectual and cultural history—it only problematises it.

The opening of Susobhan Sarkar's *Notes on the Bengal Renaissance*, which first came out as a booklet in 1946, makes clear the unease that historians felt on first using the term:

> The impact of British rule, bourgeois economy and modern Western culture was felt first in Bengal and produced an awakening known usually as the Bengal Renaissance. For about a century, Bengal's conscious awareness of the changing modern world was more developed than and ahead of that of the rest of India. The role played by Bengal in the modern awakening of India is thus comparable to the position occupied by Italy in the story of the European Renaissance.

Whether these claims are true or not is open to debate; but they're disabled by their uncritical investment in the idea of Europe as the source, paradigm, and catalyst of progress and history, both in an earlier and in the colonial age. The habit, in the context of Indian culture, of not only invoking Europe but making it the starting point of all discussion, was inculcated by nineteenth-century Orientalists: the translator and scholar William Jones called Kalidasa, the greatest Indian poet and dramatist of antiquity, the "Shakespeare of the East." To do this, Jones had to reverse history—Kalidasa preceded Shakespeare by more than a thousand years. Jones is not so much making a useful (and supremely approbatory) comparison as telling us inadvertently that it's impossible to escape "homogeneous, empty time": that as far as Kalidasa is concerned Shakespeare has already happened. This language persisted in the subsequent naming of periods in culture, and of cultural figures; and educated Bengalis followed the example of the Orientalist scholars. Thus Bankimchandra Chatterjee, India's first major novelist, became the "Walter Scott of Bengal." Both Scott and Chatterjee wrote historical novels, but when the comparison was first made, on the publication of Chatterjee's first novel, Chatterjee claimed he'd never read Scott. Even if he had, to call him the "Walter Scott of Bengal" is subtly different from, say, Barthes remarking, "Gide was another Montaigne," where a continuity is being established, a lineage being traced. In the phrase that describes Chatterjee, however, an inescapable historicism refuses a literary continuity, and turns Chatterjee into an echo. Walter Scott in Bengal is Walter Scott in the waiting-room.

The "first in Europe, then elsewhere" paradigm that Chakrabarty speaks of—what is now the developmental paradigm—is what made the process of modernisation in non-Western countries seem to many, European and non-European, like mimicry. "We pretended to be real, to be learning, to be preparing ourselves for life, we mimic men of the New World," Naipaul's narrator, Ralph Singh, says in *The Mimic Men*; Chakrabarty's friend, the exuberantly impenetrable Homi Bhabha, has an essay on mimicry and colonialism, "Of Mimicry and Man: The Ambivalence of Colonial Discourse," that has long been part of every postcolonial primer. In it he tries, using Lacan and referring in passing to Naipaul's great, intractable novel, to complicate and even rescue the idea of mimicry, to make it subversive: mimicry undermines the coloniser's gaze by presenting him with a distorted reflection, rather than a confirmation, of himself. Some of the essay's formulations about mimicry—"almost the same but not quite"; "almost the same but not white"—are close enough to the kinds of problem Chakrabarty addresses. Once again, though, as with Said, I think Chakrabarty's work gives us a richer, more penetrating language to deal with modernity and the colonial encounter. There's a barely concealed utopian rage in Bhabha against the compulsion towards mimicry, and also an unspoken nostalgia for a world in which mimicry isn't necessary. For Chakrabarty, "Europe" is a notion that has many guises, and these guises have both liberated us and limited us, whichever race we belong to. There is, therefore, a valuable element of self-criticism in his study: to *provincialise* Europe is not to vanquish or conquer it—that is, provincialising Europe isn't a utopian gesture—but a means of locating and subjecting to interrogation some of the fundamental notions by which we define ourselves.

Despite its title, it might be more productive to read *The Mimic Men* with Chakrabarty's book rather than Bhabha's essay in mind. Ralph Singh, a failed politician from the Caribbean island of Isabella, now retired at the age of forty to a boarding-house in London, and writing something like a memoir, is not so much disfigured by "mimicry" as haunted, even entrapped, by the language called "Europe." It's not a life story he wishes to compose. "My first instinct was towards the writing of history," Singh says, and he returns again and again to an analysis of a way of thinking and seeing. "I have read that it was a saying of an ancient Greek that the first requisite for happiness was to be born in a famous city," he writes. "To be born on an island like Isabella, an obscure New World transplantation, second-hand and barbarous, was to be born to disorder." "Second-hand," like "half-made," is a word weighted with the historicism that gives Singh his sense of being a failure from the start, and Singh's creator much of his pessimism. Even memory, the site of renewal for the Romantics and Modernists, is deceptive: "My first memory of school is of taking an apple to the teacher. This puzzles me. We had no apples on Isabella. It must have been an orange; yet my memory insists on the apple. The editing is clearly at fault, but the edited version is all I have." The orange exists in the waiting-room. Its historical and physical reality counts for little;

Ralph Singh's memory is "discursively constituted," and has its own truth; and, at the time of the narrative's composition, it is all he has of Isabella.

Connecting the two halves of Chakrabarty's study—the first largely a self-reflexive appraisal of social science writing, the second a critical engagement with modern Bengali culture—are not only the themes of historicism and modernity, but the figure of Benjamin. Chakrabarty picks up the key insight about the "homogeneous, empty time of history." The phrase was made current in the social sciences by Benedict Anderson in his classic discussion of the rise of the nation-state, *Imagined Communities*; but Chakrabarty's usage of it, concerned primarily with the European notion of modernity, is Benjaminesque in spirit. Yet the references to Benjamin after the introduction are relatively few. This is an interesting and intriguing elision: perhaps Chakrabarty needs him to be an invisible presence. In the second half of the book I sensed him most powerfully in the chapter "*Adda*: A History of Sociality"; and it might have been enriching to have the connection made explicit, or to know whether Chakrabarty himself was fully conscious of it. "The word *adda* (pronounced 'uddah') is translated by the Bengali linguist Sunitikumar Chattopadhyay as 'a place' for 'careless talk with boon companions' or 'the chats of intimate friends'... Roughly speaking, it is the practice of friends getting together for long, informal and unrigorous conversations." Never was *adda* so theorised and romanticised as it was in Calcutta, as both a significant component and symptom of Bengali bourgeois culture in the first three-quarters of the twentieth century. Even the usage of the word is different in Bengali from Hindi, say, where it means a meeting-place not a practice. Chakrabarty goes on:

> By many standards of judgment in modernity, *adda* is a flawed social practice: it is predominantly male in its modern form in public life; it is oblivious of the materiality of labour in capitalism; and middle-class *addas* are

> usually forgetful of the working classes. Some Bengalis even see it as a practice that promotes sheer laziness in the population. Yet its perceived gradual disappearance from the urban life of Calcutta over the last three or four decades—related no doubt to changes in the political economy of the city—has now produced an impressive amount of mourning and nostalgia. It is as if with the slow death of *adda* will die the identity of being a Bengali.

The figure who comes to mind when I read this is Benjamin's flaneur; and, though Chakrabarty doesn't explore the correspondence between *flânerie* and *adda*, the resemblances are striking. Both *adda* and *flânerie* are activities whose worth is ambivalent in a capitalist society: they rupture the "march of progress." *Flânerie* is "dawdling," and *adda* a waste of time which, at least according to one writer, Nirad C. Chaudhuri, "virtually killed family life." Neither *flânerie* nor *adda* is a purely physical or mental activity; both are reconfigurings of urban space. The flaneur, as Benjamin saw him, walked about the Parisian arcades of the nineteenth century, but as Hannah Arendt pointed out, he did so as if they were an extension of his living-room: he deliberately blurred the line dividing inside from outside. Something similar happened with *adda* in Calcutta in the twentieth century; it either took place in drawing rooms, in such a way as to disrupt domesticity and turn the interior into a sort of public space; or on the *rawak* or porches of houses in cramped lanes, neither inside the home nor in the street. For historical and social reasons, both activities are largely the preserve of the male; there are few female flaneurs and, as Chakrabarty points out, female participation in an *adda* is exceptional.

Benjamin's relationship to the flaneur and his subterranean affirmation of daydreaming in his meditations on *flânerie* lend his work an odd poignancy and ambivalence; given that Benjamin was a Marxist, the flaneur could never be wholly legitimate either outside or inside his work. Some of Chakrabarty's concerns in this book—modernity, *adda*, and the shadow of Benjamin's flaneur—occupy a similarly ambivalent position in relationship to his provenance as a subalternist historian. The subaltern is certainly an interloper in this book (especially in a terrific essay, "Subaltern Pasts, Minority Histories"), but the modern is an equally problematic one: they both challenge the historian, in this case the subalternist historian, with the limits and responsibilities of his discipline. It is the ambiguity of Chakrabarty's own position as both a critic and archivist of modernity that gives his study its poetic undertow and its intelligent irresponsibility.

The East as a Career
On "Strangeness" in Indian Writing

2006, *New Left Review*

1. Legacies of *Orientalism*

At readings by Indian writers in English, two related questions, or some version of them, will invariably be asked by a member of the audience, whatever the setting—bookshop, university seminar or literary festival. The first question is, "Which audience do you write for?"; and the second, "Are you exoticising India for a Western audience?" I'm not entirely sure why people don't tire of asking these questions; but I notice that all kinds are interested in asking them—among others, the type whose reading consists almost entirely of recent fiction, an odd mixture of *The Da Vinci Code*, Pico Iyer, and Vikram Seth; people who read almost nothing but magazines, and whose views on, and affective response to, writers derive not so much from books, but almost entirely from what's circulating about those books and their authors in print; and people in academic disciplines like cultural studies or literature, to whom, especially since the rise of the former, and the latter's surrender to the former's protocols, such questions are bread and butter.

The questions seem to arise from some residue of an idea of a moral custodianship of literature, at a time when no one—neither the reader, nor the person who attends readings because of the free drinks, nor the academic—seems to have a clear or reliable notion of what "literature" is. What is it we're trying to protect when we ask these questions? What is literature, or, for that matter, "Indian writing in English," entities largely created by writers, and apparently so susceptible to being sold and peddled like wares by them?

"Literature," as a category, has, for some time now, lost its integrity and recognisability; and there is no persuasive and intelligent debate, let alone a consensus, on the nature of Indian writing in English. Ever since the politics of representation, rather than the definition of literary practice, became a principal preoccupation of literary departments, many of us have been left with one or two tired moral gestures in lieu of a robust and ongoing discussion of, and enquiry into, what it is we're making those gestures on behalf of. And the politics of representation—for questions about a writer's audience, and his or her use of the "exotic," are political questions—has passed into the common parlance, in the way that more complex ideas from, say, Rousseau or Freud or Marx have in the past been translated into the public sphere, where they're free to be used sometimes as a knee-jerk response to the problematic.

As to the questions above, I think it's safe to say that most people who ask them—whether they're nameless literary buffs, or pillars of society, or teachers or students of literature—think the questions arose within themselves spontaneously as an immediate response to a situation or context; there's an assumption that these questions have no history or source. But surely these questions tell us more about the intellectual formations and compulsions of our time, and about this moment in Indian literary history, than their supposed answers would illuminate us about the impulses that go into the act of writing? The questioner, anyway, is hardly as interested in those impulses—that is, in the answers to the questions (for it's perfectly possible, even plausible, that there are Indian writers who conceive of their projects with something like a "Western readership" in mind; Nirad C. Chaudhuri, embarking on his great autobiography, is an example, and one that at once complicates the issue)—as in stating certain moral parameters for writing and thinking. Where did those particular parameters come from? The questions aren't timeless, but the questioner invests them with the authority of timelessness. And yet, to my knowledge, no one asked Bibhutibhushan Banerjee or Manik Bandyopadhyay whom they wrote for, or if they were "exoticising" rural Bengal for a metropolitan readership.

English, then, is part of the problem; the act of writing in English was, in India, potentially an act of bad faith, and some version of the old suspicion regarding the motives of those who write in English remains and is still at work among us. But the focus in those earlier attacks on Indian writers in English, such as the famous one led by the Bengali critic Buddhadeva Bose, was artistic practice, even if that practice entered the discussion negatively, with a metaphysical fatalism; it was apparently impossible for writers to fully and deeply address their subject except in a language that was their "own." By bringing the audience into the picture, the emphasis and the debate shift from writerly practice to cultural, social, and economic transactions—from the mystery and riddle of the creative act to the dissemination of texts and meanings, by publishers and newspapers, in the academy and in bookshops, from meaning to the production of meaning.

This is where Edward Said comes in; Said who, in a devastatingly effective substitution, replaced "meaning," in the poststructuralist enquiry (still fresh at the time) into its production, with "the Orient." The notion is brought in, almost casually, as an interjection, when Said says that his concern in his study, *Orientalism*, is to examine the "enormously systematic discipline by which European culture was able to manage—and even produce—the Orient." That "and even" shouldn't distract us from the fundamental importance Said and others after him have attached to this notion. In the last few decades, there's been a palpable but often unspoken feeling that the production of the Orient has moved beyond Europe, and Europeans, into the realm of the so-called diaspora, and of Indian writing in English. And the spread of globalisation and the free market coinciding roughly with the advent of the post-Rushdie Indian novel in English returns us to the epigraph from Disraeli in Said's book: "The East is a career." For the production of the Orient involves, implicitly, its consumption; the circle is incomplete without the "audience."

But the concern with this form of "production" has given us not so much a critical eye or sensibility, but a sense of vigilance, and, at a cruder level, a kind of vigilantism; this is where the astringency and aggression of those questions come from. More than a year after Said's death, we can reflect on the legacies of *Orientalism*—the book, not the phenomenon described within it—and say that this particular brand of vigilantism too is one of them. It's the Saidian inheritance that gives those questions their urgency; but since they seem to have no provenance, and little critical content, I'd say they are vulgarised legacies of *Orientalism*, among the many by-products of that great polemic that are both ubiquitous and don't bear close scrutiny. This doesn't prevent those questions from being reiterated, as a constant, irrefutable challenge, and their standpoint from remaining unexamined; vulgarisations permeate language, and become a habit of thinking.

2. The Storyteller

Maybe we could enquire about what sorts of presuppositions these questions—"Which audience do you write for?" and "Are you exoticising your subject for a Western audience?"—are based on. Take the first question first, which accuses, by implication, the Indian writer in English of being removed from his or her "natural" readership: an Indian one. The question relies on utopian ideas which are present everywhere and all the time in the way we think of these matters.

For instance, the "Indian audience" is itself a utopian idea; and, like all utopian fictions, it makes us flushed with emotion, and fills us, according to the situation, with a sense of pride or injustice or protectiveness. Yet it's difficult to construct an ideal readership, waiting to receive or judge new works by writers, in a country in which even the Anglophone urban middle class—a minority—is divided and differentiated by disharmonies of interest: political, social, intellectual, not to speak of pettier reasons for disagreement. Possibly the question arises from an Arcadian vision of Indian history—India as a womb of storytelling and myth, where audience and storyteller or performer are umbilically united. And possibly it comes from a particular view of other cultures, including modern ones, where writers are perceived to write for a bourgeois constituency that also provides them with a "natural" habitat—so that the problem of the audience is seen to be a problem special to the deracinated, dislocated Anglophone Indian (a belief shared by many Anglophone Indians themselves), who has, as it were, stepped out of, or turned against, nature.

Yet the dissonance between audience and writer goes into the heart of modernism, and the modern, itself: not only as a form of elitism, a high-handed, inhumane rejection, by the modernists, of the ordinary person. I mean that the dissonance is written into the text; that it's a profound and complex resource for the writer. For instance, the rift between reader and writer not only surrounds the novel, *Ulysses*, and its reputation; it's a powerful component in the work. We know that the Ulysses-figure in the novel, Leopold Bloom, the petit bourgeois copywriter, is not the kind of man who'd read *Ulysses*, or is exactly the sort who wouldn't. Bloom's reading comprises the trashy magazine, *Titbits*, which he peruses in the lavatory, "seated calm above his own rising smell." Later, as if it were a modernist "readymade" that had unsuspected uses, he turns it to toilet paper: "He tore away half the prize story sharply and wiped himself with it." A great gap, in terms of writer and audience, divides Joyce from Bloom. Stylistically, artistically, Joyce, in writing his novel, had no intention of closing that gap, but only of widening it; but imaginatively, he needed to make the journey toward Bloom so that his novel might move outward into the world from the circumference of Stephen's persona, and onward from the *Portrait*. In writing it, Joyce defines no clear-cut, consoling relationship to his audience; the novel is built upon a paradox, upon both the necessary embracing and the necessary rejection of Bloom by his creator.

Let me cite another instance of this dissonance, this time in a story from a vernacular Indian literature, where (so the person who asks the Indian English writer the question about the audience implies) author and reader are at one in prelapsarian harmony. The story is "Suryana Kudure," or, in A. K. Ramanujan and Manu Shetty's translation, "A Horse for the Sun," by the Kannada writer U. R. Ananthamurthy, whom I very much admire, but whose public pronouncements have got him into a sort of critical rut. These pronouncements largely consist of repeated airings of the belief that the vernacular or "*bhasha*" writer has an immediate and organic access to his readership and community that the Anglophone Indian writer doesn't and, really, can't. Yet his own finest work tells us something quite different about the location of the modern Kannada writer, and the tensions latent in the latter's relationship to his or her readership. In "A Horse for the Sun," the narrator, a person very like the author, even down to his name, "Anantha," a city-dwelling intellectual, a disillusioned Marxist, returns briefly to his village, and, accidentally, runs into a childhood friend, Venkata—a bit of a clown, a buffoon, a person who hasn't moved on or achieved anything; by Anantha's social and moral standards, a failure.

Anantha is disappointed in, even repelled by, his old friend; but, oddly, he's also attracted to his air of sensuousness and freedom, his apparent unburdenedness. Venkata's domestic life is a mess; but he embodies an elemental, physical joy. Later in the day, in his house, he tells a reluctant and tired Anantha that he'll administer him a head-massage; while doing so, he launches into a near-meaningless, extraordinary soliloquy. Newsprint and faeces mingle with one another in Bloom's toilet; in Venkata's bath, Anantha's various tortured cerebral speculations dissolve into Venkata's rapturous preverbal utterance and the body's sensations. Venkata is the story's subject, but, as Anantha knows, he will not be its reader; and it's precisely the physical closeness and intellectual disconnectedness that Anantha feels toward Venkata that impels and shapes the story, that gives its sense of thwarted desire and its calamitous ending. Ananthamurthy, the spokesman and propagandist for Kannada literature, and flagellant of Indian English writing, believes the "bhasha" writer belongs to an organic community; the vision of Ananthamurthy, the artist, arises compellingly from the conviction that no organic community is possible.

No writer has a given and recognisable audience, except, perhaps, in our fabular reconstructions of antiquity or medieval history. A writer, sooner or later, has to come to terms with this, in a much more painful and thoroughgoing way than the questioner in the audience will understand. The reader too needs to come terms with it, if they are to have more than a passing interest in what literature does; for the writer not only speaks to the reader, but interrogates the unbridgeable gap between themselves. Any theory of reading that doesn't take this into account will leave itself open to question. Benedict Anderson's narrative of nations coming into being through "imagined communities" of readers is, for instance, yet another utopian conflation of nationality with readership, which never incorporates, into its study, the notion that discontinuities are as important to the formation of the modern imagination as collectivities. It's not only the reader who takes the decision of rejecting or accepting a writer; the writer, too, depending on what his objective is at that moment, and how he means to achieve it, gives himself to, or withholds himself from, the reader.

3. Life Itself

What does the "exotic" in "Are you exoticising your subject for a Western audience?"—a question asked indefatigably of Indians who write in English—what does the word mean, or in which sense is it meant?

Dictionaries will give you a range of meanings, such as "foreign"—where "foreign" is usually "tropical"—and "strange" and even "bizarre." But the dictionaries' interpretations are almost entirely positive; the exotic has to do with a certain kind of allure, the allure of the strange and faraway. They still haven't taken into account the post-Saidian registers of the word, by which it has become a habitual term with which to count the spiritual costs of colonialism: "inauthentic" and "falsified" are still not options among their list of meanings. The word's stock had never been very high, but its reputation has declined in the way the reputation of "picturesque" had earlier; although the latter never transcended its status of being a minor aesthetic term into becoming the populist catchphrase that the former has become.

Said, of course, feels compelled to use the word in the first page of *Orientalism*, where he notes that a French journalist, on "a visit to Beirut during the terrible civil war of 1975–1976 . . . wrote regretfully of the gutted downtown area that 'it had once seemed to belong to the Orient of Chauteaubriand and Nerval.'" For the European, for the French journalist, to mourn the demise of this Orient was almost natural, for, as Said goes on to say, this Orient "was almost a European invention, and had been since antiquity a place of romance, exotic beings, haunting memories and landscapes . . . Now it was disappearing"—in the Middle East, especially, as the French journalist saw it, into the tragic mess of contemporary history. In a salutary reminder, characteristic of Said both in his study and his political work, the reader is told of the simple but, till then, often ignored, irony of the fact that the Orient was also a real place, even in the time Chauteaubriand and Nerval; that, even then, "Orientals had lived there, and that now it was they who were suffering"; however, "the main thing for the European visitor was a European representation of the Orient and its contemporary fate . . ."

Characteristic, too, of Said in much of his literary critical work (his political writings and activism are almost a compensation for this), is, as he fleetingly admits himself, his own study's turning away from the

Oriental, except in his or her itinerary in European texts, and from the Oriental representation of the Orient. This—the Orient's representation of itself—is presumably what the "almost" in "the Orient was almost a European invention" refers to, and also suppresses; that the Orient, in modernity, is not only an European invention, but also an Oriental one, an invention that has presumably created and occupied an intellectual, cultural, and political space far larger and more important than its European counterpart. The book about the Oriental invention—and I mean that word in both senses, as "creative" and "spurious" production—of the Orient is still to be written; for now, we have to be content with that "almost." Dipesh Chakrabarty, in his *Provincializing Europe*, wryly observes that a literary commentator, while describing the provenances of *Midnight's Children*, its mixture of "Western" and "Eastern" elements, makes specific references to what she considers the Western resources of Rushdie's novel (*The Tin Drum*, *Tristram Shandy* etc.), but refers to the Eastern ones only in blurred and general categories: "Indian legends, films and literature." Chakrabarty gives this sort of critical viewpoint a hilarious definition: "asymmetric ignorance." While one should hesitate before ascribing to Said an ignorance of modern Oriental cultural traditions, that "almost" in his sentence certainly constitutes an asymmetry—an asymmetry whose logic he pursues implicitly but quite relentlessly in his study.

What does this asymmetry mean to our understanding—our specifically Said-inflected understanding—of the "exotic"? In the sense that we use the term today, the "exotic" doesn't just mean "foreign," but a commodification of the foreign: an intrinsic part of the "production" of the East that Orientalism entails, and which is, crucially, made possible by the spread of capitalism and of markets. When the person in the audience asks the Indian writer in English about exoticisation, he means to say that the writer is a sort of deracinated Oriental who, in an act of betrayal, has become involved in the production of the Orient. We've inherited the Saidian asymmetry along with the Saidian critique;

it leads us to believe that Oriental and, for our purposes, Indian history was a bucolic zone untouched by the market until, probably, the Indian novelist in English came along; that the Orient has been in a state of nature in the last two hundred years, translated into the realm of production and consumption only by Western writers and entrepreneurs. And in this way, we exoticise exocitisation itself, making it impossibly foreign to, and distant from, ourselves.

A glance at the cultural history of our modernity, however, tells us that we've been "producing" the Orient, and exoticising it, for a very long time; that the exotic has been a necessary, perhaps indispensable, constituent of our self-expression and political identity, as given voice to in popular culture, in calendar prints, oleographs, the "mythologicals" of early Hindi cinema, as well as the lavish visions of Indian history in the latter—these are the signatures of the cultural and political world of the anonymous; a "production" of the East more challenging or significant than anything the word "Orientalism" can hope to encapsulate, and part of whose inheritance, as seen in the core of kitsch in the BJP's version of Hindutva, is ambiguous. So persuasive is this production and its peculiar language that outsiders, and even Indians, often see it—say, in its incarnation as the genre today called, inexactly, "Bollywood" cinema—as essentially or even immemorially Indian, not realising that these forms emerge at a crux and juncture in the nineteenth and early twentieth centuries when religion and tradition begin to respond to the incursion of capital; that the forms are quite different from the highly impersonal, stylised variations of folk art prior to capitalism; and that they make, for the first time, the notion of "bad taste" a powerful contender in Indian cultural life.

A certain sort of middle-class flirtation with the exotic goes back to the formation of our modernity: in some of the paintings of, say, Abanindranath Tagore, or especially those of Ravi Varma. This particular strain of exoticism, which appears in the late nineteenth century, is marked, really, by an appropriation of realism, of photographic and naturalistic detail; a commodification of the native, in the case of Ravi Varma, in the terms of Western, sometimes pre-Raphaelite utopias, each mythic scene depicted the outcome of both mental and actual journeys made between India and Europe, in particular, Germany (Varma set up his printing press outside Bombay in collaboration with German print-technicians). This new utopian naturalism distinguishes Varma's (and others') vivid exotica from the Kalighat *pats* and oils of the early decades of the nineteenth century, which, with their combination of stylised figures in the folk style and their greedy assimilation of elements of the colonial world (hairstyles, attires), represent a vital, mischievous, and self-critical pupal phase in modern popular culture, and especially in the local artist's early response to capital; a genuine deflection of the exotic through the sensuousness of the line itself. But, of course, the Indian production of the exotic also later becomes important—far more so than its Western counterpart—to canonical artists like the filmmaker Satyajit Ray as something they define their art, even their very sense of the "real," against: what's stifling to the young apprentice director in 1948, in an essay called "What is Wrong with Indian Films," is not his burden as a postcolonial, but his burden as a modern—the presence, on all sides, of a powerful home-grown "exotic" in cinema, a descendant, in the moving image, of Varma's utopian realism*; what Ray calls elsewhere the "mythologicals and devotionals" that "provide the staple fare for the majority of Bengal's film public."

This "production" of the East in cinema has already quite a long history in India, he notes dourly in 1948: "Meanwhile, 'studios sprang up,' to quote an American writer in *Screenwriter*, 'even in such unlikely lands as India and China.' One may note in passing that this springing up has been happening in India for nearly forty years." The call to turn

*I mean to imply, by this term, a mixture of an openness to markets and a fidelity to the conventions of Western art that's quite different from the partly ironical and belligerently playful intentions of "magic realism" in post modernity.

away from this home-grown production is quasi-religious, Vivekananda-like: "The raw material of the cinema is life itself. It is incredible that a country which has inspired so much painting and music and poetry should fail to move the filmmaker. He has only to keep his eyes open, and his ears."

"Life itself": this brings us to the second part of what's so problematic about the recent history of the term "exotic" in our country. When Ray speaks of "life" and the "raw material" of life, he's speaking of a refutation of the spectacular that comprises the exotic, in favour of the mundane, the everyday, and the transfiguration of the mundane. "Life," "the everyday," "reality" or "*vastav*," rather than "reality" as "*satya*," with its connotation of spiritual "truth": all these are invented by the modernist bourgeois Indian imagination in the nineteenth century as categories inextricable from "Indianness"; and then the "real" is transfigured by the artist in the new, secular domain of culture emerging at the time. The crucial role of the transfiguration leads, in the forties, to Ray's directive to the filmmaker to "keep his eyes open, and his ears": the words not only echo Vivekananda, but Tagore, who, in a song invoking the givens of nature—light, air, grass—says, "kaan petechhi, / chokh melechhi"; "I have kept my ear peeled, / I have gazed upon." The act of "seeing," or "recognising" the "real," once it has emerged, becomes a secular act full of spiritual urgency, sacred and yet displaced from and mostly unconnected to religious topoi, antithetical in its own eyes, importantly, to the equally vital project of commodifying and "producing" the local.

That transfiguration involves a making foreign or strange the "raw material" of the commonplace; a process that is, indeed, for artists like Ray, a critique of the "strangeness" of the "mythologicals," of popular culture, of the exotic. Tagore defines it at the conclusion of the same song: "janaar majhe ajaanare korechhi sandhaan"; "I've searched for the unknown / in the midst of the known." The "raw material" of estrangement, for the modern artist, is *not* the extraordinary, but as much light, grass, air as it is the dross that surrounds us: verandahs, advertisement hoardings, waiting-rooms, pincushions, paperweights.

All these, in a process both elusive and fundamental to art, are made new and distant—but, in India, critical language, especially in English, has for some time lacked a vocabulary with which to engage with this transformation and its contexts and questions. Even much of the bafflement that attended Ray's early and middle work in India, and the complaint that he lacked political content, has probably something to do with the inability to understand the defamiliarised in art.

4. On Strangeness

It's the matter of strangeness in art—what Viktor Shklovsky called, almost a century ago, "defamiliarisation"—that brings me to the late Arun Kolatkar, and to a short and unique book, called *Jejuri: Commentary and Critical Perspectives*, edited and, in part, written by Shubhangi Raykar. *Jejuri* is Kolatkar's famous sequence of poems which was published in 1976, and won the Commonwealth Poetry Prize the following year. It mainly comprises a series of short lyric utterances and observations through which a narrative unfolds—about a man, clearly not religious, but clearly, despite himself, interested in his surroundings, who arrives on a bus at the eponymous pilgrimage-town in Maharashtra where the deity Khandoba is worshipped, wanders about its ruined temples and parallel economy of priests and touts, and then leaves on a train. In some ways, the sequence resembles Philip Larkin's "Church Going"; except that, where Larkin's distant, sceptical, bicycle-clipped visitor "surprises" in himself a "hunger to be more serious" inside the church, the hunger to be more curious is characteristic of Kolatkar's peripatetic narrator.

Kolatkar was a bilingual poet who wrote in both Marathi and English; in Marathi, his oeuvre is shaped by a combination of epic, devotional, and weird science-fiction and dystopian impulses. In English,

Kolatkar's impetus and ambition are somewhat different: it's to create a vernacular with which to express, with a febrile amusement, a sort of urbane wonder at the unfinished, the provisional, the random, the shabby, the not-always-respectable but arresting ruptures in our moments of recreation, work, and, as in *Jejuri*, even pilgrimage. Kolatkar was, in the fledgling tradition of Indian writing in English, the first writer to devote himself utterly to the transformation and defamiliarisation of the commonplace; given that Indian writing in English has, in the last twenty years or so, largely taken its inspiration from the social sciences and postcolonial history, that avenue opened up by Kolatkar has hardly been noticed, let alone explored, by very many contemporary writers. By "defamiliarisation" I mean more than the device it was for Shklovsky; I mean the peculiar relationship art and language have to what we call "life," or "reality." "Realism" is too inexact, loaded, and general a term to suggest the gradations of this process, this relationship, and its perpetual capacity to surprise and disorient the reader. In India, where, ever since Said's *Orientalism*, the "exotic" has been at the centre of almost every discussion, serious or frivolous, on Indian writing in English, the aesthetics of estrangement, of foreignness, in art have been reduced to, and confused with, the politics of cultural representation. And so, the notion of the exotic is used by lay reader and critic alike to demolish, in one blow, both the perceived act of bad faith and the workings of the unfamiliar.

Kolatkar died last year, and his death means he's safely passed into the minor canonical status that India reserves for a handful of dead poets who wrote in English. But the present consensus about him shouldn't obscure the fact that his estranging eye in his English work has been problematic to Indian readers. Shubhangi Raykar's commentary was published in 1995 with, she says, "the modest aim of helping the undergraduate and graduate students in our universities." Her book is, of course, indispensable to any reader not wholly familiar with the references to various myths and legends, especially those to do with the deity Khandoba, that recur in the poem. But there's another difficulty, one to do with reading, that Raykar draws our attention to:

> Yet another aspect of *Jejuri* is that it is a poem that can be fully understood and enjoyed only when the reader is able to "see" it. *Jejuri* is, thus, a peculiarly visual poem. Repeated references to colour, shapes, sizes, textures of objects and many other details . . . are outstanding aspects of *Jejuri*. And yet these very aspects bewilder the students.

Among the "critical perspectives" included in Raykar's book is the Marathi critic Bhalchandra Nemade's essay, "Excerpts from Against Writing in English—An Indian Point of View," originally published in 1985 in *New Quest*, a journal of ideas published from Pune descended from the influential *Quest*, which itself was modelled on *Encounter*. Nemade's opening paragraphs are fortified by a range of allusions to linguistic theory; but the nationalistic tenor of the essay doesn't demand too much sophistication or imagination from the reader: "A foreign language thus suppresses the natural originality of Indian writers in English, enforcing upon the whole tribe the fine art of parrotry." The typo-ridden text has "ant" for "art," and the juxtaposition of "tribe," "ant," and "parrot" gives both the sentence and its subject matter an odd anthropological texture. Unlike the Bengali writer and critic Buddhadeva Bose, who worried that the Indian writer in English would have nothing either worthwhile or authentic to say, Nemade is as interested in the realm of consumption, in the possibility of the East being a career (to adapt Disraeli's epigraph to Edward Said's great polemic), as he is in the validity of the creative act itself: "An Indo-Anglian writer looks upon his society only for supply of raw material to English i.e. foreign readership." He mentions three instances of what, for him, are acts of "aesthetic and ethical" betrayal: Nirad C. Chaudhuri's *The Autobiography of an Unknown Indian*, Narayan's *The Guide*, and Kolatkar's *Jejuri*. And the now-familiar question, still relatively fresh in 1985, is asked and sardonically answered: "What kind of audience do these writers keep in mind while writing? Certainly not the millions of Indians who are 'unknown' who visit Jejuri every year as a traditional ritual . . ."

Here is the mirage of the organic community that so haunts our vernacular writers—the idea that those who write in their mother tongue are joined to their readers in Edenic harmony; anyhow, Nemade doesn't ask himself if the readership of *New Quest* is an extension of, or an interruption in, that community. Kolatkar's poem he classifies as a form of "cynical agnosticism" and "philistinism." Quoting one of the most beautiful lines in the sequence, "Scratch a rock and a legend springs," where the narrator is noting, with evident detachment, the incorrigible way in which the apparently barren landscape generates mythology, Nemade says "he writes with little sympathy for the poor pilgrims, beggars, priests and their quite happy children at Jejuri"; instead, "Kolatkar comes and goes like a weekend tourist from Bombay." Nemade's a distinguished critic and writer, but this isn't a particularly distinguished offering. Yet it's interesting because of its rhetoric, in the way, for instance, it uses the word "tourist," to create a characteristic confusion between estrangement as a literary effect, and the threat of the "foreign," with its resonances of colonial history. The aesthetics of wonder is inserted into, and enmeshed with, a politics that is partly nationalistic, partly xenophobic.

That interpreting the operations of the random or the unfamiliar in the work of the Indian writer in English is a problem beyond malice or wrong-headedness becomes clear when we look at Raykar's notes, which give us both sensitive close readings of the poems and a great deal of enlightening information about the local references and terrain. Yet, Raykar, who is obviously an admirer of Kolatkar's, seems oddly closed to the experience of estrangement. In fact, estrangement becomes, once more, a form of cultural distance, and the notes a narrative about alienation; a narrative, indeed, of semi-articulate but deep undecidedness and uncertainty about what constitutes, in language, poetic wonder, citizenship, nationhood, and in what ways these categories are in tension with one another. Examples abound, but I'll give only two. The first concerns her note to "The Doorstep," a poem short enough to quote in its entirety:

> That's no doorstep.
> It's a pillar on its side.
>
> Yes.
> That's what it is.

For Raykar, these lines betray a "gap between the world of the protagonist and the world of the devotees." For "a traditional devotee," she says, "every object in the temple exists at two levels. One is the material level which the protagonist can see and share with the devotees. The other level transforms a mundane object into a religious, spiritually informed object." Raykar points out that this "level is not at all accessible to the protagonist." But surely there's a third level in the poem, in which a significance is ascribed to the mundane, the superfluous, that can't be pinned down to religious belief; and it's this level that Raykar herself finds inaccessible, or refuses, for the moment, to participate in.

My second example is her note on "Heart of Ruin," the poem that precedes "The Doorstep" in Kolatkar's sequence. As Raykar tells us—and this is the sort of information that makes her book so useful, and, since it's one of a kind, indispensable—the poem is "a detailed description of the then dilapidated temple of Maruti at Karhe Pathar." From the first lines onward, Kolatkar gives us a portrait of a casual but passionate state of disrepair: "The roof comes down on Maruti's head. / Nobody seems to mind. / . . . least of all Maruti himself." This is how Kolatkar catalogues the dishevelled energy of the scene, as well as his bemused discovery of it:

A mongrel bitch has found a place
for herself and her puppies

in the heart of the ruin.
May be she likes a temple better this way.

The bitch looks at you guardedly
Past a doorway cluttered with broken tiles.

The pariah puppies tumble over her.
May be they like a temple better this way.

The black eared puppy has gone a little too far.
A tile clicks under its foot.

It's enough to strike terror in the heart
of a dung beetle

and send him running for cover
to the safety of the broken collection box

that never did get a chance to get out
from under the crushing weight of the roof beam.

Morosely, the narrator concludes—and Kolatkar's abstemiousness with commas serves him well in a sentence in which the second half is neither a logical extension nor a contradiction of the first—"No more a place of worship this place / is nothing less than the house of god."

Raykar's gloss, again, translates Kolatkar's laconic, estranging sensibility into the neocolonial, or at least the deracinated, gaze: "To a visitor with an urbanised, westernised sensibility it is always an irritating paradox that the almighty god's house . . . should be in such a sorry state of disrepair... Hence the ironic, sardonic tone." I think Raykar's and Nemade's response to the superfluous and random particular in *Jejuri* (comparable, in some ways, to the impatience Satyajit Ray's contemporaries felt with the everyday in his films) is symptomatic, rather than atypical, of a certain kind of postindependence critical position, which obdurately conflates the defamiliarisation of the ordinary with the commodification of the native. With the enlargement of the discourse of postcoloniality in the last two decades, the critical language with which to deal with defamiliarisation has grown increasingly attenuated, while the language describing the trajectory of the East as a career has become so ubiquitous that, confronted with a seemingly mundane but irreducible particular in a text, the reader or the member of the audience will almost automatically ask: "Are you exoticising your subject for Western readers?"

The two poems by Kolatkar I've quoted from, as well as Nemade's criticisms, remind me of a short but intriguing essay by the social scientist Partha Chatterjee, called "The Sacred Circulation of National Images," and I'd like to end by dwelling on it briefly. Chatterjee is puzzled and engrossed by what has happened to these "national images"—for instance, the Taj Mahal; Shah Jahan's Red Fort—as they've been represented in our textbooks in the last forty or fifty years: that is, in our relatively brief, but palpably long, history as a republic. He discovers that early photographs and engravings found in textbooks dating back, say, to the twenties, are gradually replaced in textbooks after 1947 by a certain kind of line drawing. He finds no economic *raison d'être* for this change: "Are they cheaper to print? Not really; both are printed from zinc blocks made by the same photographic process." But the more telling change occurs in the nature of the representations themselves, as the pictures of certain monuments are transformed into "national icons." The earlier pictures and photos, Chatterjee finds, have an element of the random in their composition—an engraving of the Taj Mahal has a nameless itinerant before it; an early photograph shows a scattering of "native" visitors before the same building; early pictures of the Red Fort or the *ghats* in Benaras have the same sort of "redundant" detail—a group of men, a dog—in the foreground.

As these monuments are turned into "national icons" in post-Independence history textbooks, the pictures are emptied of signs of randomness, emptied, indeed, of all but the monument itself, and a new credo and economy of representation comes into existence: "There must be no hint of the picturesque or the painterly, no tricks of the camera angle, no staging of the unexpected or the exotic. The image must also be shorn of all redundancy..." We all know what Chatterjee is talking about from our own memories of the textbooks we studied as children, from the functional but implicitly absolute representation of monuments they contained. Although the impetus behind the "emptying" of the textbook image seems partly Platonic—a nostalgia for the ideal likeness, unvitiated by reality's unpredictability—Chatterjee places it in the context of the Indian nation-state, identifying it as the process by which national monuments are turned to "sacred" images.

It seems to me that both Nemade's and Raykar's literary responses to *Jejuri* are, with different degrees of intensity (and, in Nemade's case, belligerence), really part of a larger discussion of what constitutes nationality and the nation-state; that the sacredness they invest in and are anxious to protect in Jejuri is less the sacredness of Khandoba and of religion, and more that of an absolute idea, or ideal, of the nation. Kolatkar's doorstep, his broken pillars, roofs, and beams, his mongrel puppy and dung beetle, violate that idea and its space, as I think they're meant to, just as much as the itinerant or animal the anonymous engraver introduced into his representation was at once accidental and intentional. Defamiliarisation not only renovates our perception of familiar territory; it dislocates and reframes our relationship of possessiveness to that territory in ways that the discussion on nationality, on what is authentic and what foreign, what's exotic and what native, not only cannot, but actually suppresses. For Kolatkar, the break that the superfluous brings about in the telos of Nemade's and Raykar's unstated but undeniable national narrative is a small ecstasy; for Raykar, and Nemade especially, a source of puzzlement and unease.

Women in Love as Post-Human Essay

2006, introduction to the Penguin Classics edition

I WAS IN MY FINAL YEAR at University College London in 1985, when my tutor, the South African novelist Dan Jacobson, told me that I'd read a great deal of poetry but not enough prose. He asked me to read four novels, the earliest of which was *Moll Flanders*, the most recent *Sons and Lovers*. I remember reading the Lawrence in my studio apartment on Warren Street, my days lit by the glow of the fires in the pit, my unremarkable room overlooking the street changed by the smell of Mrs. Morel's ironing. Afterwards, I felt I'd made a discovery; not so much as a student, but as a reader and a writer-aspirant groping for his true subject.

At twenty-three, I was in awe of the modernists, especially Eliot. A very different sort of poet preoccupied me as well: Philip Larkin. What must have drawn me to them, as a young man ill-at-ease in England, in the Bombay he'd left behind, and even in the early 1980s, was, I think, their nostalgia for and sense of loss in relation to certain utopian sites of culture—Europe, antiquity, middle England. Their political conservatism (which I innocently thought of in purely aesthetic terms), where the urge to preserve and cherish, as well as to exclude, informed even the experiments in language and tone they undertook, must have also appealed to me; as did their transcendental longing for an elsewhere, a hereafter, a longing which, I think, permeates Larkin's work despite his rejection, in "Aubade," of the notion of an afterlife, and of religion as a "vast, moth-eaten brocade."

What I found in the writer who had composed *Sons and Lovers* was an extraordinary refutation of this anguished longing, an anguish I'd thought I must at least vicariously make my own. On several levels, it opened my eyes to my own temperament as a writer, and even (though I use the term with the utmost wariness) as an "Indian." It wasn't the Oedipal paradigm in the novel which interested me; it was its profound rejection of tragedy (which my own creativity, too, was turning away from in order to discover itself), a rejection which I sensed was (though I dared not say it of this most "English" of novels) fundamentally non-Western. Already, in this great, early work, Lawrence is delineating, in the most immediate imaginative terms possible, a refutation and, at once, a celebration whose nature he'd describe not long before his death in *Apocalypse*, and which was to mark him out from his modernist contemporaries: "Whatever the unborn and the dead may know, they cannot know the beauty, the marvel of being alive in the flesh. The dead may look after the afterwards. But the magnificent here and now of the flesh is ours, and ours alone, and ours only for a time." This isn't just a Dylan Thomas-like statement about the heroic poignancy of carnality; "life," for Lawrence, is a complex and loaded word, denoting neither a continuity, nor a spontaneous occurrence, but a historical crisis, a break between the old and new, and between cultures. It is part of his polemic against European humanism and its metaphysics, as the "here and now" too is; but to see how Lawrence's ideology, his anti-metaphysic, is also an aesthetic, we must turn to his poetic manifesto, "Poetry of the Present," where the religiose "unborn and the dead" of *Apocalypse* is translated into literary terms—"the perfected, crystalline poetry of the past and the future"—from which the "poetry of the moment," the "here and now" (the poetry Lawrence believes he's written), constitutes a radical departure. In *Sons and Lovers*, that break has begun to be effected; the "magnificent here and now" is vividly present in the novel, but it already has an unprecedented revolutionary sharpness (in this, the least strident of his works) quite different from the "here and now" invoked by his famous modernist contemporaries.

This becomes clear when we read the essay on poetry which became Lawrence's introduction to his *New Poems* (1918), written, it seems, around the time he was completing *Women in Love*. And what Lawrence is working towards in the novel, in terms of formal and spiritual ambition, informs his discussion of poetry; "poetry," which becomes a metaphor for Western literature in general, and for the "classics" of English literary tradition:

> The poetry of the beginning and the poetry of the end must have that exquisite finality, perfection which belongs to all that is far off. It is in the realm of all that is perfect. It is of the nature of all that is complete and consummate. This completeness, this consummateness, the finality and the perfection are conveyed in exquisite form... Perfected bygone moments, perfected moments in the glimmering futurity, these are the treasured gem-like lyrics of Shelley and Keats.

Against this, Lawrence posits an aesthetic which relinquishes "perfection" and "exquisite form"—relinquishes, in a sense, both *Sons and Lovers*, which possessed these qualities, as well as the canonical definition of what comprises a "work of art."

> But there is another kind of poetry: the poetry of that which is at hand: the immediate present. In the immediate present there is no perfection, no consummation, nothing finished. The strands are all flying, quivering, intermingling into the web, the waters are shaking the moon. There is no round, consummate moon on the face of the running water, nor on the face of the unfinished tide... There is no plasmic finality, nothing crystal,

permanent. If we try to fix the living tissue, as the biologists fix it with formalin, we have only a hardened bit of the past, the bygone life under our observation.

At first glance, this might seem like a somewhat febrile, overwritten version of the Joycean "epiphany," or any of those modernist preoccupations that trace their history to the Romantic "privileged moment," the Wordsworthian "spot of time," in which an extraordinary, transformative experience is made available to the artist. Another look at Lawrence's essay tells us, however, that he's speaking of something that lacks the repose and self-containedness of Wordsworth's "emotion recollected in tranquillity" or Pound's "emotional and intellectual complex in a moment of time," or the elevated status (Joyce is careful to introduce an element of the sacred with his choice of term: "epiphany") that the Romantic or modernist moment has. The latter renovates the banality of the present by opening it, almost randomly, and yet fortuitously, onto the past; thus Proust's narrator, tasting the "petite madeleines," ceases to feel "mediocre, contingent, mortal," and is transported to a realm where he has "infinitely transcended those savours" of "the tea and the cake," although he's still unsure of what that realm might be. Lawrence's moment deliberately claims its "difference" from this poetic rehabilitation of the world through an instant in time: he rejects Proust when he rejects the "hardened bit of the past, the bygone life under our observation," and when, in the same essay, he says: "Don't give me the infinite or the eternal: nothing of infinity, nothing of eternity. Give me the still, white seething . . . the moment, the quick of all change and haste and opposition: the moment, the immediate present, the Now." Lawrence is struggling to take the Romantic/modernist moment out of its canonical, humanist lineage; and the overwriting in these passages is at once a sign of that struggle, as well as a gesture towards the radical incompatibility of that Lawrentian "here and now" in the English canon. (This incompatibility is something I'll continue to return to, later, in this introduction.) Much of the imagery in the extracts I've quoted above is, as it happens, common to the language he's fashioning in *Women in Love* at that time to deal with his preoccupations; the face of the "quivering" moon upon the water also appears in the strange, coded dreamscape in the famous "Moony" chapter in *the novel.*

•

After the relative tentativeness of his first two novels, Lawrence discovered a remarkable visual style in *Sons and Lovers*, only to muddy it (I use the word advisedly, for "mud" is an integral Lawrentian trope in the assault upon transparency and clarity that became so important to him) in the next two novels, *The Rainbow* and *Women in Love*. "I shan't write in the same manner as *Sons and Lovers* again," he said in the famous letter to Edward Garnett. And in another letter to Garnett defending his new style:

> I have no longer the joy in creating vivid scenes, that I had in *Sons and Lovers*. I don't care much more about accumulating objects in the powerful light of emotion, and making a scene of them. I have to write differently.

One shouldn't underestimate, in spite of this, the break that *Sons and Lovers* itself represents, nor ignore the continuities the novels he wrote after it, and the rhetoric he'd develop about "art" and "life" in his later writings, have with that early work. What's fascinating, though, is Lawrence's sense that the novel is an artistic moment he must leave behind, and what this departure, this apparent severance of ties, this dissolution might comprise. Certainly, one might say that, with *Sons and Lovers*, Lawrence had grown into some of the key aspects of modernism—to do with language and its mediation and renovation of reality, in a style quite unlike his precursors or even contemporaries like Arnold Bennett, but in many ways consonant, in the novel's response to sensory perception, and its use, especially, of the image, with the modernist project. One of the characteristics of modernism is that it doesn't simply take "reality" as a fact or a given to be reported upon, as naturalism does, but as a potential transmitter of value to the self, or the subconscious. This value is not obvious or visible, but, in many ways, has to be recovered or "created" by the artist. It's a transaction that has its origins in Romanticism, of course, but which modernism relocates from the natural world to the bourgeois city. The value in question is residually, but indisputably, religious, although, since the "spot of time" is secular, its religious provenance must remain at once hidden and palpable. This contradiction marks the oxymoron with which Wordsworth describes the quality of the "spot of time" in *The Prelude*: "visionary dreariness." Proust makes apparent the simultaneous suppression and indispensability of religious wonder in modernist sense-perception in his metaphorical construction of a scene in which the narrator stops at a hawthorn-hedge:

> I found the whole path throbbing with the fragrance of hawthorn blossom. The hedge resembled a series of chapels, whose walls were no longer visible under the mountain of flowers that were heaped upon their altars; while beneath them the sun cast a checkered light upon the ground, as though it had just passed through a stained-glass window; and their scent swept over me . . . as though I had been standing before the Lady-altar, and the flowers . . . held out each its bunch of glittering stamens . . . in the flamboyant style like those which, in the church, framed the stairway to the rood-loft . . . How simple and rustic by comparison would seem the dog-roses which in a few weeks' time would be climbing the same path in the heat of the sun, dressed in the smooth silk of their blushing pink bodices that dissolve in the first breath of wind.

As a midpoint and phase of transition between English naturalism and modernist suggestion, *Sons and Lovers* is an extraordinary example. Take the passage below, which struck me even the first time I read it, and which is startlingly reminiscent, in its deliberate evasions and in the way in which it insinuates a sense of wonder, of the one I've quoted from Proust; here, the pregnant Mrs. Morel has been locked out of her house at night by her drunken husband; wandering about, she's exhausted and angry but constantly distracted by the world around her:

> Languidly she looked about her; the clumps of white phlox seemed like bushes spread with linen; a moth ricochetted over them, and right across the garden. Following it with her eye roused her. A few whiffs of the raw, strong scent of phlox invigorated her. She passed along the path, hesitating at the white rose-bush. It smelled sweet and simple. She touched the white ruffles of the roses. Their fresh scent and cool, soft leaves reminded her of the morning-time and sunshine.

Here are the wholly unexpected, but, once made, supremely apposite associations between physical outline and memory, combined with the strategic, irrelevant detail—"the clumps of white phlox . . . like bushes spread with linen; a moth ricochetted over them"—that are characteristic of modernism's off-kilter transaction between language, reality, and the subconscious (the metaphor of clothing and domesticity—"linen," "ruffles"—taking us back to Proust's "silk" and "blushing pink bodices"). The association is sometimes stated, as in the "cool, soft leaves" reminding Mrs. Morel of the "morning-time and sunshine," but not explained, as it would be in a metaphor or simile. But sometimes it is suppressed, as in the observation about the rose-bush (which again recalls, but also extends further, Proust's "simple and rustic" dog-roses): "It smelled sweet and simple." These adjectives struck me when I was an undergraduate: "sweet," yes, but in what way "simple"? How could a smell be "simple"? Proust, the pioneer of the olfactory in modern literature, was referring, after all, to a thing and not a smell when he used the word. Something had been suppressed, and "simple" was anything but simple; it was an ambiguity. Lawrence, then, had learnt the same lessons the modernists had, and learnt them exceptionally well: of control over the conflicting registers of language and memory, over expression and concealment. With *The Rainbow*, and especially *Women in Love*, he loosened, for some reason, that control, and muddied (a very different project from making ambiguous) his language. Why he should have done so, and with conscious, intellectual, and spiritual intent, remains intriguing and significant, and distinguishes him further from the other major practitioners of the time.

Like certain other writers, Lawrence believed he was living during a time of crisis and unprecedented historical change, a change that has a peculiar charge in Lawrence's work because it's made available to us not only in spite of, but in, the element of the banal in the lives of, say, Birkin, Ursula, Gudrun, Gerald, and Hermione in *Women In Love*; in the flirtations, arguments, conversations, confessions of love, teas, parties, and visits to country houses. What emerges from our reading of this novel is a sense of two seemingly conflicting impulses explored simultaneously: on the one hand, an absolute commitment on the author's part to his characters, and, therefore, an unspoken taking for granted of the humanist basis from which the idea of "characterisation" emanates; on the other, the impulse to make the crisis of the human a condition for the conception and the inner life of the work. There was, of course, the personal crisis: *The Rainbow* had been banned because of obscenity, and for four years Lawrence worked on his next novel without being assured of a publisher or an audience. Then there was the war, which Lawrence, with his relentlessly inverted diagnostic analyses, his constant, almost compulsive, redefinitions of what was the disease and what the cure, would probably have seen as one of the symptoms of a crisis rather than a crisis itself. As he says in a foreword he wrote later for *Women in Love*:

> It is a novel which took its final shape in the midst of the period of war, though it does not concern the war itself. I should wish the time to remain

> unfixed, so that the bitterness of the war may be taken for granted in the characters.

That "crisis," nevertheless, was on his mind in regard to the novel Lawrence makes clear in the penultimate paragraph; though here, too, he allows its historical provenance and features to remain "unfixed":

> We are now in a period of crisis. Every man who is acutely alive is acutely wrestling with his own soul. The people that can bring forth the new passion, the new idea, this people will endure. Those others, that fix themselves in the old idea, will perish with the new life strangled unborn within them.

That last sentence is, of course, among other things, a reference to the musical orchestration of unnatural deaths in the novel, from the prophetic death of the drowned child who strangles, underwater, the schoolteacher who tries to rescue her, which sets off two other deaths: the deceptively "natural" death of the elder Mr. Crich, the owner of the mines who dies mourning the child, and of his son, Gerald, who, despite his new ideas about the business, is even more "fixed" in the "old idea" of control than his father is; his death, then, appropriately, has a frozen immobility.

These powerful symbolic, even allegorical, impulses in Lawrence are made at once complicated and material to us, in *Women in Love*, by being translated into the realm of style; style is where the concerns of the abstract symbolic order of the novel are turned into actual process. Lawrence is deliberate about his intentions, and it is the reason why he could not "write in the same manner as *Sons and Lovers* again"; both before and after the paragraph in which he declares "We are now in a period of crisis," and speaks of the struggle with the "soul," he's busy commenting on the business of translating that struggle into the processes of language, thereby making material, in the act of writing, the conflicts explored in the novel's mental symbolic order. It's no accident that, in the preceding paragraph, Lawrence points out that the "struggle for verbal consciousness should not be left out in art"; and, in the final paragraph, the theme of "crisis" is, once and for all, related to his preoccupation with style:

> In point of style, fault is often found with the continual, slightly modified repetition. The only answer is that it is natural to the author: and that every natural crisis in emotion or passion or understanding comes from pulsing, frictional to-and-fro, which works up to culmination.

Most modernists felt, of course, they were in a time of historical and spiritual crisis: David Jones and T. S. Eliot to do with the war, and with the disappearance of cultural resources, both pan-European and, in Jones's case, local and Welsh. For Ezra Pound, the crisis had to do with the contemporary scene in literary culture, a scene at once radical and dispiriting, as explored in *Hugh Selwyn Mauberley*; but also with the spread of the free market, resulting in the anti-Semitism that informed his championing of culture. (Art and culture, for Pound, as for others, were prey to the market and to business: "Usura rusteth the chisel," he said in the famous "Usura" canto, "It rusteth the craft and the craftsman / It gnaweth the thread in the loom . . ." And the stereotypical Jew, as the title of the canto itself hints at, is, for Pound, a figure for the threat of the market.) For Virginia Woolf, the crisis had to do with reality itself, and its representation in literature, a taking stock that directed both her experiments in fiction and her critique, in her essay, "Mr. Bennett and Mrs. Brown," of the sort of "realism" practised by Arnold Bennett. These are significant, sometimes disturbing, points of departure, and responses to the changed world; and, above all, they are significant because they're of their time and are characteristic of how we think of that time. Lawrence's crisis is significant, on the other hand, because it is odd and out of place and seems to occur some fifty or sixty years prior to its recognised moment; it has to do with a loss of faith in the

Enlightenment, with the fact that the "human," in its European construction, is finished, and that new epoch is defined by transactions of both power and fecund exchange between the self and the "other," which, for Lawrence already, and increasingly, is the non-West. He is almost the first modern writer anywhere, let alone the first English one, to respond to the fact of what we now understand as "alterity" and "difference," and in a way that's at once more demanding, exhausting, moving, and less pat than the manner in which postcolonial writers (for whom "difference" might be seen to be, at least in the eyes of the current orthodoxy, a legitimate concern) have often responded to the same things.

What's extraordinary about Lawrence's reaction to the crisis he perceived, to the inroads of the "other," and to what he saw as the end of humanism, is that it's undertaken not only as prophecy and insight, but, especially since *Women in Love*, made deliberately material on the level of style. In particular, his constant testing, after *Sons and Lovers*, of the notion of "good" or "fine" writing, perplexing earlier admirers, is itself an attempt to breach paradigms like the "literary," which make features, and even departures and experiments, in language recognisable within humanist conventions of reading. Indeed, to many of the earlier admirers, Lawrence appears to be marring, or, as I said before, "muddying" his own work. And so, the struggle for, and spiritual negotiation of, power that the critic Hugh Stevens, for instance, sees as characteristics of both this novel and the story "The Prussian Officer" (composed before it), can be seen to be played out not only in narrative, in the characters' lives, but in the act of composition itself; the author's relationship to language is not symbolically disjunctive or alienated, as it was with Eliot or Kafka, but agonistic.

For the modernists, language—and by implication, the act of creation—is often a metaphysical, Sisyphean burden, as well as compulsion. Kafka's work, thus, is full of images of fruitless and mysteriously obsessive labour; Beckett's narrator, at the end of *The Unnamable*, confesses, "... in the silence you don't know, you must go on, I can't go on, I'll go on"; and Eliot, in beautifully controlled language, speaks of the betrayals of language:

> . . . Words strain,
> Crack and sometimes break, under the burden,
> Under the tension, slip, slide, perish,
> Decay with imprecision . . .

But Lawrence isn't interested in the metaphysical tension between language and silence, saying and not saying; what absorbs him is the relationship of power between author and material: "Never trust the artist, trust the tale." The implications of this are what preoccupy Lawrence when writing his review of Thomas Mann's *Death in Venice*, and in his view of Flaubert. The review was published in 1913, after he'd made his "break" with *Sons and Lovers*, and begun to fashion the new language he'd explore first in *The Rainbow* and then, more comprehensively, in *Women in Love*. Mann's novella, for Lawrence, is an example of the "will of the writer" striving "to be greater than and undisputed lord and master over the stuff he writes which is figured to the world in Gustave Flaubert." And further:

> Thomas Mann seems to me the last sick sufferer from the complaint of Flaubert. The latter stood away from life as from a leprosy. And Thomas Mann, like Flaubert, feels vaguely that he has in him something finer than ever physical life revealed. Physical life is a disordered corruption against which he can fight with only one weapon, his fine aestheticism, his feeling for beauty, for perfection, for a certain fitness which soothes him, and gives him an inner pleasure, however corrupt the stuff of life might be.

Once more, "physical life" or "life" is, for Lawrence, a complex oppositional weapon in his attack upon the old language of humanism; it represents an opening out in that language, and not just a grand disavowal of the aesthetic, as, say, Wilfred Owen's declaration in his manifesto for his war poems, "Above all, I am not interested in poetry," is. Lawrence himself, in *Women in Love*, is interested in opening himself to the "other," not only in terms of subject matter, but on the experiential and material level of style. He wishes to open out, unprecedentedly in the strategic deliberateness of this ambition, style on to its "other," "bad" style (one thinks of Eliot's innocently supercilious, "To me, also, he seems often to write very badly: but to be a writer who had to write often badly in order to write sometimes well"), on to overwriting, to the "continual, slightly modified repetition." It's not a question, any more, after *Women in Love*, of writing "badly" or writing "well" —"I shan't write in the same manner as *Sons and Lovers* again," he'd said—but of involving both author and material in an agonistic relationship that would exist on various levels: between writer and craft ("Never trust the artist, trust the tale"), the self and the "other," the West and the non-West, style and "bad writing." "The latter stood away from life as from a leprosy," he said of Flaubert; Lawrence not only wanted, it seems, his work to be *about* life, but strange as it may sound, to, as style, *become* it. One should add immediately that he didn't want to anthropomorphise style ("How stupid anthropomorphism is!" reflects Ursula; Lawrence detested anthropomorphism, as another attempt to impose a human paradigm upon the nonhuman, and, by metaphorical extension, the non-Western), nor to organicise it, to "breathe life" into it; by turning style into "life," he wished to effect a radical break between it and its humanist conception.

The shrewd Mann, whom Lawrence underestimated, would have been one of the very few novelists at that time who'd have seen, in a more accurate way than Eliot, what it was that so profoundly exercised Lawrence—not perhaps to pursue the latter's example himself, but to allow that vantage point to transform his own thoughts, especially in *Dr. Faustus*. At one point in that late work, Mann implicitly critiques his own work in the terms that Lawrence had earlier; critiquing it, that is, not from the emergent position of the modernism of the time, where style and form are caught between the poles of the conventional and the experimental, but where they are situated on the dividing line between culture and its "other." And so, when the academic Serenus Zeitblom points out to the composer Leverkühn that "the alternative to culture is barbarism," Leverkühn replies that "barbarism is the antithesis of culture only within a structure of thought that provides us the concept. Outside of that structure the antithesis may be something quite different or not even an antithesis at all." For Lawrence, the oppositional friction between man and woman in *Women in Love* is only one part of its constant argumentation on what's culture and its "other"; as is, crucially, style. Here, in this brief, animated discussion in the chapter "Moony" between the two sisters, the schoolteacher Ursula (who's in love with Birkin, the Lawrence-figure in the novel) and the artistic Gudrun, we are reminded of the "impossibility" of Lawrence's quest ("impossible" both in the literal sense, and in the social one, meaning "wearing" or "frustrating")—to move toward the "antithesis" that is "something quite different or not even an antithesis at all":

> "Yes," cried Ursula, "too much of a preacher. He is really a priest."
>
> "Exactly! He can't hear what anybody else has to say—he simply cannot hear. His own voice is so loud."
>
> "Yes. He cries you down."
>
> "He cries you down," repeated Gudrun. "And by mere force of violence. And of course it is hopeless. Nobody is convinced by violence. It makes talking to him impossible—and living with him I should think would be more than impossible."
>
> "You don't think one could live with him?" asked Ursula.
>
> "I think it would too wearing, too exhausting. One would be shouted down every time... He cannot allow that there is any other mind than his own. And then the real clumsiness of his mind is its lack of self-criticism—. No, I think it would be perfectly intolerable."

Lawrence is ironicising himself, of course, as he does brilliantly in the chapter "Gudrun in the Pompadour," in which a group of Birkin's bohemian acquaintances read out and mock one of his high serious, exhortatory letters in a café. But self-mockery, comedy, characterisation, are as indispensable to the economy of the novel as is its utter investment in the notions and experiences of "clumsiness" and the "intolerable," notions which these staged scenes expertly introduce. Certainly, the openness to the "other" brings, from this novel onwards, an element of "clumsiness" and the "intolerable" to Lawrence's writing; in his response to the "other," to the non-West, even to "primitive" art, and in the way he responds to them, Lawrence both belongs to, and departs radically from, the modernist temper. *Women in Love* is scattered with references to, and encounters with, African art; but the "primitive" is not brought into the domain of "high" culture, as it is with modernism—it remains a wonder, but also a breach, an "obscenity" (and it was obscenity, as defined then in England, that had got Lawrence's previous novel into trouble); "obscenity" not only as vulgarity, but as the incongruous, the "intolerable."

> It was an ordinary London sitting-room in a flat, evidently taken furnished, rather common and ugly. But there were several negro statues, wood-carvings from West Africa, strange and disturbing, the carved negroes looked almost like the foetus of a human being. One was of a woman sitting naked in a strange posture, and looking tortured, her abdomen stuck out . . . The strange, transfixed, rudimentary face of the woman again reminded Gerald of a foetus, it was also rather wonderful, conveying the suggestion of the extreme of physical sensation, beyond the limits of physical consciousness.
>
> "Aren't they rather obscene?" he asked, disapproving.
>
> "I don't know," murmured the other rapidly. "I have never defined the obscene. I think they are very good."

Gerald's interlocutor is the Russian who, with the members of the bohemian set described in this chapter in the "rather common and ugly"

London flat, will arraign and ridicule Birkin's letter in the Pompadour Café; will arrive, through the letter, at a definition of the "obscene." In the "Pompadour Café" chapter, Lawrence implicitly, but palpably I think, connects the question of "otherness," the "rather wonderful" but "rather obscene" statues in the London flat, to the question of style and language, in this case in Birkin's letter, which Halliday, the one reading it out, calls, sneeringly, "absurdly wonderful." The "other" or the non-Western does not figure in the economy of *Women in Love* as the African mask does in Picasso, or the Japanese prints in Van Gogh, as a fresh and untapped vernacular resource; or as the directives from the *Upanishads* at the end of *The Waste Land* do, transformed into a cosmopolitan, high cultural utterance. In each of these cases, the non-Western enters, and then is domesticated, in a humanist / modernist economy of representation; in *Women in Love*, the "other" figures as a relinquishing of Flaubertian "control," a feature of language that's "impossible," "clumsy," "obscene," "absurdly wonderful," "intolerable."

Here, in *Women in Love*, Lawrence begins to create a critical language of binaries that he'd develop thenceforth till the end of his life; but these binaries are made problematic and aesthetically challenging—they aren't "fixed," to use a common Lawrentian pejorative, but are in a state of bewildering but intriguing realignment, and for a number of reasons. One of them is the curious but astonishing way in which Lawrence manages to insert his overarching quest, the quest to go outside of Western humanism, into the English novel of the great tradition, so making that novel "different" from itself. He doesn't "move on" from the great tradition, or break it up formally, or introduce, paradoxically, the epic into everyday bourgeois space, all of which the modernists do; instead of abandoning the language of the great tradition, he turns it, in *Women in Love*, upon itself. Never have the English realist novel and post-humanist essay come together in this way before or since. The binaries are caught and embedded, always, in this transition, and meshed in the language's turning upon itself; they are never quite available outside it. Often his very imaginative powers as a novelist give to whatever seems negative or "fixed," on the level of the narrative's relentless theorising, an incomparable elegiac force. Gerald is such a character, cast in the Flaubertian mould of being "greater than and undisputed lord and master over the stuff" of "life" and its "disordered corruption," emblematising, then, part of the architecture the novel wants to shake off—yet in the contradictory pull we, and Birkin, and, indeed, Lawrence, feel toward him, he's essential to that act of "shaking off" remaining "unfixed" and in a Lawrentian way "impossible." Lawrence's polemic never lets up, but neither does the performance of its compositional dynamics and writerly emotion; and this is what makes reading *Women in Love* such an unsettling and unique experience, where we're constantly traversing the distance between resistance and awakening. The resistance is caused by the odd, heavy proximity between the writing and the ideas; between the insistence of the style, the argument, and the very world that's being described. It is not a "novel of ideas," though it's nothing without them, and nor is it the opposite of such a novel, the novel of style and sensation and psychology, such as Eliot ascribed to James, when he said that the latter had a mind so fine that it was never marred by a single idea; our awakening as readers comes in the midst of our grudging realisation that *Women in Love* is "difficult" in a Lawrentian, rather than modernist, way, that it is perverse and will not accept the common ground on which such distinctions are erected.

•

Lawrence's binaries, to do with "light," "the sun," the "crystalline," the transparent, and the "fixed" on the one hand, and with the "melting," the "muddy," "flux," "corruption," and especially "darkness" on the other, are complicated by the fact that at least some of them derive from a common pool that has been made use of before, and would continue to be used by the modernists and the symbolists. "Light" and "dark," the binary that derives its immemorial authority from religion, is powerfully co-opted, as we know, into the secular metaphysics of symbolism and, later, absurdist literature; but Lawrence's use of the binary, which might seem to locate him in the common pool I mentioned, is actually quite different, and is part of an antimetaphysic. Claiming to abandon the visual mode after *Sons and Lovers*—"I have no longer the joy in creating vivid scenes . . . I don't care much more about accumulating objects in the powerful light of emotion, and making a scene of them"—Lawrence speaks in a curious and striking rhetorical language that leads us to Derrida's insight about "light" and "seeing" being foundational tropes for Western metaphysics. Something like a premonition of the Derridean critique about the controlling dimension of the visual is already at play in the uneasy statement about "accumulating objects in the powerful light of emotion." Derrida, of course, notes the tropes of light in the language of what he calls "Western metaphysics"—for instance, when we speak of the "clarity" of an idea, or of "seeing" the way in which an argument makes sense, or an idea as an "illumination," or of understanding something in the "light" of an idea. A source of metaphorical light in language makes it possible for us to think of the mental and actual worlds we inhabit in terms of clarity, perspective, distance, transparency, as well as of their absence; as M. H. Abrams, a critic of Derrida, but one of his most lucid commentators, remarks in *Doing Things with Texts*, the "sun . . . serves Derrida himself as a prime trope of the founding presence, or logos." The visual as a medium of power, and a metaphor for absolute knowledge: this is what Lawrence means when he speaks about "accumulating objects" in a "powerful light"—"powerful" in a theological and authoritative sense. Again and again, the image of water at night-time, "unfixed" and refractive, preoccupies the novel, as in the "Water-Party" chapter, in which people in boats move about with lanterns on the lake:

> The dark woods on the opposite shore melted into universal shadow. And amid this universal undershadow, there was a scattered intrusion of lights. Far down the lake there were fantastic pale strings of colour, like beads of wan fire, green and red and yellow. The music came out in a little puff, as the launch, all illuminated, veered into the great shadow, stirring her outlines of half-living lights, puffing out her music in little drifts.

Here is a chapter that begins as an eerie celebration of community and ends as a doom-laden record of the individual consciousness, with the drowning of a child and a young man. If light is humanist consciousness, the chapter becomes an essay in which argument is translated into experience, event, and form—never rejecting the visual, but grappling with it—while uncannily foreseeing Lawrence's own words in *Apocalypse*: "There is nothing of me that is alone and absolute except my mind, and we shall find that the mind has no existence by itself. It is only the glitter of the sun on the surface of the water."

Indeed, sun and daylight and consciousness are brought together in the story of the Crichs, the powerful mining family, as it's gradually transformed from a moving realist tale about the vicissitudes of English economic power into an apocalyptic narrative about humanism. The elder Crich, Thomas, dies more than midway into the novel, "slowly, terribly slowly . . . only half-conscious—a thin strand of consciousness linking the darkness of death with the light of day." That consciousness is to be inherited and sustained by the son, Gerald; and Lawrence's uncharacteristic pun on "son," as Gerald stands at the dying man's bedside, restates his insistent polemic against light: "Every morning, the son stood there, erect and taut with life, gleaming in his blondness." Birkin, on the other hand, is "wavering, indistinct, lambent."

Again, these dualities between the principal characters culminate in the chapters at the end, beginning with "Snow": familiar modernist symbolic terrain rewritten in the terms of Lawrence's antimetaphysic as Birkin, Ursula, Gudrun, and Gerald come to Innsbruck for what will be a tragic vacation for the latter: "Birkin was on the whole dim and indifferent, drifting along in a dim, easy flow, unnoticing and patient, since he came abroad, whilst Gerald, on the other hand, was intense and gripped into white light, agonistes." (Indeed, the words from *Apocalypse* are echoed again, in regard to Gerald, after the friends' arrival at their hotel: "When they had bathed and changed, Gerald came in. He looked shining like the sun on frost.")

After *Sons and Lovers*, Lawrence would recurrently explore the relinquishing of the visual (in spite, or perhaps because, of being such an astonishingly visual, even visionary, writer), and what that implied in terms of "contact"—both literal "contact," or touch, as well as the metaphorical but profound confrontation with "otherness." In the story "The Blind Man," the eponymous protagonist, thus, "seemed to know the presence of objects before he touched them":

> It was a pleasure to him to rock thus through a world of things, carried on the flood in a sort of blood-prescience... So long as he kept this sheer immediacy of blood-contact with the substantial world he was happy, he wanted no intervention of visual consciousness. In this state there was a certain rich positivity, bordering sometimes on rapture. Life seemed to move in him like a tide lapping, lapping, and advancing, enveloping all things darkly.

In the story, touch leads to an inadmissible form of "contact"—between the blind protagonist and another man, a visitor to the house. The abnegation of the visual, tellingly, leads to a fluid and liquid state, a "flood... of blood-prescience," "a tide lapping, lapping... enveloping all things darkly." We begin to understand now what Lawrence is attempting with his images of darkness, water, and the moon (contrasted always with images of fixity, frozenness, and solidity) in *Women in Love*: not so much to abandon the visual, as to turn the visual against itself.

All the while, in this novel, but especially in the last chapters set in snow country, Lawrence is developing the poetics of an antihumanist style. To this end, he reiterates and orchestrates here a series of what will become increasingly familiar contrasts. On the one hand, we are told of the crystalline ("For Gudrun herself, she seemed to pass altogether in the whiteness of snow, she became a pure, thoughtless crystal"), and the deathly, as well as of the culture of the "late eighteenth century, the period of Goethe and of Shelley, and Mozart," which Gudrun and Loerke take a "sentimental, childish delight in" praising as "by-gone things . . . the achieved perfections of the past"; and, on the other, we are shown Ursula's longing to escape the "terrible static, ice-built mountain-tops" into "earthy fecundity" and "dark earth." Here, Lawrence is citing fixity, conflict, and process not only as the novel's preoccupations, but its very language and form. Soon after he completed *Women in Love*, he would, in attempting to arrive at a radical definition of poetic form in "Poetry of the Present" (written between 1918–19), seem to refer to the snowed-up landscape and its tragic denouement, its vision of crystalline fixity in ice and Gerald's frozen corpse, again:

> The ideal—what is the ideal? A figment. An abstraction. A static abstraction, abstracted from life. It is a fragment of the before or after. It is a crystallised aspiration, or a crystallised remembrance: crystallised, set, finished. It is a thing set apart, in the great storehouse of eternity, the storehouse of finished things.

As I've said, it's difficult, in this great novel, to discuss his binaries as if they were categories that preceded or stood outside the language they were formulated in. Lawrence's crucial oppositions in its final chapters, between the "static, ice-built mountain-tops" and "earthy fecundity," are, "Poetry of the Present" reminds us, to be found in language, while at once being *of* language:

> There is poetry of this immediate present, instant poetry, as well as poetry of the infinite past and the infinite future. The seething poetry of the incarnate Now is supreme... In its quivering momentaneity it surpasses the crystalline, pearl-hard jewels, the poems of the eternities.

The "poems of the eternities" are, the essay tells us, the "treasured, gem-like lyrics of Shelley and Keats," the products of the "late eighteenth century, the period of Goethe and of Shelley, and Mozart" that Gudrun and Loerke spend hours discussing in the snowed-up hotel. With this novel, Lawrence departs, as Birkin and Ursula do briefly toward the end, before returning to the scene of tragedy, the "great storehouse of eternity, the storehouse of finished things"; and the binaries that govern the narrative become problematised by becoming entangled in his exploration of, and struggle with, style.

Notes on the Novel After Globalisation

2007, *Meanjin*

Sometime in May in 2005, I was sitting in a flat in Cambridge, England, and watching television—the expected plug for the Hay on Wye Festival. A programme on books, with three novelists, Kazuo Ishiguro, Julian Barnes, Jonathan Coe, in conversation: so rare are these today that I was willing to forget—perhaps was hardly aware of—the fact that almost every discussion on culture on contemporary television (interviews with authors, readings from books) is connected to a publishing or media moment and is, in essence, a plug. Critics and authors have succumbed to this arrangement and its conveniences, and negated, almost unknowingly, the irrelevant, expansive, and almost purposeless space for literature in the media. The waywardness and surprise of literary discussion have largely disappeared with that space; because the plug is a deeply ritualistic activity, a totemic observance, in which you know in advance what you're supposed to do and say.

In retrospect, this might be why the discussion in which Barnes, Coe, and Ishiguro (three admirable writers) took part was respectful, low-key, and slightly peculiar. At one point, the interviewer promised that he'd ask them, after a commercial break, about what the free market was doing to the novel; once the break was over, though, the discussion veered toward a predictable direction—the life and health of the novel. "Is the novel dead?" asked the interviewer. "V. S. Naipaul said it is."

"And then he wrote another one," said someone wryly. No, the rumours of its death were hugely exaggerated; the novel was alive and well, all agreed.

This wasn't the first time I was witness to this ritual—and what can one call it but a ritual of obeisance, and, like all rites, an occasion of empty, terrified praise as well as prevarication? Why, after all, should a genre that's flooded shelves in bookshops, that has flourished almost monstrously while other genres—poetry, the short story, the essay—have been buried or prepared for burial—why should the novel, of all things, require a periodic certificate of health, a circumlocutory announcement, every few months, that it is ailing and, then, that it was always well? Surely this is behaviour characteristic of closed, tyrannical kingdoms, in which the despot is pronounced ill and well at regular intervals, leading to a constant cycle of mourning and celebration; while other deaths and annihilations go unnoticed?

•

The novel's been around for a long time, but only in the last thirty years has it achieved a curious sort of preeminence, in that it's the one literary genre in which certain convergences possible only after globalisation—between "serious" and "popular" culture, between theoretical or intellectual validation and free-market or material investment—take place. The reception of the novel reminds us that there are no real oppositions and dichotomies in the globalised world, and that the celebration of narrative is also a confirmation of the intolerance of oppositionality.

The dismantling of binaries was one of the primary moral functions of the poststructuralist, postmodernist moment, because of the hierarchies of power that, historically, they at once concealed and expressed. The rise of narrativity has been intriguingly continuous, or concomitant, with the decline of the binary. As I've already said, in the cultural politics of the free market, the *reception* of narrative—or the novel—is also involved in the overturning of the binary that separates "serious" writing from "popular," commercially successful from critically acclaimed writing. For the larger narrative of the globalised free market in which the smaller one, the novel, is located, that dichotomy is a nuisance and an inconvenience. Faced with the engulfing, all-embracing, narrative-like movement and proclivities of globalisation, is it time to recuperate the binary, and give it back a measure of polemical strength and moral dignity?

•

Let me go back, briefly, to another memory, one that precedes, by a couple of years, my sighting of these writers on television. I was in New York, teaching; it was the autumn of 2002. I made several trips outside the city, some, to Pennsylvania and Boston, on Greyhound buses. The mythology of the Greyhound bus, memorialised in so many popular songs, faded quickly; as did the mythology of travel, the American romance of the highway. It was on one of these trips that I realised how difficult it was, in the globalised world, to escape, to convincingly take refuge in namelessness and anonymity. I was going through all the motions of travel; as the bus took the highway in the evening, I sought to be cocooned by movement and invisibility. But there was a false note. I could never bring myself to believe I was completely alone (this had nothing to do with the strangers on the other seats, who, typically, contribute to the traveller's aloneness rather than take away from it). I gradually understood that the problem was the sense of my own identity being constantly linked to and inescapably meshed with numberless gestures of disclosure I was half-aware of and constantly involved in: if I were to use my credit card, for instance, to buy a packet of crisps and a newspaper at a "gas station," or if I were to call a friend on a hypothetical mobile phone which I didn't actually possess. The highway, and darkness, provided no assurance of melting away; and none of the lanes in the small towns we rushed past really dissolved into the unknown; the magic of concealment was no longer a tenable one. It was only two years after the bombing of Afghanistan, and recent coverage told us that even the most obscure settlements in the least known parts of the world could be recorded, studied, and, if it proved necessary, destroyed. There is no "outside" in the globalised world.

•

Globalisation, then, is a text, in the special but influential meaning that the word "text" has taken on in the last thirty years: a fabric of lateral connections and intersections that abhors, and negates, verticality. The lens of the satellite studying us from above is not really an instance of verticality, or of the Foucauldian godlike panopticon, because it's as much *in* the text as we are. Space, too, is part of the text; "pure" emptiness isn't possible in free-market globalisation, and neither, as a result, is a sense of dissolution. There's no escape for us from an infinitely lateral and discursive grid of connectedness; nor is there any escape from it for the satellite.

•

The philosophical underpinnings of globalisation as a form of lateralness can be found in theories, or vulgarised versions of those theories, that have predominated thought in the last three or four decades, some of them originating in radical developments in philosophy, or in the social sciences, or in cultural history, often finding a new life when transposed to literary departments. These theories, of course, play a significant, even definitive, role in the way we think of the novel today, in our privileging the narrative and discursive over the poetic, the fragmentary, and the unfinished; but they also, I think, prepare in some measure the intellectual ground on which our larger acceptance of the lateral and of narrativity, and of the moral rightness of narrative, is based; and they explain our suspicion—a suspicion the free market implicitly shares and nurtures—of the poetic, of verticality, of a breach in the narrative.

Among the first theorists to give a moral and political value to—and speak up in the cause of, as it were—narrative was the Russian formalist and philosopher, Mikhail Bakhtin. The "novel" was not a genre for Bakhtin (Forster's humorously anodyne and pointed description of the novel as a work of fiction exceeding fifty thousand words would hardly have sufficed for him); instead, he fashioned it, unprecedentedly, as a polemical term. It's clear that, when he referred to the novel, it was a particular *kind* of novel he was interested in reinventing, a text that was marked by lateral and sideways movements, "a system of intersecting planes," to which end he created a vocabulary suggesting simultaneity and socialised space—heteroglossia, polyphony, dialogue, carnival—all conjuring a radius within which more than one voice was speaking, more than one person moving. The "dialogic" novel, whose paradigmatic proponent was Dostoevsky, was then part of an attack on the "high" cultural, enclosed, monological nature of the "poetic": represented, in Bakhtin, not so much by a poet as, oddly, by the novels of Tolstoy. This is perhaps the first time the "poetic" falls into disrepute not because of the layman's usual impatience with obscurity or irrelevance, or the Platonic disdain of daydreaming and the untrustworthiness of the poet, but because of a new antimetaphysical politics to which privileging a certain notion of narrative is crucial. Later, important modulations on Bakhtin, such as Julia Kristeva's "intertextuality," also involve a refutation of the essentially metaphysical notion of anteriority; Kristeva warns us that "intertextuality" is not a "banal study of sources" or influences, but an attempt to engage with the way sign-systems interpenetrate one another, in effect, laterally. Bakhtin was, one might recall, largely unknown outside his own country for much of his life, but his work was made available in France after his death in

1975, and gradually canonised in the American academy in the eighties; that is, his critique of the "poetic" remained, when he was actually formulating it, unknown to the practitioners and theorists of "high" modernism and existentialism in Europe (just as their work seems largely ignored by this student of, among other things, the seventeenth, eighteenth, and nineteenth centuries). It's only in the eighties that his particularly weighted celebration of narrative began to circulate in academia, and became one of the coordinates in preparing the groundwork for how we see narrative today; how we find it unnecessary to critique it, partly because we still think of it, in the light of the Bakhtinian legacy, of itself being a subterranean and indispensable critical tool: of the old enemy, "high" culture.

•

What are some of the other coordinates responsible for preparing what I've called the "intellectual groundwork" for narrativity? Among the most considerable and stimulating is, surely, Benedict Anderson's subtle and probing *Imagined Communities*. In taking pains (though "taking pains" is probably not the most apt way of speaking of a book with such a light, alchemical touch) to differentiate the old kingdoms from the modern nation-states, Anderson makes an essentially Bakhtinian distinction, between centripetal societies converging towards a vertical, monarchical point, divinely sanctioned, and centrifugal ones, held together by the observance of secular time—the clock and the calendar—and what he calls "print capitalism." Because Anderson is interested in rewriting (the punning figurative usage is, I suppose, inescapable) the nation as a form of narrative, the activities of reading and of producing novels become not only important examples of evidence shoring up his argument, but metaphors for discursivity. That is, reading novels isn't just something that people who live in nations happen to be doing; for Anderson (and for Bakhtin), the novel isn't only *about* society, or a mirror of it, but the most typical instance, and a tissue, of the conditions of narrativity in which it, the novel, is located. It's important to see that the novel, despite the physical characteristics of its being—pages bound within a hardback jacket—is not an enclosed, bounded entity within another enclosed, bounded entity, a book sealed by its cover within a nation defined by its borders, but (like the nation itself) something in constant transaction with the narrativity it's produced by, and to which it constantly contributes. (I say this in spite of Anderson's contrast of the physically circumscribed condition of the book with the loose nature of a pound of sugar; for his study is not a humanist exploration of how the novel might reflect the conditions of a nation, or how the latter might come together to produce a certain kind of novel. These dividing lines are really untenable for Anderson, and untenable because the way he views both nation and novel are in some fundamental way informed by the idea of the "text.") In this sense, Anderson's "nation," too, in spite of its bounded nature, is, like his "novel," a precursor of globalisation, an infinitely lateral web of intersections, and print-capitalism a brilliant metaphor for—and, once again, a precursor of—the sort of technology that not only produces narrative, but is imbricated in it. Anderson's book was published in 1983, and it's clearly marked, despite bearing all the animating characteristics of the European cosmopolitan imagination, by the new postmodern affirmation of the lateral and discursive. The point at which this shows up most interestingly is in his influential gloss of Walter Benjamin's notion of "homogeneous, empty time." Anderson's interpretation is really proto-postmodernist, invoking narrative through an imagery of lateralness and "simultaneity," a "simultaneity [which] is, as it were, transverse, cross-time, marked not by prefiguring and fulfilment, but by temporal coincidence, and measured by clock and calendar." Add to the last two, as Anderson does in the next paragraph, the novel and the newspaper, and the reinterpretation of "homogeneous, empty time" as a continuum that makes narrativity or textuality possible is complete. Anderson's choice of word—"imagining"—in relation to the two printed material objects mentioned is curious, given the "imagination" is private, vertical, nonmaterial, and often, in its self-absorption, at odds with narrative; the implications of this slight, but fundamental, incongruity of phrasing are never fully investigated in the book. Certainly, Benjamin's own concept of "homogeneous, empty time" is a modernist one—a utopian linear flow (where clock and calendar not only stand for simultaneity, but for an unfolding) which makes possible the idea of development and the "concept of the historical progress of mankind." Benjamin's attack on "homogeneous, empty time" also takes on its revolutionary Marxist purpose (inveighing against historicism) through a characteristically modernist aesthetic—the aesthetic of the present moment, the messianic "*Jetztzeit*," in which present and future come together, and create a rupture in linearity. In Anderson's "homogeneous time" of nationhood, narrative, and discursivity, the "imagination" in his title could have plausibly fulfilled that messianic / romantic role, but will not, or perhaps cannot.

•

The parameters for narrativity were already put in place, of course, by the time Anderson was writing, by Foucault and Derrida. This was done, as we know, in different ways by the two philosophers, but, in both cases, by eroding the border separating language from what was putatively "outside" it; by using linguistic terms—"discourse" and "*écriture*"—in a particular way, so as to suggest that "reality" (largely ontological and phenomenological in Derrida; political and institutional in Foucault) was inextricable from the language that purported to convey or represent it. All this gradually brings into motion, or creates the moral context for, the banishing of the "outside" that is so much an unquestioned part of existence in the globalised world. "There is nothing outside of the text," said Derrida in *De la grammatology*; or at least he did in Gayatri Chakrabarty Spivak's translation. In his essay, "Ideas of the Book and Histories of Literature: After Theory?," Peter D. McDonald, looking again at the original, "*Il n'y a pas de hors-texte*," calls Spivak's version "clumsy," a clumsiness that "Derek Attridge's 1992 version ("*There is no outside-the-text*") improved only slightly... Both missed the punning force of the original, which set *hors-texte*, a technical bookmaking term roughly translated as "plate" (as in "This book contains five colour plates") alongside *hors texte*, which Attridge's translation comes closest to capturing. This play on words (or on a hyphen), which reflects Derrida's lively bibliographical imagination... does not, of course, provide a key to the talismanic sentence's meaning. What it does indicate is that "*Il n'y a pas de hors-texte*" announced neither a triumphant nor a culpable break with history." The word "text," though, in the way Derrida uses it, involves a radical demolition of an "outside" to narrativity. A "text" is not a "book"; a book, like language itself in the old days of humanist criticism, is delineated physically and symbolically from the world around it; the book is *about* the world. After Derrida's "text," narrative no longer refers to, reports on, describes, or captures the world; it becomes the system of lateral transactions by which we understand what we used to call "the world" is.

•

I've spent some time looking at these formative, often ubiquitous, works because of the role they played in transforming narrative into a critique that decisively overturned the old hegemonies and pedagogies: metaphysical, European, masculine. (There is, as we know, a powerful version of Derrida that can be enlisted in the cause of the "poetic"; however, the populist version involves the Derrida of lateral interconnections, the never-ending chain of signifiers.) It must be at least partly because of this that narrative, today, brings up not so much the associations of rationality, logic, and factuality that prose did earlier, but those of liberation, delight, celebration, and radical freedom. And so, even the early chapters of Anderson's study (whose intentions are hardly as pointedly antimetaphysical as those of the philosophers who must be responsible, to a significant extent, for giving his book its particular timbre) are infected by an excitement about the march of narrative; the celebration of print-capitalism turns narrative from a mode of telling into heroic actor. Anderson's excitement comes, surely, not only from his discovery of how nations were formed by narrative, or from the inexorable and elegant development of his argument, but has something to do with being part of larger critical campaign in which narrative plays an exemplary role, and, therefore, with the *timeliness* of his project.

•

With the consolidation, in the nineties, of extraordinary changes in the realms of politics, culture, and economics, the truth is that the pernicious bygone elitisms have been rendered largely obsolete—turned into shibboleths. In the meanwhile, the postmodern conception of narrative, an infinitely lateral web, with its abolition of the "outside," has become a form of (often seemingly benign) control enforced through a series of disclosures and constant transactionability in the domains of "information" and the "market." The air of celebration that surrounded, in intellectual debate, the anti-Enlightenment thrust of narrativity in the last four decades has merged, subtly but indelibly, with the orchestrated, upbeat tone of globalisation.

After poststructuralism, "nostalgia" became a dirty word; it pointed to a longing for hieratic, repressive totalities, a malaise that could affect, at once, the fascist, the humanist, and the member of the old Left. Globalisation has appropriated the inadmissibility of nostalgia in its own robust way; globalisation is about "being at home in the world" in a wholly unprecedented manner—not in the "poetic," Heideggerean sense, nor in the mode familiar to mystics, conflating the earthly and the paradisial, but in a way peculiarly sanctioned and authored by the market. For the first time, with globalisation, we have not so much the West's familiar investment in the idea of the future, and of development, but an apotheosis of the present—again, an unprecedented apotheosis, quite unlike the modernists' quasi-religious recuperation of the "present moment" or the epiphanic in their work. No, the "now" of globalisation has little to do with—indeed, is inimical to—the epiphanic, with its potentially disruptive, metaphysical resonances.

•

Another coordinate that should be mentioned in this mapping of narrativity as a crucial critical and political conceit is the idea of "storytelling." It's a notion that didn't really exist in any persuasive way on the intellectual landscape thirty years ago. Its rise is related to the fashioning of the discourse of postcoloniality; "storytelling," with its kitschy magic and its associations of postcolonial empowerment, is seen to emanate from the immemorial funds of orality in the non-Western world, and might be interpreted as a critique of the inscribed word, and its embeddedness in Western forms of knowledge. "Storytelling," then, is also an alternative to disciplines like history in the Western humanities; if it is now an ingredient in history-writing, it is so precisely to mark a break with the Eurocentric, the literate, the elite. No wonder that the notion is invoked almost always with an air of glamour and celebration. Both the concordances and the distinctions between this invocation and Walter Benjamin's recovery of the figure of "the storyteller" are instructive; for Benjamin was by no means an unequivocal advocate of narrativity. Thus, in the first paragraph of "The Task of the Translator": "No poem is intended for the reader, no picture for the beholder, no symphony for the listener." Benjamin is expressing the profound modernist desire for disjunction, a breach in the lateral weave of the fabric; it's an image strikingly different from the one of simultaneous readership that comprises Anderson's nationhood. Today, in the early twenty-first century, we've entered yet another cultural and political phase, after the shifts and reappraisals represented, in their time, by modernity and postmodernity. This shift asks us to look at narrative once again; and it asks the novelist to be careful about the point at which "storytelling" begins to collude with the narrativity of globalisation.

•

In the breach, in the notion of the "outside," in the poetic, probably lies the much-maligned question of value. Like the poetic, like verticality, like "high" culture, value is one of those elitist, metaphysical bastions that have been exposed by, and replaced with, the discursive engines of postmodernity. The position of critical theory in relation to value—that it was a crucial tool for the bourgeois elite in exercising control and exclusion; that the contrast between a transcendental value in the sphere of culture and a contingent material value in the marketplace was a sham, and that both forms of value were complicit with one another, often operating and being disseminated in strategically dichotomous but essentially similar ways—the position of theory on this, at the moment its critique began to be formed, was both accurate and timely. Pierre Bourdieu, with his legacy of conceiving of culture as a "field" (comprising publishers, literary prizes, book reviews, and literary networks) provides another significant coordinate in the mapping of lateralness and narrative; and Bourdieu played, in introducing the term "cultural capital," an important role in the demystification of literary value. Despite the unworldly, "high" cultural pretensions of literary and artistic value, it is, for Bourdieu, a symbolic form of material advantage (itself engendered by all kinds of materialist networks that deal in the currency of this symbolism) with which the beneficiary can make their way up and through society.

This was, for the latter half of the twentieth century, an apposite intervention. It is now, in 2007, a dated one, just as the idea of a critical, demystifying narrativity is. "Value," "high" culture, and "verticality" are no longer centres of, or metaphors, for power; narrative is. We're living in a world "after theory," not because theory has died out and we could, if we chose, return to a measure of humanist sanity, but because the problem of globalisation has less to do with theory's familiar villains than with the process of reification that globalisation entails.

•

There is, for instance, the reification of value; and it's what makes the symbolic power of what Bourdieu calls "cultural capital" anachronistic. Even fifteen years ago, it was possible to say, "Stocks in Elizabeth Bishop were relatively low in her lifetime, but shot up remarkably in the eighties," and refer, in speaking of an underrated poet by means of a financial metaphor, almost entirely, and figuratively, to the domain of "high" culture. The specific use of the words "stocks" reminds us that the structure of signification within which literary value operated in bourgeois modernity was always related to the structure of signification wherein market value was decided. And yet there's a powerful, subversive irony in the sentence, in the way "stocks" is used to describe a poet who was, and is, a writer's writer, and a genre that never had a huge public. Value in the domain of culture may have been complicit with market value, but it contained a residue of the ironic sensibility that pervades, for example, much of religion, and which devotional poets have frequently tapped into. So the Indian saint-poet Khaalas could say, "Why did you abandon chanting the Name? / You didn't abandon anger, you didn't abandon desire, / Why did you abandon the real treasure?" The "real treasure" here— "*asli ratan*" in the original—is ironical usage, the word "treasure," or "*ratan*," in straddling two worlds, that of the marketplace and eternity, carrying with it a polemical doubleness, and the word "real" ("*asli*") emphasising the irony.

George Herbert structures his sonnet "Redemption" around the doubleness of the notion of value, and the two possible registers of the word:

Having been tenant long to a rich lord,
    Not thriving, I resolvèd to be bold,
    And make a suit unto him, to afford
A new small-rented lease, and cancel th' old.
In heaven at his manor I him sought:
    They told me there that he was lately gone
    About some land, which he had dearly bought
Long since on earth, to take possessiòn.
I straight returned, and knowing his great birth,
    Sought him accordingly in great resorts:
    In cities, theatres, gardens, parks, and courts.
At length I heard a ragged noise and mirth
    Of thieves and murderers: there I him espied,
    Who straight, *Your suit is granted*, said, and died.

It's impossible to express, or put to argumentative use, this scouring sense of how related but antithetical registers of value operate in different spheres of the world unless the domain of culture reserves a degree of verticality to itself, unless it's both situated within the narrativity of the world, "in great resorts: / In cities, theatres, gardens, parks, and courts," and outside it. There is, however, no "outside" in globalisation; and, as a consequence, both culture and value have largely lost their doubleness. When I, at this moment, say, as a published writer, "My stock is high," or "It's low at present," I may seem to echo the comment on Bishop, but I'm speaking, really, much more closely according to the logic and metier of the market. Today's writers *are* stocks and shares; the ironical register of the term "value" is, on the whole, no longer available to us.

•

Let me recapitulate briefly and look at where we stand in relationship to narrative at present. The dominant tone of modernism was, I think, poetic; that is, it was haunted by totalities—to do with culture, mythology, religion, and nature—that seemed to have been available organically to premodern man, although it couldn't, itself, approach those totalities except in a state of ambivalence, and through the fragment and allusion. Modernity is the last phase of humanism, and is caught between its two resonances: between progress and the perfectibility of the human on the one hand, and nostalgia and loss on the other. Modernism aestheticises this in a new and influential way: the *avant garde*, for instance, is enmeshed in the vocabulary of development, in the idea of the "breakthrough," of being at the forefront, at the vanguard—and, at the same time, it ironicises development, for its experiments rehabilitate broken, unfinished forms, at odds with the social completeness that the world around the artistic community strives for.

Postmodernity is the age of narrative, in a quite different sense from Arnold's characterisation of Dryden's time as the "age of prose." Narrative levels out the binary of prose and poetry, as well as the latter's, and culture's, doubleness, its situatedness in humanist ideals of development and meaning as well as its special abnegation of them. The transcendental and "disinterested"—Arnold's word—are always imbricated with the material, and narrative is the principal constituent of a critique that, once and for all, draws our attention to this fact, while also being the primary instance, the tissue, of this imbrication. In fashioning this critique, postmodern theory still relies, I think, on a crucial degree of irony; as Derrida points out, there is, in fact, no new antimetaphysical language to replace old metaphysical language with; you must turn the old language "upon itself." And yet the insight, or strategy, suggests that the formulation of this critique takes place in a domain somehow separate from, or outside of, the spheres in which language is ordinarily at work; it's that space, that significant gap, that makes the critique manoeuvrable.

Globalisation represents a new phase—that of the rapid, incremental reification of the special postmodern notion of narrative. The postmodern philosophers, obsessed with the hubris of modernity, couldn't have foreseen how the on-and-on lateral movement of narrative, perpetually eschewing closure and delaying the finality of a fixed "meaning," would turn from ironical critical strategy into, increasingly, the context for lives in free-market globalisation. Neither could they have predicted what free-market reification would do to the "old" humanist language; rather than simply turn it upon itself, the "old" language has been transmuted by the market into an ideological discourse to whose tonalities contemporary criticism is only beginning to alert itself. The ideological language of globalisation is made up of terms from older discourses, terms such as (to name a few) "freedom," "democracy," "popular," "people." These words, once located in antithetical worldviews and rival interpretations—in liberal as well as socialist ones—still carry, confusingly, echoes of their old, conflicted meanings while never really referring to them; they lack anteriority, depth, verticality, and, in effect, disruptiveness; they're catchwords in the new-found reification of the discursive. Let me touch upon, very briefly, perhaps cursorily, what's happened to the language of culture and literary criticism in this context of discursiveness.

Just as ellipsis and disjunction were the signatures of modernism—and, to a considerable extent, of modernity—in characteristic "poetic" tension and timbre, a rhetoric of excess, plenty, and a relentless engulfing inclusiveness is the hallmark of globalisation, with its powerful narrative and prolix impulses. Globalisation is the tragicomic rhetoric of putative plenty overwhelming the awareness of palpable want. In India, for instance—as is the case, I'm sure, in Europe and America—want is all around us; and yet we don't really need to do business with it, as we did in modernity, because it can no longer occupy a definitive, oppositional space "outside" us; it has been incorporated into and domesticated in the narrative of abundance. This is not an "ideology" in the old sense, in that it is not a propagation of a point of view; it's a self-referential form, for narrativity is the instrument of globalisation, as well as its sole repository of value. And we're now at a moment when the theories of narrative abundance in the last forty years—the infinite play of *écriture*, the notions of "carnival" and "dialogue," the tide of print-capitalism and the communal imagination, the inexhaustible fund of postcolonial "storytelling"—begin to collude with globalisation's text and script of ever-increasing plenty. It's here, in the reified plenitude of narrativity, that we must situate the statements and announcements of exponential abundance: not only about the spread of democracy and "freedom," but claims such as, "More and more people are reading the novel." Narrativity, as postmodern critical theory has demonstrated, is self-generating; it can produce abundance without the bogeys of privation, struggle, or development. This does something odd to linear time where the market's version of "culture" is concerned; it either compresses it extraordinarily, or *anticipates* it. Thus, "masterpieces" are announced before they're published, and it's also because of this lateral generation of plenty, this disposal of linear development, that we have such an unprecedented number of first-time novelists publishing "masterworks." At no point in history when value and accomplishment were related to linear development could such an efflorescence of immediate, readymade talent—an efflorescence of the "now" of globalisation—be possible.

•

A quick glance at the itinerary, superannuation, and rewriting of the word "world" in the new language. It's a word, again, that possesses a certain post-Enlightenment doubleness, in that it refers to a horizontal, physical entity, the sum total of the geographical mass we inhabit, and, in embodying profound universalist aspirations, has a verticality and interiority premised on ideals common to the human subject everywhere. We sometimes use "global" and "world" as if they were interchangeable, without taking into account that the two are not only at odds with one another, but related hierarchically. Globalisation abhors verticality and the universal, except when it reconfigures the latter on its own terms; and it negates the old-style internationalisms and cosmopolitanisms that worked like barely visible networks between the "high" cultures of different nations. The principal tool and figure for globalisation is the English language; if we're insufficiently aware of this, it's because one is never fully conscious of the material contexts and drives of universals when one is living in the midst of them. But it is, for instance, always a task to enter a mainstream music and DVD store and search for the corner that displays "world" cinema. It reminds us that the "world"—which, in the case of cinema, still represents, across languages, the persistence of a "high" modernist internationalism that once occupied centre stage in "culture"—that the "world" is now a poor suburb of the global, or even an unacknowledged squatter who's annexed a section of globalisation's large and ever-increasing mansion. Similarly, "world" music, which is largely a postglobalisation construct comprising a mishmash of classical, folk, and popular traditions from non-Anglophone countries. In this case, the "global" anthropologises the "world"; makes it remote, ornamental, tribal.

•

Here are two comic analyses of the writer in the midst of plenty—the narrative of abundance, which is not unrelated, as I've attempted to show, to the abundance of narrative. The first instance comes from the maladroit, disturbing, faintly unsavoury French novelist Michel Houellebecq, from his first novel, *Extension du domaine de la lutte*; what drew my attention to it, really, was Theo Tait's shrewd article on Houellebecq in the *London Review of Books*. According to Tait: "All Houellebecq's books have some theoretical underpinning: a modest extension of the argument of the *Communist Manifesto*, proposing that what we call sexual freedom is in fact the last stage in the free market's resolution of personal wealth into exchange value." And he quotes a droll section of the novel, which, he says, "explains its ironically grandiose title":

> Just like unrestrained economic liberalisation, and for similar reasons, sexual liberalism produces phenomena of *absolute pauperisation*. Some men make love every day; others five or six times in their life, or never. Some make love with dozens of women; others with none. It's what is known as "the law of the market." In an economic system where unfair dismissal is prohibited, every person more or less manages to find their place. In a sexual system where adultery is prohibited, every person more or less manages to find their bed mate. In a totally liberal economic system, certain people accumulate considerable fortunes; others stagnate in unemployment in misery. In a totally liberal sexual system, certain people have a varied and exciting erotic life; others are reduced to masturbation and solitude.

This is, in effect, Houellebecq's attempt to place not only the sexual human being but also the writer in what I've called globalisation's "tragicomic rhetoric of putative plenty overcoming the awareness of palpable want." Compare this with the Croatian novelist Dubravka Ugrešić's essay, "How I Could Have Been Ivana Trump and Where I Went Wrong." Many of Ugrešić's essays are to do with the strange transformation of the East European writer after the disappearance of the Soviet bloc, and are related to the sense of dislocation she experiences on stepping out into the "free world" and being confronted with another, less expected disappearance—that of the domain of the literary, and of culture. This leads to a comedy of misreadings and thwarted desires. "Who is Ivana Trump?" Ugrešić asks us, and answers her own question: a fellow East European, a champion skier and a model who emigrated to Canada in 1973, and, "three years later... traded up her brief career as a model and [the skier George Syrovatka's] wife for the career of being Donald Trump's." After her divorce from Trump, Ivana inherited the Plaza Hotel on Fifth Avenue, New York, and "lavish severance pay, and became a successful businesswoman, writer, and active participant in the international jet set."

None of this would have much to do with Ugrešić had she not read a "lengthy review of Ivana Trump's novel" in the *New York Times Book Review*, in the same issue that published "an unjustly malicious review" of Joseph Brodsky's *Watermark*. "One reviewer vilified Brodsky for his language 'jammed with metaphors,' and the other praised Ivana for her analytical intelligence." Ever since, Ugrešić has been following Ivana's trajectory with bemused interest; her return to Croatia, her purchase of "hotels, casinos, department stores..."; her purchase of the "Split daily newspaper *Free Dalmatia*. She would not get involved in editorial policy, she said, she would just take a column that she would write herself." These days, when students in Ugrešić's creative writing class ask her "how one becomes a writer," she, by her own account, replies with "complete authority": "Take up a sport and train like hell. Anything else could lead you in the wrong direction." For, "having become a writer of world renown, it would have been difficult for Joseph Brodsky to become a brilliant skier, while it was easy for Ivana Trump to go from being a skier to a writer, even a brilliant analyst of political conditions in her former communist homeland..." Moreover, "[h]aving myself become a writer, I have little prospect of ever becoming a soccer player, but every soccer player can easily occupy my territory: literature. Thus the well-known soccer player, Davos Suber, announced after 1998 World Cup, when the Croatian team won third place: *No offence to Croatian writers, but we have probably just written the greatest fairy tale in the history of Croatian literature.*"

These sardonic-surreal observations are located, as a gesture of defiance, within the narrative of abundance, and within, as well, the illusory abundance of narrativity. They also alert us to the fact that the market for the novelist, the purveyor of representation, and his or her relation to the erstwhile "reader" has changed with the reification of narrative. If, as Walter Benjamin claimed in "On Some Motifs in Baudelaire," the "crowd," in the democratising nineteenth century, wanted to see and read about itself in the novel ("It became a customer; it wished to find itself portrayed in the contemporary novel, as the patrons did in the paintings of the Middle Ages"), the situation today is somewhat different, as not only Ivana Trump, but the various versions of Pop Idol, as well as the high levels of tolerance for tuneless singing on the two-decade-old Indian television show *Close Up Antyakshari* remind us. The "crowd" no longer wants to consume its representation; the spectator wants, now, to "be" the artist. In the plenty of globalisation, this transposition is not just possible; it's logical. Meanwhile, the "real" writer, whoever he or she might be—someone who can do nothing else, who cannot, by an act of the will, escape their writerliness, who has nothing to show for themselves but their craft and their work, whose identity as a writer, in other words, has an anachronistic ontological weight—may well be subjected, in Houellebecq's term, to "pauperisation"; be reduced to "masturbation and solitude"; in other words, to being, in English slang, a "wanker."

•

It's impossible, one will have noticed, to speak up these days for art. Academic criticism and paid-up scholars are silent, for reasons I've already discussed and enumerated, about the question of art and its value; while the *language* of "disinterested" valuation has been relocated in the marketplace with an entirely new intentionality and purpose. "High" art has been made to take responsibility for twentieth-century history; specifically, for the excesses of Western man. In the process, held hostage, as it were, it's been made indefensible. The shifting of "blame" from the human being to the "work of art" began as an ostensibly tragic, but conveniently exculpatory, gesture within late modernity itself; this is what informs, for instance, George Steiner's fraught and slightly grandiose and self-congratulatory reply to Christopher Bigsby's question "about the question and value of art itself," a reply that, unwittingly, gives the entire onus of valuing art—and then the urgency of dismantling that value—to history, specifically Western history:

> Why did the great culture of Europe not resist more effectively when the inhuman came? Why did the nation of Beethoven and Bach, of Kant and of Goethe, become the nation of Auschwitz?
>
> ....I kept asking the question and was forced to the conclusion that people trained to love art supremely, people like you and I for whom a great play, novel or poem was of true significance, must acknowledge that the cry in fiction blots out the cry in the street...that imagination trained to imagine, to fictionalize, is lamed in the face of actual, concrete inhumanity.

•

At first, the ritual genuflection toward, and defence of, the novel (which I described at the beginning of this piece), might seem curious in the present climate. It needs, straightaway, to be distinguished from a defence of the artistic; the defence of the novel by Ishiguro, Barnes, and Coe is *not* a defence of art. Its tone of moral seriousness and piety is different from the piety of the custodians of culture and aesthetics in modernity; it's a piety that (despite Coe's interest in bygone cultural spaces that made possible the work of experimental novelists like B. S Johnson) arises not from the patrician certainties of "high" culture, but from the contemporary aggressiveness, and righteousness, of narrativity. Here, Naipaul's curmudgeonly, possibly mischievous, pronouncement about the death of the novel serves as a provocation; it contains, perhaps, a concealed nostalgia (barely admissible to Naipaul himself) for the superannuated realm of "culture." The mere utterance causes disruption; it reminds us of the low tolerance for, and the marginalisation of, the disruptive, the poetic, and the antinarrative in globalisation.

•

What I've been struggling to articulate is my strong and returning sense of globalisation's reinvention and appropriation of narrative. And I'm also trying, I suppose, to dwell and pause with my own puzzlement, a puzzlement arising from my suspicion that there is no critique of this reinvention, but only a dogged and dated critique of hierarchy. Like all people on the cusp of something, or at a crossroads, the lack of urgency and focus in the language we use, as well as an intimation of its subtle and far-reaching transformation, trouble me; for that particular critique of hierarchy has largely lost its immediacy because of the way hierarchies have relocated and radically reframed themselves. This is the thing, one gradually learns, about hierarchies and absolutes; that they are not only static—they are at once static and fluid, and their absoluteness is not incompatible with their constantly taking on new guises; becoming, even, their own opposite as they do so.

This is not, by any means, an essay against popular culture. We do need to continue to take popular culture seriously; we also need to reframe a language to understand what "popular" culture means in the context of the present—for the word, like "freedom," has been re-formed and almost made theological in the unipolar world. How do we develop a critique of the global without at the same time pretending that globalisation hasn't happened? It is impossible—untenable—to formulate a critique which says, "All this is terrible, globalisation is bad, let's go back." I have no intention of subscribing to the violence of "going back"; at the same time, how do we make our knowledge of globalisation, of discourse, of power, negotiate, in a way different from ever before, the close reading, the specificity, that gave us pleasure?

Ray and Ghatak and Other Filmmaking Pairs

The Structure of Asian Modernity

2009, Satyajit Ray Lecture, Nehru Centre, London

IT SEEMS that there are all kinds of unresolved problems to do with Satyajit Ray—to do with thinking about him, with finding a language to speak about him that doesn't repeat the indubitable truisms about his humanism and lyricism. How does he fit into history, and into which history—the history of India; the history of filmmaking; some other—do we place him first? We don't ordinarily talk about Ray "fitting in," because he is an icon and a figurehead, and figureheads don't generally have to fit in; traditions, schools, and oeuvres emanate from them. Glancing toward Ray, we see, indeed, the precious oeuvre, but it's more difficult to trace the tradition—either leading up to Ray or emerging from him. People closer to home will mention something called the "Bengal Renaissance," and Tagore, when thinking of lineage; and even those who aren't students of film know who some of the precursors are: Jean Renoir, Vittorio de Sica, John Ford. As to inheritors of the style, you could, with some hesitation and prudence, point to Adoor Gopalakrishnan, and, a bit further away, to Abbas Kiarostami. But what does this constellation of names and categories add up to? For, in the end, we're reduced to looking at Ray as if he were alone, as someone who possessed, as Ray said of *Rashomon*, "just the right degree of universality."

To me, it's increasingly clear—especially in the light of the changes in politics and culture in the last quarter of a century—that Ray is the only embodiment of an Indian "high" modernity, specifically a vernacular "high" modernity, that the world has had to deal with. The "world," in this instance, refers to places in Europe and America where film festivals were hosted, the great metropolitan centres in which debates to do with "culture" were decided, and even sections of the Indian intelligentsia: Ray's humanism was noted in his heyday, but the encounter with Indian modernity that watching his films constituted was hardly mentioned, or only inadvertently experienced by the viewer. And yet Ray's work did occupy the consciousness of the second half of the twentieth century, and, to be understood, must have required a different set of rules from those applying to the paradigmatic, "authentic" India of either the Orient or, later, of postcoloniality—the India of chaos, crowds, empire, resistance, voices, irresistible self-generation, and colour. Ray's India, or Bengal, was not, in this sense, paradigmatic—but, as with Apu's room overlooking a terrace and railway tracks in *Apur Sansar*, it was strangely recognisable and true. Were we being shown, then, that, it was, after all, "recognisability," rather than cultural "authenticity," that was a feature of modernity? And how aware was the audience, as they discovered Apu's world, of that distinction?

Let's go back at this point to Ray's own record of his encounter with Japanese cinema in the form of Kurosawa's *Rashomon*. Ray is writing about this in 1963, probably a little more than twelve years after its release—for Kurosawa's film went to the Venice Film Festival in 1951, winning the Golden Lion there, and Ray says, "I saw *Rashomon* in Calcutta soon after its triumph in Venice." He adds—for Japan seems as far away from Bengal as it is from Venice, and Venice probably closer to his Calcutta—"This is the point where I should confess that my knowledge of the Far East is derived largely from Waley and Lafcadio Hearn; and that while I know my Shakespeare and Schopenhauer, I have yet to know Murasaki and the precepts of Lao-tzu." This is not just the prototype of the colonised subject airily declaiming his allegiances; it's the modern as revisionist, impatiently estranging himself from a fundamental constituent of his identity: that is, the Orient as a point of origin. For Ray, I think, the prism of this revisionism is his particular understanding of "Bengaliness": Ray once offended readers of the *Illustrated Weekly of India*—and I speak from living memory—by saying that he didn't think of himself as a Hindu, but as a Bengali. This revisionist view of Bengaliness is not so much a sub-nationalism, or even just a residue of his father's Brahmoism, as an opposition to cultural identity as we understand it today. It's an opening out onto a secular, local, even regional sense of the everyday, cohabiting, at once, with a constant premonition of the international, which defines the "Bengaliness" of the first half of the twentieth century.

In the same essay on Japanese cinema from which I've just quoted, "Calm Without, Fire Within," Ray, still discussing *Rashomon*, makes a shrewd observation, to do with the culture of filmmaking certainly, but also the sort of questions that the sudden appearance of a compelling cultural artefact raises. "It was also the kind of film that immediately suggests," says Ray, "a culmination, a fruition, rather than a beginning. You could not—as a film making nation—have a *Rashomon* and nothing to show before it. A high order of imagination may be met with in a beginner, but the virtuoso use of cutting and camera was a sort that came only with experience." Those first two statements are among the cleverest statements I've read on the reception of the product of one culture into another, a cautionary reminder of how the critical language of reception simplifies and caricatures, even while occasionally applauding, the encounter with the foreign artwork or phenomenon, and ignores certain blindingly obvious problems. Remember that Ray is not speaking here of the classic encounter with "otherness," with the savage or the peasant, the staple archetypes of postcoloniality, but of something—in this case, *Rashomon*—that only occurs in the economy and theatre of modernity, of a moment of dislocation, of revaluation, taking place within that terrain of film festivals, film societies, and educated—maybe even cinematically educated—middle-class audiences. Why is it that, when a clearly modern non-Western phenomenon emerges globally—say, Mandela, or Ray himself, or Arundhati Roy's environmental activism, or a liberation movement—he or she or it is seen as a "beginning" rather than a "fruition" or "culmination," as if they belonged to an intellectual environment without texture or entanglements or process, a history composed, astonishingly, of supermen or women who rise without explanation from the anonymity around them? Even more than Western history after Carlyle, non-Western history still seems, at least in the popular imagination, condemned to be an account of exceptional men and women and events springing out of an undifferentiated, homogeneous landscape: the site of development. In coining the wonderful rubric, "film making nation," with its conflation of a specialist activity with a political entity, Ray is not so much being a cinema geek as he's reminding us of the nitty-gritty, the materiality, the processes, of history, and of crafting history.

The opening sentences of Ray's next paragraph give us an important key to understanding the sort of encounter he's talking about, but end in a somewhat conventional formulation: "Later revelation of Kurosawa's past work and the work of other Japanese directors has confirmed what *Rashomon* hinted at: the existence of an art form, western in origin, but transplanted and taking root in a new soil. The tools are the same, but the methods and attitudes in the best and most characteristic are distinct and indigenous." Is that all, however, that the encounter with *Rashomon* hints at—a transplantation of an art-form, and its subsequent indigenisation? Is the history of the modern artwork simply a history of its production in the West, and its indigenisation elsewhere? (These are questions, of course, that have been raised by historians such as Dipesh Chakraborty and others in other contexts, to do with the nature of the "modern" itself, but not, I think, in connection to the specific business of genre.) We must remember that, crucially, Ray's own response to *Rashomon* could not have come out of nowhere; we couldn't, to paraphrase his words on Kurosawa's film, have had that response and "nothing to show before it." It—that response to *Rashomon* in 1963 in Calcutta—is not so much a beginning as a "fruition, a culmination" of something; and the history from which it emerged at that moment, in the context of *Rashomon*, cannot be summed up as a history of Western origination, colonial dissemination, and, finally, indigenisation; of import and export. Yes, it's a history that involves travel, but travel as a means of unravelling meaning rather than just moving forward in a landscape; modernity, in the realm of culture, appears to consist of a series of interchanges and encounters in which the putatively initiating meeting—such as the one between Ray and Kurosawa's film—is also a "culmination, a fruition," of interchanges that have already taken place.

One is reminded of this if one thinks back to the emergence of Iranian cinema in the late eighties. There was that initial moment of surprise when, in London and other cities, audiences viewed the films of Abbas Kiarostami and Mohsin Makhmalbaf and, in the nineties, Jafar Panahi and others, for the first time. There was fairly widespread acknowledgement that a form of art-house cinema that was at once deeply humane and innovative was coming out of a country about which the secular middle classes around the world knew relatively little, and about which they knew already whatever they needed to know. Into this frame, the frame of preconceptions, entered, for instance, the engineers, film directors, and drifting professionals who drove through Kiarostami's tranquil but earthquake-stricken landscapes, with middle-class children sitting, often, beside them in the car, journeying towards families in houses in remote villages; also in that frame appeared Makhmalbaf's weavers, village primary schoolteachers, Afghan daily wage-earners, carnival bicyclists. Objects came into the frame as well—apples; fabrics; the blue tile on the wall of a village house; shoes in a shop window in Tehran. The audiences noted these people and things with a mixture of delight, surprise, and recognition, seeing them as elements of what they hadn't known before, as well as of the already known. The quality of the already known gave to these details their recognisability, their authenticity; viewers knew almost straightaway that what they were watching was indisputably "real" cinema, with cinematic values of a high order; the details possessed not just universality, but the pacing and aura of the modern, particularly modernism, with certain modulations on that sensibility that these very gifted filmmakers' works introduced. So, "foreignness" wasn't the crux and core of Iranian cinema; the crux was its enlivening and dislocating recognisability. The fact that this cinema had its impact at a time when the infrastructure and *raison d'être* of the art-house cinema movement was, worldwide, being dismantled was an irony that was either not noticed, or not considered worth commenting on. Yet the most important question regarding these films still remains unaddressed. Here was a kind of cinema that "immediately suggested," as Ray had said of *Rashomon*, "a culmination, a fruition, rather than a beginning." What was it a fruition of? What had happened, or was happening, in Iran, and, for that matter, elsewhere, that these films were powerfully hinting at—not through their subject matter, but through the culmination of a certain practice, and all the more powerfully for that? Not knowing leaves a gap in our understanding, and also leaves us dependent on that model of transplantation and indigenisation. And what happens when something that's purportedly been indigenised is carried back to the land it was transplanted from—an occurrence such as the first showing, say, of Iranian films in New York? Whatever the answer to that might be, it cannot approximate the frisson that the actual event—the New York audience watching the Iranian film—would have involved. The emergence of Iranian cinema represented not just a culmination of certain filmic styles and values, but a convergence of links, hitherto unnoticed, that came together to create a new-minted but unexpected, even unlikely, experience of the "modern," in that decade when modernity, apparently, had finally begun to wane. "Modernity" was the unlooked-for culmination through which New York and Iran momentarily came together.

And yet this experience of the "modern," which arises not from a canonical history of modernity written solely by and in the West, but through a series of interchanges and tensions (such as Ray's encounter with *Rashomon* embodies)—this continual experience of the "modern" is almost always, if it involves a non-Western artist, subsumed under the categories of "East" and "West," and within issues of cultural authenticity. Everyone collaborates in this emotive and persistent haziness to do with cultural characteristics, including the commentators and the artists themselves. That is, they fit their thoughts and justifications into one of two compartments: that either the artwork, if it was produced in the East, bears the unmistakable and ancient imprint of its cultural lineage; or that it transcends all those marks into the convenient domain of the universal. Only the artwork itself refuses to collaborate in this formula, insisting that the intersection between cultural lineage, foreignness, and recognisability must, in the time of modernity, be arrived at as, in Ray's word, a "fruition," that is, as a radical moment of awareness of underlying histories, and, at once, as an unpremeditated but considered acknowledgement of that "fruition." By "fruition" Ray means, as we have seen, not something static, not a pinnacle of development, but a sudden intimation of intelligibility, and modernity as a language dependent on, and constantly illuminated by, such intimations. But then Ray himself, in his essay, goes on to speak in the terms of the same dichotomy that I just described. "Of all the Japanese directors, Kurosawa has been the most accessible to the outside world," he says. "There are obvious reasons for this. He seems, for instance, to have a preference for simple, universal situations over narrowly regional ones . . . But most importantly, I think, it his penchant for movement, for physical action, which has won him so many admirers in the West." Ray then clarifies that he isn't overly bothered by whether the "penchant" for action is a consequence of a "strong Occidental streak" in

Kurosawa, or whether it springs from something "within the Japanese artistic tradition"; for he is still "able to derive keen aesthetic pleasure" from Kurosawa's work. However, he points out that "there is no doubt that he is a man of vastly different temperament from Ozu and Mizoguchi, both of whom come nearer to my preconception of the true Japanese filmmaker. Here, too, I may be wrong, but a phrase of my dear old professor sticks in my mind: 'Consider the Fujiyama,' he would say; 'fire within and calm without. There is the symbol of the true Oriental artist.'"

Ozu and Mizoguchi are actually, as far as filmmaking temperament and subject matter go, quite different from each other: in contrast to Ozu's subtle suburban idylls, Mizoguchi's work, in fact, shares with Kurosawa a fascination with premodern Japan and its distinctive artistic resources. I suppose what Ray is talking about—and the basis of the comparison he's making—has more to do with pacing: the "movement" and "action" of Kurosawa's kind of cinema, the slowness of Mizoguchi's and especially of Ozu's universe. Slowness, who knows, may well be an Oriental characteristic; it may also be part of the colonialist construction of the Orient, as well as of the response of Western critics to directors like Ozu. Ray points out, bringing his own metier, at this point, into the picture, that the "complaint is frequently heard that some Japanese films—even some very good ones—are 'nevertheless very slow.' Some of my own films, too, have drawn this comment from Western critics." (Chandak Sengoopta, in an issue of *Outlook* magazine, reminds us of the sort of early criticism that Ray is talking about here.) Ray points out that "a slow pace is, I believe, as legitimate to films as it is to music. But as a director I know that a slow pace is terribly hard to sustain. When the failure is the director's fault, he should be prepared to take the blame for it. But it is important to remember that slowness is a relative thing, depending on the degree of involvement of the viewer." With the phrase "a relative thing," Ray is, I think, gently refuting the "universal" cultural situation presumed by Western critics, and arguing, somewhat diffidently, for his Easternness. But he doesn't remind us that slowness is also a principal, even sacred, feature of modernism, which privileges the image over narrative, the individual moment over the overarching timespan, thus holding up the way a story ordinarily unfolds. It's possible, of course, that Ray's pacing is the result of an Oriental identity that he's usually at pains to distance himself from. For instance, the sequence in Ray's first film *Pather Panchali* (based on Bibhutibhushan Banerjee's 1928 novel of the same name) in which the camera spends a noticeably large amount of time observing the movement of water insects upon a pond during the monsoons might be, as Max Lerner said of the Apu trilogy in the *New York Post* in 1961 (and this kind of opinion is obviously still fresh in Ray's mind in 1963), "faithful to the Indian sense of time, which is actually a sense of timelessness." Or it could, more plausibly, be at once a sideways reference to the long descriptions of Apu reading by a pond in Banerjee's novel (which Ray makes no attempt to invoke directly), as well as a homage to and a reworking of the forty seconds or so (a considerable amount of time in a film, even more considerable when the film is about half an hour long) in Renoir's *Partie de Campagne* given to the swirls and eddies of river-water as the holiday-makers paddle downstream. The eddies of water in Renoir's river and the agitated pool in Ray on which the narcissistic water insects jump, absorbed, not to mention the mysteriously alluring pool by which Apu keeps his vigil, are part of the gluey, nonlinear substance of modernism, its flow and pattern of consciousness. We don't need to decide, for now, whether or not the pond sequence in Ray's *Pather Panchali* is "faithful to the Indian sense of time," or is another instance of "transplantation and indigenisation." I see it as a "fruition" of something, giving way to a moment of recognition that undermines these polarities, and ramifying into an awareness of other moments and histories available to us in modernity, which we didn't necessarily think of until that moment. Renoir's own shots of the river, too (in a film based on a Maupassant story that comes from a different impulse: to narrate the arc of a lifetime without abandoning economy and compression), I'm sure, must have appeared to Ray a "culmination, a fruition, rather than a beginning."

It's interesting, though, that, when Ray worries briefly about whether Kurosawa's predilection for "action" comes out of a "strong Occidental streak" in the filmmaker, or whether it arises from "within the Japanese artistic tradition," he doesn't mean by the latter the work of Ozu and Mizoguchi, or the constituents of a "film making nation," but an older, perhaps a purer, tradition. Yet, barely a paragraph ago, when speaking of the "culmination" that *Rashomon* is, he'd appeared to be locating that film (and, by implication, his encounter with it), in a context more complex, more impinging, and less pastoral than a Japan seen through the eyes of Lafcadio Hearn. In fact, it was *Rashomon* that had led Ray to the idea of a modern Japanese cinema, and to discover and uncover the different perspectives and convergences that Ozu and Mizoguchi represented. If we take stock today, we see that Kurosawa is still the best-known Japanese filmmaker outside of Japan; and, almost as well-known in the West, but certainly a slightly larger presence in Japan than outside it, is Yasujirō Ozu. What's noticeable about this confluence—between Ozu and Kurosawa—is how it brings into play two very distinct styles of seeing, two different approaches to time and movement, with the flow of the confluence weighted more in one direction—Kurosawa's—than the other. And, because of this difference of temperament (Kurosawa's polyphonic, sometimes mythopoeic; Ozu's urbane, quiet, and still), and also because, for a long time, we'd come to identify Kurosawa with Japanese cinema—for these reasons, Ozu must, for us, even now retain the air and freshness of a secret, of a personal discovery: almost as much as, in fact, he would have for Ray. He is the hidden coordinate in that "fruition" and "culmination," the one that lies behind the revaluation and opening that *Rashomon* involves, implicating us in a sense of the modern that is deceptively simple and immediate but far-reaching. To contain this pairing by saying that Kurosawa is less

Japanese than Ozu is to miss the many-sided way in which we receive and interpret modernity. If we look at the countries I've cited in the course of this talk—Iran and India—we see how this pattern, in the context of film, repeats itself strangely but tellingly, and even, sometimes—challenging our preconceptions about cultural authenticity—inverts itself. In India, for instance, Ray himself is part of a pair, and the other half of the pair is the prodigiously gifted, but self-destructive, Ritwik Ghatak, who died in the seventies probably as a result of his alcoholism. There are many ways in which this pairing could be described and contrasted; one could call Ray a classicist, and Ghatak the possessor of an operatic sensibility. One could also describe Ray as a progeny of the Enlightenment and its flowering in Bengal, and Ghatak as an errant son, someone who turned the Enlightenment inside out in his movies. More characteristically, however, Ray's temperament has been called "Western" by some Indian critics, and Ghatak the more genuinely "Indian" of the two, and for reasons completely opposite to those pertaining to Ozu and Kurosawa. I think that, in this formulation, Ray's slowness, which in Ozu is a mark of recondite "Oriental" stillness, his air of "calm without, fire within," is seen as a kind of European reserve, and associated, in particular, with Western-derived realism; while Ghatak's narrative energy, his melodrama, his fascination with mythic grandeur (all of which in Kurosawa can be seen to be driven by a "strong Occidental streak" that prefers declamation to suggestion, "action" to stillness), is, in the Bengali filmmaker, often supposed to emanate from authentically Indian, and oral, modes of storytelling. One can imagine a parallel planetary configuration in which Ghatak is more famous in the West than Ray, and Ozu than Kurosawa, and sense that, in that universe, the terms would be adjusted, and mirror each other, accordingly, and essentially remain unchanged.

Similarly, Iran: the two major filmmakers from that country, Abbas Kiarostami and Mohsin Makhmalbaf, have strikingly contrasting sensibilities, the former presenting a very interesting development on neorealism, where nuance, bourgeois ordinariness, and leisureliness, along with odd but rich self-reflexivity, create the lens through which Iran appears; the latter, Makhmalbaf, making use of folklore, bright colours, and fairy tales. This sort of dichotomy rehearses one that's been familiar to us for more than twenty years now: the one that identifies suggestiveness, compression, and realism with canonical Western traditions, and storytelling, fantasy, orality, and passion with postcolonial ones. When we are viewing Ray or Kurosawa or Kiarostami, however, we are really witnessing a "fruition" which always suggests more, which, at that moment, we are capable of sensing but not grasping. Not necessarily more of the same—other Kiarostamis and Rays and Kurosawas, confirming, thereby, these filmmakers' traditions and cultural identities—but of their opposites and others: Ozu and Makhmalbaf and Ghatak. All these form the hidden coordinates of what that moment of "fruition" gestures towards: tensions and contestations that form the fabric around, and of, the artwork, and of which we too are a part. They make, in a sense, the old opposing categories of "East" and "West" seem cumbersome—even, in the limited but pervasive roles ascribed to them, redundant.

The Alien Face of Cosmopolitanism

An Indian Reading of Cynthia Ozick on the Woolfs

2009, *New Left Review*

LET ME BEGIN with a series of recent conversations. In fact, these are snatches of conversation from larger discussions, in almost all of which the subject of cosmopolitanism and modernity—in their locations both in and out of Europe—were broached, explored, and argued over. In one of them (the venue was a bookshop), I was trying to articulate my unease with the term "postcolonial writer"; not only as a description of myself, but as a description of a generic figure. Both the affiliations and the oppositionality of the "postcolonial writer" seemed too clearly defined; while, for most of the more interesting canonical writers of twentieth-century India, the complexity and unexpectedness of their oppositionality took their affiliations to unexpected territory—for the Urdu writer, Qurratulain Hyder, therefore, there was Elizabeth Bowen; for the Bengali poet, novelist, and critic Buddhadeva Bose, who adored Tagore and also adored Eliot, there were the compensatory, contrary figures of the poet Jibanananda Das, a contemporary he did much to champion, and of D. H. Lawrence and Whitman. The richness of the various power struggles to define the literary within India in the time of modernity, and the robust, often contradictory creative opportunism that took place in the interests of that struggle, is, alas, considerably reduced and simplified by the terms "colonial" or "postcolonial." If one were to map the strategic affinities of these writers, those terms would gradually lose their mythic integrity; what would begin to appear (almost accidentally, as not every point of the map would be known to the other) is a sort of trade route of vernacular experimentation, a patois of the concrete, an effervescent cherishing of the idiosyncratic. If we were to trace the lines radiating from one writer or location to another on this map, we might, for instance, find that, often, a high degree of attention and erudition had been brought to bear upon the commonplace.

Of course, no such map exists. But the fact that these forms of "commerce" (Pound's word for his curious relationship with Whitman) did characterise literary activity in the late nineteenth and in the twentieth centuries comes back to us even today, in, as I've just suggested, unpremeditated instants. One of them occurred at the end of the discussion I just referred to, when, in that bookshop in Oxford, a young Bangladeshi graduate student said to me: "I've spoken to Indian writers who write in Bengali"—and, here, he mentioned Sunil Ganguly, the leading poet, novelist, and aging enfant terrible who lives in Calcutta, and Ketaki Kushari Dyson, poet, translator of Tagore, erstwhile star student, who lives in the Oxford she was an undergraduate at, and who was in that audience—"I've spoken to these people, and they aren't happy with the term 'postcolonial.'" He suggested this might be because of the sort of transverse mappings and affiliations I'd mentioned, and which these writers had pursued in the interests of arriving at the recognisable tone and metier of their enterprise, lines of contact that couldn't be contained by the orthodox demarcations of the "postcolonial." But it was, still, chastening and something of a salutary shock to be reminded of actual, specific individuals, and to become conscious of them in a new way, as I began to become aware of Ketaki Kushari Dyson that evening, sitting not a great distance away from me, in her seventies now. In constructing my argument, I'd thought about myself, about history and the great canonical writers of the Indian past, and even, in general terms, of writers like Ketaki Dyson; but I hadn't thought of her in particular, and, for whatever reason, it had never occurred to me to speak to her, or to query her, about the subject. I knew her opinions on a range of things; but, on this, there had been an inadvertent silence. Now, to hear from another source, during a public conversation (she, wordless, as if she had some of the sphinxlike instructiveness of history or the archive), that she was unhappy at being termed a "postcolonial" was at once vindicating and, as I've just confessed, disconcerting.

In attempting to think about the alien face of cosmopolitanism, I've had to have recourse to moments such as this one, to impressions rather than hard historical fact. Something not spoken of, a question not asked, something you thought you'd forgotten, and remembered later in a different way: these are almost all that are left of the residual cosmopolitanisms of the world—an odd sense of discomfiture, and, in lieu of a definitive language, personal reminiscences that appear to have implications, but remain isolated and arbitrary. I'm interested in exploring whether these moments—essentially afterthoughts from itineraries that have almost been erased—can mark the beginnings of an admittedly desultory enquiry, as much as the assignation of an actual historical date might: a date such as the Indian art historian Partha Mitter fixes, for instance, when he argues that the Bauhaus exhibition in Calcutta in 1922 led to the formation of an artistic avant-garde in India. The exchange that evening in Oxford, and my failure to follow up with Ketaki Dyson, who disappeared quickly after the event, have made me alert to the conversations I've had since with writers in, for the want of a better term, the Indian vernaculars—they being, often without quite knowing it, the sole remnants in our country of those vanished cosmopolitanisms. But there are remnants adrift everywhere—and, so, overheard remarks and incomplete confessions from people, especially writers and academics, from various parts of the world also shape my interpretation. I'm not, in doing this, hinting that the rumours of the death of the cosmopolitan are exaggerated; nor am I simply arguing for his or her survival. I am registering the persistence of a worldview as an angularity, resurfacing constantly, at a time when the old dichotomies that defined and animated it (for instance, the "cosmopolitan" in relation to the "provincial") have become largely irrelevant. How does one think of the cosmopolitan in the global world?

Let me cite three conversations, beginning with the most recent one. Not long ago, I had dinner with C. S. Lakshmi, who was visiting Calcutta from Bombay, where she lives; Lakshmi is better known by her pseudonym "Ambai," and is one of the most sensuous and experimental short story writers in the Tamil language. My wife had begun to talk about a little, comical altercation Salman Rushdie had initiated with me recently in print, while I, without irony, protested my admiration for *Midnight's Children*. "But you can't just bring in these forms by force," said Lakshmi, scolding an invisible third party. "Firstly, you have to see if there's any such thing as 'magic realism' in your tradition or not." She'd clearly decided this was doubtful. She confided, perturbed, scandalised: "Do you know, it's begun in the languages as well." By "languages" she meant the Indian ones. "Even Tamil and Kannada writers are now trying to be 'magic realist.'"

Before I reflect on these statements, let me quickly move on to the second conversation. This took place over the telephone, again in Calcutta; my interlocutor was Utpal Kumar Basu, probably the most accomplished and—if I might use that word—interesting living poet in the Bengali language. We were discussing, in passing, the nature of the achievement of Subimal Misra, one of the short-story writing avant-garde in sixties Bengal. "He set aside the conventional Western short story with its idea of time; he was more true to our Indian sensibilities; he set aside narrative," said Basu. "That's interesting," I observed. "You know, of course, that, in the last twenty years or so, it's we Indians and postcolonials who are supposed to be the storytellers, emerging as we do from our oral traditions and our millennial fairy tales." "Our fairy tales are very different from theirs," said Utpal Basu, unmoved. "We don't start with, 'Once upon a time . . .'"

In both cases, Basu's and Lakshmi's, a cultural politics to do with a more or less unexamined category, "Indianness," was being used to advance a politics of the modernist avant-garde; both writers, in effect, were offering a throwaway polemic against what the postmodern and the postcolonial had largely rehabilitated—narrative and the fairy tale. A second glance at their remarks, and the suggestive way the word "our" is used in them—"our tradition," "our stories," "our sensibilities"—tells us that it's not the essential and changeless that's being gestured towards, but the contingent and historical; a cosmopolitanism of the avant-garde that had been located in an India which, since the late nineteenth century, had been making those transverse mappings across territories in the pursuit of certain objectives: the fragmentary, the concrete, and a certain quality of the aleatory that narrative couldn't accommodate. If the didacticism of the postmodern and the postcolonial had taught us that narrative—especially in its guise as epic—was liberating, that storytelling was "empowering" in its expression of identity, the cosmopolitan avant-garde all over the world in the twentieth century had repeatedly drawn our attention to the tyranny, the enforcements, of narrative: it was to the latter that C. S. Lakshmi and Utpal Basu were referring when using that pronoun, "our."

Using the rhetoric of cultural nationalism in the service of the interests of the avant-garde has a long history in the non-West, almost as long a history there as that of modernity itself, and I've written about this elsewhere. There is, for example, Tagore's strategic celebration of the fourth-century Sanskrit poet Kalidasa, as a great, possibly the supreme, describer of the "real" (Tagore's word for the "real" is "nature"), a celebration undertaken while demonstrating that Western poetic language—especially Shakespeare's language—repeatedly falls short of the Flaubertian task of description. This praise is formulated in the first decade of the twentieth century; but even earlier, in 1894, to be precise, Tagore is already attacking rationality and teleology, and enshrining the aleatory, in his essay on Bengali nursery rhymes. Here, drawing the reader's attention to the presence of random associations that so-called "grown up" writing often lacks, he borrows from, or echoes remarkably, William James's famous essay in *Psychology*, which had been published just three years earlier. The rubric of Tagore's meditation is shored up by forms of cultural nationalism (the invention of a literary tradition with regard to Kalidasa; the construction of a Bengali childhood in connection with the nursery rhymes), but the interests are the interests of the avant-garde (through Kalidasa, a privileging of the image and the "here and now"; through the nursery rhymes, a celebration of the disruption of linear time, and of the mysterious importance of the "superfluous"). And these interests, intriguingly, are being articulated right at the inception, worldwide, of the avant-garde, and, coincidentally, at the crossroads, or confluence, at which both political nationalisms and cosmopolitanisms are everywhere coming into being. The nationalism makes possible Tagore's cultural politics as a colonised subject, and the cosmopolitanism a certain kind of journey and mapping (for instance, the crucial and unprecedented borrowing of the notion of the "stream of consciousness," "*nityaprabahita chetanar majhe*," the first known literary transposition of the idea, in fact). Against what the nationalisms of the colonies are being fashioned we are certain, but to what end, and against exactly what, the anarchic play, the space for the superfluous, promoted by the various cosmopolitanisms are being posited we are still not entirely clear about; but it's clear that the urgency of the mission leads to an intricate and intense reciprocity over and across the values imposed by colonialism.

Here, I should also mention the Japanese writer Junichiro Tanizaki's brief, dreamlike manifesto, *In Praise of Shadows*, where a civilised cultural politics carries forward an essentially modernist programme. Tanizaki is speaking of Japanese, even, occasionally, Eastern, architecture, habitation, allocation of domestic space, and domestic appurtenances in opposition to Western conceptions and traditions of the same things; in doing so, he's positioning shadows, indefiniteness, a desire for decrepitude and recycling, against the definiteness, the clarity, the newness treasured by the West. It's really a modernist dichotomy, a modernist polemic; in speaking of the East and the West, Tanizaki is subtly, richly, delicately, conflating the Japanese with the modernist. We should remember that, from the late nineteenth to the early twentieth century—when neither modernism nor the avant-garde had been ascribed the denominations, the locations, the histories and epiphanic moments by which we know them today—the West, for both European radicals and non-Western artists and thinkers, was identified with linearity, rationality, and naturalism. The Bauhaus painters' works—Klee, Kandinsky, and others—were brought to Calcutta on Tagore's behest; the latter had, Partha Mitter tells us, seen these paintings on a visit to Austria, and recognised a concordance, a convergence, of temperament and intention with his own; Mitter also reminds us of Klee's secret but deep absorption in Indian philosophy. Once the paintings were exhibited, they were reviewed in Calcutta's major English-language daily, the *Statesman*, by Stella Kramrisch, an art historian of Austrian-Jewish descent, who was also spending time in India at Tagore's invitation. In her review, Kramrisch told her readers that these paintings might reveal to them "that European art does not mean naturalism and that the transposition of forms of nature in the work of an artist is common to ancient and modern India." The attack on linearity and naturalism cannot be characterised as a Western development alone, with occasional epiphanic and opportunistic uses of "other" cultural resources by Western artists: Picasso with his African mask, Gauguin and Van Gogh with their Japanese prints.

A history of cosmopolitanism and modernism has to take into account both the incursion of the Japanese print into Van Gogh's painting and the peculiar mixture of identity-making, cultural politics, and modernist rhetoric in people like Tanizaki and Tagore: that both were happening at the same time, and, importantly, that the modernism we're aware of in different ways today was being fashioned in the same world. What is common to Picasso, Gauguin, Kramrisch, Klee, Tagore, Tanizaki, and others is an impatience with a certain kind of hard and finished object, a cosmopolitan profligacy and curiosity, a renewed, all-consuming attention directed to the contingent, the "here and now," the particular, and a stated or secret flirtation with "otherness" or "difference," at a time when no language exists to do with "difference," except the one dealing in terms like "East," "West," "progress," "materialism," and the "primitive." It is no historical coincidence that the avant-garde and the modernist were created everywhere in the time of colonialism. One exists in the other, in hidden ways—but not interred simply, as, in Edward Said's reading, the West Indian plantation is hidden in Jane Austen's work; a suppressed, indubitable truth that, once brought to light, would clarify and redress at once.

•

I had mentioned a third conversation. More enigmatic comment than conversation, I remember it dislocated me because of its suggestive rather than categorical nature, and because it gave me an intimation of lines of contact I should have known more about. It also hinted at a problem of language which is always with us, and prohibits a discussion of modernity without the use of certain catchwords and oppositions: "Western," "derived," "mimicry," "elitism." The context here is my visit to the Wissenschaftkolleg in Berlin for lunch almost three years ago, as a preamble to a talk I would deliver in early 2006. My very generous hosts that afternoon all happened to be, fortuitously, Egyptian academics: probably because, given my own interests, all three—two women and a man—were from cultural studies or postcolonial studies or literary departments. Predictably, at some point, the conversation hovered around and then moved gently, but headlong, towards Indian literature, Salman Rushdie, and "magic realism"; as predictably, my contribution introduced a note of uncertainty in relation to the question of unacknowledged modernisms. The women nodded; I sensed that their own trajectories and career choices would have ordinarily distanced them from my preoccupations, but that erstwhile literary investments, perhaps (who knows) buried family histories, and, more noticeably, Rushdie's recent pro-American politics in relation to Iraq had also alienated them from the project of epic fantasy. The man, however, was slightly different; unlike the women, at least one of whom seemed to have spent a lot of time in America, he taught in a department of literature in Egypt; his dilemmas, his biography, would have been somewhat unlike theirs, which is probably why it was in private that he told me: "We have the same problem in Egypt. We find it difficult to talk about the cosmopolitanisms and modernisms in our tradition." As I revisit the scene now, I become aware of distinctions and contrasts that my mind had suppressed at the time. The women were globalised individuals, and spoke English fluently: one of them, I think, was a naturalised American. The man, on the other hand, with all his unprepossessing sophistication, evidently spoke and wrote English as a second language. This reminded me of certain parallels in India, and the way the English language inflected histories there: the women, with their possibly elite and global backgrounds, their command of English and their smattering or more of Arabic, echoed the contexts in India in which postcoloniality and notions of hybridity had been consolidated; the man, comfortable in Arabic, with more than a cursory knowledge of English, deeply engaged, in fact, with European literature, reminded me of an earlier, superannuated context in my country, in which, largely, our cosmopolitan modernity had been formed, and from which, with cultural inflections very similar to the Egyptian man's, writers like the poet Utpal Basu and the short-story writer C. S. Lakshmi had emerged.

•

What do I mean, or, for that matter, understand by the word "cosmopolitan"? The primary sense that's operational in India is, as I've pointed out elsewhere, a constitutional one: it's related to a governmental guarantee that heterogeneous faiths, communities, and cultures might cohabit peacefully, even vibrantly, within a visible space—usually, the city—in the nation. In this, it's not unlike "multiculturalism," or the special Indian post-Independence version of the "secular": a domain not outside of religion, but a constitutionally protected space of inter-religious, intercommunal coexistence. Perhaps the word "cosmopolitan" also makes a gesture towards the urban middle classes; and, as a result, it's often Bombay (where I grew up), whose educated middle class encompasses a multifariousness of faiths and provincial identities—Gujarati, Maharashtrian, Parsi, Tamil, Bengali, Bohri Muslims, "East Indian" Christians, to name some of them—that's called the most "cosmopolitan" of Indian cities.

I, however, for the purposes of this piece, have an idea of the word somewhat different from the constitutional one; it has to do with the notion of inner exile at the core of the "high" cultures of the twentieth century. If one were to keep this notion in mind, the city of Calcutta would come powerfully into the frame; and a history of Bombay cosmopolitanism beg to be written that is more than, or distinct from, an account of variegated urban coexistence. I will return to these two cities later. But the theme of "inner exile" reminds us that the bourgeois cosmopolitan (most profoundly, in our imagination, the European cosmopolitan)—whether artist or intellectual or writer—was never entirely at one with himself or herself. Let's stay with the European cosmopolitan for a moment, as an apparently founding, fundamental type. He or she presents a characteristic twentieth-century embodiment of Europeanness, but also an intriguing modulation upon it; in fact, a testing of the very limits and recognisable features of Europeanness, because the cosmopolitan, by his or her very nature, is constantly telling us they belong nowhere. In what way? One of the main reasons for this, as we know, is that at the heart of the hegemonic "high" cultures of modernity is the Jewish artist or intellectual; simply put, the Jew, the Other. With the crucial involvement of the figure of the Jew—and I use that term metaphorically as well as literally, introducing all its specific physical dimensions—in the shaping of cosmopolitanism, European modernity becomes, at once, characteristically itself, with its unmistakable eclectic tenor, as we know it today, and deeply alienated from itself. All that is canonically strange about the European twentieth century—its avant-garde, its artistic disruptiveness, its experimentation—opens up, if we linger with the figure of the Jew for a while, into the strange that is not canonical, that is not European, that always carries within it the unrecognisable texture of the minority. But this pursuit can't be an exercise where we eventually rip off the mask to reveal the true face underneath, fair or dark; because we have to reconcile ourselves, in a new way, to the fact that cosmopolitanism does not, and never had, a true face; its characteristic domain, and achievement, is the defamiliarised.

•

Before I go any further, I should quickly distinguish what I'm doing here from the many excellent scholarly studies available on the role of Jewishness in modernity. My attempt is less rigorous and more impressionistic, and has, inescapably, to do with facets of who I am: raised in Bombay, a middle-class Bengali, located, as both a writer and a reader, in the histories of modernism in a putatively postmodern age. Chancing upon an old essay by Cynthia Ozick, "Mrs. Virginia Woolf: A Madwoman and her Nurse," from her 1983 collection, *Art and Ardor*, set into motion a train of thoughts that had been with me for a while, to do with Jewishness as well as the India I'd grown up in. It also made me think further into what, in the context of the conversations I've reported, I'd already been thinking about: who is the non-Western cosmopolitan? Did he or she, as it were, vanish thirty years ago into postcolonial identity and ethnicity? Or does the dichotomy of the Western and the non-Western, as we understand it today, actually fall apart in the cosmopolitan?

Ozick's essay is a review of Quentin Bell's biography of his aunt Virginia; and it is, as the title implies, an account of a difficult marriage held together by significant companionship. But it also contains a surprisingly large digression on Leonard Woolf's Jewish identity in particular, and Jewishness in general, the compulsive reflections of a commentator who, a privileged insider in American letters (and, increasingly, a passionate proponent of Zionism), must, at this moment of all moments, confront the spectre of non-Europeanness. Ozick, however, doesn't speak of herself directly; instead, she dwells on the ministering husband in the very heart of Bloomsbury, and, specifically, on faces and appearances. She introduces the theme, the hiccup, the rupture, after briefly sketching the educational background of the Bloomsbury set, and then narrowing upon Leonard: "Cambridge was not natural to him, Bloomsbury was not natural to him, even England was not natural to him—not as an inheritance; he was a Jew." And then these comments, on the biographer's failure to properly imagine Leonard Woolf, leading to an unexpected consequence, an opening up; for, Ozick would have it, Bell's inability to "get" Leonard makes him present to us, while aunt Virginia, whom Bell might understand intuitively, becomes distant: "Quentin Bell has no 'authority' over Leonard Woolf, as he has over his aunt; Leonard is nowhere in the biographer's grip... The effect is unexpected. It is as if Virginia Woolf escapes—possessing her too selectively, the biographer lets her slip—but Leonard Woolf somehow stays to become himself."

And in what way, in Ozick's essay, does he "become himself"? She describes the strange courtship, the really very distinct worlds, domestic parameters, and lineages the husband-and-wife-to-be belonged to, Virginia's trademark enervating uncertainties, the careful and polite abstention, in their set, from any remark being passed either on Leonard's religion or his agnosticism, and, in spite of this, Virginia's bewildered admission: "You seem so foreign." Now, Ozick begins to discuss the inescapable marks of Jewishness, and, in doing so, almost accidentally touches upon an element in the fashioning of the cosmopolitan in the twentieth century that is rarely acknowledged; the way the cosmopolitan could, poetically, "belong nowhere," be in a state of inner exile, while the subconscious responded to a register, an actual mark, in her or him, which it could never express itself about with the candour that Virginia Woolf, from her position of agitated intimacy, could: "You seem so foreign." This is the mark of alterity or difference: not antithetical to cosmopolitanism's homelessness, its internationalism, but, I hope to suggest, fundamental to it. Ozick brings us to the incontrovertible piece of evidence, the face, tracing its passage and vicissitudes from Woolf's paternal grandfather's time to his own. In connection, again, with his contemporaries, Ozick points out that "if his own origins were almost never mentioned to his face, his face was nevertheless there, and so, in those striking old photographs, were the faces of his grandparents." Ozick quotes Leonard Woolf's own words, from his autobiography, on his paternal grandfather: "a large, stern, black-haired, and black-whiskered, rabbinical Jew in a frock coat" with a "look of stern rabbinical orthodoxy." According to Ozick, he preferred his Dutch-born maternal grandmother's face, "the round, pink face of an incredibly old Dutch doll," and he also wondered if this grandmother might have had "a good deal of non-Jewish blood in her ancestry. Some of her children and grandchildren were fair-haired and facially very unlike the 'typical' Jew." About his grandfather, though, he was resolutely without illusions: "No one could have mistaken him for anything but a Jew. Although he wore coats and trousers, hats and umbrellas, just like those of all the other gentlemen in Addison Gardens, he looked to me as if he might have stepped straight out of one of those old pictures of caftaned, bearded Jews in a ghetto..." And so, in his unconvincing "coats and trousers, hats and umbrellas," Leonard's grandfather is already working his way towards that secular modernity that his grandson will come to inhabit, almost naturally, but whose neutral "Englishness," in turn, even in the temporary persona of the colonial officer, a figure of authority, does not deceive Ozick. She is, again inadvertently I think, gesturing towards a history of the secular from the nineteenth century onwards that is as characteristic of the non-West as it is, as we see, of the heart of Empire itself; the fusing of ethnic identity, as in the case of the grandfather, with a European paradigm, an almost proud fusing, one can't help feeling, in spite of the grandson's misgivings; and then, two generations later, with the fashioning of the cosmopolitan, the modern, and the modernist, we have the grandson's invisibility, which, as Ozick shrewdly points out (without unfolding any of its consequences), is also a form of visibility. The process was taking place, let's say, in Bengal as much as in London; it is often called "Westernisation," which is an almost meaningless term, not only because the process meant very different things to, say, to Leonard Woolf's grandfather and to Woolf himself, but because it does not catch the intricacy, the cultural and emotional complexity, of the way "difference" directs the process. It's something that could equally, and as validly, be called "non-Westernisation," without any of the assertiveness of the postcolonial discourses.

Ozick now turns to a photograph, part of what she calls a "pictorial history of Bloomsbury." Before she offers her reading, she offers her caveat: "One is drawn to Leonard's face much as he was drawn to his grandfather's face, and the conclusion is the same. What Leonard's eyes saw [that is, when they confronted his grandfather] was what the eyes of the educated English classes saw [that is, when regarding Woolf]." Ozick is right to alert us to this; but there is also the question of what her eyes see, and what ours do. Ozick studies the "arresting snapshot" of Leonard Woolf and Adrian Stephen, brother of Virginia Woolf. "They are," says Ozick, "both young men in their prime; the date is

1914 ... They are dressed identically (vests, coats, ties) and positioned identically—feet apart, hands in pocket, shut lips gripping pipe or cigarette holder ... Both faces are serene, holding back amusement, indulgent of the photographer." At this point, we come to the anticipated turn in the portrayal: "And still it is not a picture of two cultivated Englishmen, or not only that. Adrian is incredibly tall and Vikinglike, with a forehead as broad and flat as a chimney tile; he looks like some blue-blood American banker not long out of Princeton; his hair grows straight up like thick pale straw. Leonard's forehead is an attenuated wafer under a tender black forelock, his nose is nervous and frail ..." After a moment's reflection on what the correct analogy might, Ozick decides to be, as she puts it, "blunt": "he looks like a student at the yeshiva. Leonard has the unmistakable face of a Jew."

Ozick is absolutely right, I think, in her preternatural and prickly sensitivity, to exhume the Jewish identity of the "cultivated Englishman"; but she is perhaps wrong to give it such fixity. There is another kind of movement taking place in this image, this picture, which Ozick says nothing about, and which would consign Adrian Stephen's type—blonde, tall, "Vikinglike"—into history just as Woolf's grandfather had been consigned to history; it involves, in the unwitting figure of Woolf, the emergence of the cosmopolitan—the person who belongs nowhere, the person whose alterity and state of exile are hidden but unmistakable. The old distinction between the "student at the yeshiva" and the "cultivated Englishman" may have been true of Woolf's grandfather's time, but it is, already, no longer of Woolf's: to be modern, increasingly, will be to be impure, to both conceal and exhibit that impurity. The great project of "high" modernity, defamiliarisation, and the principal discourse of postcoloniality, alterity, had always, we'd presumed, been distinct from each other, belonging to distinct phases of twentieth-century history, and even embedded in worldviews at war with one another. A second glance at the cosmopolitan—especially at the Jewish writers and artists who lived in Europe, many of them transplanted to America from around the time of the Second World War, or who died shortly before (Walter Benjamin, Kracauer, Adorno, Schoenberg, Bloch, Hannah Arendt, to name a few)—reminds us that alterity is an indispensable and intimate constituent of the "high" modern, that it is the hidden twin of what is already hidden but powerfully definitive of "high" modernity—the defamiliarised. To be modern, Ozick accidentally reminds us, is to be foreign, to be "different": not only figuratively, but, in significant ways, literally; and it is of course the literal, for obvious reasons of her own, that Ozick is here fiercely concentrated on. As far as appearances are concerned, the misfit in the picture, the one who is already beginning to date, is Adrian Stephen, not Leonard Woolf.

Let me, here, address my own recollections of cosmopolitanism; for Ozick's essay is of interest to me because, primarily, it makes me realign what I already know. I wish to refer to faces and styles of appearance in Bombay that gradually decided for me, as I was growing up in the sixties and seventies, what the lineaments of cosmopolitanism and bohemianism might be. In the light of Ozick's essay, I am led to wonder what made me take those decisions: for no clear or definitive catalogue of features had been put down. Of course, one identified an artist or writer of the avant-garde through their work, but there was clearly another realm involved, or else I wouldn't have registered the adolescent shock I did at the discrepancy between T. S. Eliot's appearance and his poetry, the canonical unfamiliarity and experimental nature of the latter, and the unfamiliar or unexpected conventionality of the former. We are aware, certainly, that Eliot made deliberate comic use of this discrepancy, in "Prufrock," of course, but pointedly in "Lines for Cuscuscaraway and Mirza Murad Ali Beg": "How unpleasant to meet Mr Eliot! / With his features of clerical cut, / And his brow so grim / And his mouth so prim . . ." Here is the American exile, in middle age, a man who has, for long, deliberately emptied his appearance of signs of exile, and who seems to be mocking the visible features of cosmopolitanism (not in his poetry, but in his personal style), who seems to be refuting (and I'm making no easy connection with his publicised anti-Semitism) the subterranean ethos of alterity.

The realm of the visible, then, is an important one in recognising the cosmopolitan, because it comprises both carefully orchestrated markers and intrinsic lapses. Visible signs also help us to distinguish between cosmopolitanism as inner exile, and the other, constitutional form of cosmopolitanism I mentioned earlier, a state-sponsored multiculturalism. As the decades after Independence went past, this second form became the authoritative one in India, and especially definitive, in a clichéd way, of society in Bombay; what the history of cosmopolitanism as a state of inner exile might be in that city has become increasingly difficult to remember or articulate. The visible markers of constitutional cosmopolitanism were symbolic and straightforward, as in a Hindi film set in the seventies, signifying sub-nationalisms that added up to the nation: there was the Sikh in his turban, there was the Muslim in his skull cap, there was the Christian crossing herself, and there the hero, at once Hindu and everyman, embodying the secular space—the film, the story, the nation—in which, despite tribulations and challenges, these particular elements unite. With the cosmopolitan as exile, the visible elements—the blue jeans, the hand-spun khadi kurta, the sandals, the filterless cigarette between the fingers, the copy of Lorca in one hand—did not add up; they did not cohere, as the constitution had foretold the heterogeneous fragments of the nation would; they were casual signs of belonging nowhere. I will elaborate on this in a moment.

I realise that, as I was growing up, I began to identify the cosmopolitan avant-garde and the bohemian artistic community in seventies Bombay not only by their practice, but also as a consequence of what they looked like. That tutoring had come to me from desultorily studying members of this sub-class from a distance, as well as both the works and faces of the American, especially, the New York, artists and poets; in fact, a certain kind of American person who happened to be quite distinct from the "tall, Vikinglike" American banker prototype Ozick compares Adrian Stephen to. In this group, whose features I'd been subconsciously absorbing, I'd include a whole range of practitioners, whose work, at the time, I didn't necessarily admire: Allen Ginsberg (who'd visited India in the sixties and hung out with the Bombay and especially the Calcutta poets, including Sunil Ganguly, whom I earlier described as an "aging enfant terrible"), as well as figures from pop culture and entertainment, like Bob Dylan, Woody Allen, Groucho Marx, and, with his diverse racial background and his benign belligerence, a sort of honorary Jew, Frank Zappa. There seemed to be an air of the outsider, of difference, about these people: I ascribed this to their practice, and to the persona being an extension of that practice. To be an outsider, in the twentieth century, was also to often have a curious combination of, on the one hand, the awkward, the pedagogical, the pedantic, and, on the other, the anarchic and comic, and, often, the two were interchangeable: thus, the anxious academic air of Woody Allen and Groucho Marx, and the quietly comic appearance of Albert Einstein. These were signs of the fine balancing act through which alterity was shaping modernity: a seriousness that was out of place and therefore foreign, mirroring a foreignness that was altogether too serious. The result could be comic, as is evident from Ozick's pitying, acerbic: "he looks like a student from the yeshiva." The modern, marked and pursued by difference, also makes a mess of things: "under the sign of Saturn" is how Susan Sontag describes the condition in connection with Walter Benjamin, who is less than adept at the technology of everyday life ("my inability even today to make a cup of coffee"), botching up too, with the yeshiva student's seriousness, his final, attempted escape to the United States. In India, this seriocomic figure of the modern, singled out at once by modernity and difference, emerges in the nineteenth century with the Bengali babu, and is parodied by Bengalis and Englishmen alike—most savagely, for the Anglophone reader, by Kipling in *Kim* at the beginning of the new century.

As for myself, I didn't dwell on the fact that many of the faces I was studying, by some coincidence, belonged to Jews, though this was often a part of their self-advertisement; Jewishness, hidden or anxious, if ineluctable, in the Europeans, seemed to have become, with these Americans, a more acknowledged secular component, sometimes a subversive one, of defamiliarisation. Many of the poets who lived or studied in Bombay, and wrote in English in the sixties and seventies—set apart in those relatively early decades after Independence, therefore, by the curious double prestige and disgrace of writing in a colonial language and an international one—this strange microcosmic minority (comprising, among others, Arun Kolatkar, Arvind Krishna Mehrotra, Nissim Ezekiel) were unmistakably cosmopolitans. They reminded me in some ways of the Americans, but this I might have taken to be a family resemblance, integral to the texture of the time. I may have also assumed that there were elements in their visible and intellectual make-up that they'd fashioned after the Americans; certainly, Kolatkar and Mehrotra had studied, respectively, William Carlos Williams and Pound in order to create a vernacular that would allow them to move away from both Orientalist poetry and King's English, a language of defamiliarisation, of finding the uncanny in the Indian mundane. Something in them also very powerfully echoed the Jewishness of American artists; but I was not conscious of this fact—nor do I think were they—except subliminally. The Jewish artist created a space that many non-Western cosmopolitans, especially in Bombay in the sixties, came to rework seamlessly in their own milieu, without anyone either clearly noticing it, or being able to remark on it except in inadequate terms such as "Westernisation." I say "inadequate," because the Jew had almost unknowingly introduced a dimension of racial and physical alterity to the modern, which, almost unknowingly, the sixties Indian English poets and bohemia presented their modulation upon. It was not simply towards the European or the Western that poets like Kolatkar and Mehrotra were aspiring, but a condition of twentieth-century modernity that crucially brought together what are seen to be incompatibles: defamiliarisation and difference, modernist experiment and ethnicity, Europeanness and non-Europeanness. It also occurs to me here that the modernities and cosmopolitanisms that I am familiar with were all shaped by disenfranchised elites; that is, by groups of people who, in the contexts they found themselves in, had no natural—or had a somewhat ambivalent and subterranean—access to political power. This was true of the Jews in Europe and even America; it was true of the Bengali in the time of colonialism; it was true of the odd minority position of the Indian poets who wrote in English in the sixties, at a time well before English was the "boom" Indian language it would become twenty five years later, being reproached by the canonical writers in the Indian vernaculars and Ginsberg alike for employing a foreign tongue. It was in these contexts of disenfranchised elitism that other, cultural modes of power were fashioned by these cosmopolitans. The question of legitimacy raised by each of the elites I've mentioned finds its odd, and possibly logical, counterpart in the constant question of the legitimacy of the artwork itself in modernism—is this art?—a challenge which has, of course, been domesticated in the triumphal narrative of European modernity.

Among the Bombay poets were a number of people who belonged to liminal religions: for instance, the founder poet of the group, the late Nissim Ezekiel, was Jewish, a descendant of the Bene Israel sect that had sought refuge in Gujarat in the 2nd century BCE; and there was Adil Jussawalla, one of the most intellectual of that set, a Zoroastrian and a Parsi. I'll only point out here that their minority status played itself out in two ways: firstly, in a semi-visible relationship to the secular, largely Hindu nation, and, secondly, in connection to the prism of cosmopolitanism, where it also merged into their roles as sometimes derided deracinated writers in the English language. Occasionally, and this is only a hunch, being part of a minority seems to have given them, particularly Ezekiel, privileged access to international cosmopolitanisms; at least, this what these lines from Ezekiel's autobiographical poem, "Background, Casually," seem to indicate: "The Indian landscape sears my eyes. / I have become a part of it / To be observed by foreigners. / They say that I am singular, / Their letters overstate the case." "Singular" is a word Ezekiel uses more than once; it encompasses both the resonance of the minority and of the privileged cosmopolitan. Living in India, being Indian, you almost feel that Ezekiel is aware of Jewish cosmopolitanism, but has forgotten the problem of Jewish alterity.

Interestingly, all these artists and poets—whether they were Hindus, Muslims, Parsis, Jews, Christians—made cosmopolitanism visible in a new way in the sixties and seventies, in that brief period when the old disenfranchised vernacular elites began to lose their intellectual hegemony in India, and before a new empowered post-Nehruvian ruling class emerged in the eighties with Rajiv Gandhi; they fashioned a style called the "ethnic," and, in doing so, complicated the relationship between the Indian and the deracinated, between authenticity and foreignness. "Ethnic," at the time, used to indicate, generally, non-Christian, non-European identity; with the bohemian set in India, it denoted the condition of belonging nowhere. Among the visible symbols of the ethnic were hand-spun khadi kurtas, sometimes worn in conjunction with long churidar pyjamas, sometimes blue jeans, cotton Bengali tangail saris, and, on the foreheads of bohemian women, large vermilion Fauvist bindis or dots, the feet of both men and women in Kolhapuri chappals or sandals. The conventional Western clothes of the Indian middle class—shirts, trousers, suits, shoes—were set aside, not in the interests of nationalism, but for a combination of clothing which, individually, could be overdeterminedly "Indian," but were now suddenly transformed into a signature of deracination. The "ethnic," then, is a peculiarly sixties' Indian modulation of alterity's delicate relationship to the cosmopolitan and the defamiliarised.

On this matter of the visibility of the cosmopolitan, and its surprising allocations of the recognisable and the unrecognisable, I wish to end with a tiny coda on the city of Calcutta, and on the Bengali bhadralok or bourgeois—the descendant of the babu. The Bengali bhadralok emerges more or less parallel to the Jewish cosmopolitan in Europe; in him, once again, as in the Jew, we find the "high" cultural defamiliarised merging with the irreducibly non-European. Unlike, for instance, the Japanese modern, the bhadralok eschews the Western suit; the suited Bengali, in fact, is often seen to be a government official, or a functionary of the Raj. The bhadralok's visible mark of deracination, of defamiliarisation, is the once-feudal costume, the white dhuti and panjabi or kurta; at what point the transition took place from the feudal to the cosmopolitan is difficult to pinpoint, but once it had, it became increasingly difficult to mistake, from a distance, the wearer of that costume as anyone except a person belonging to a particular history that was, indeed, unfolding worldwide. The fact that—unlike the flowing Persian or Oriental robes worn by Rammohun Roy or the Tagores, or, for that matter, the club-goer's suit—the dhuti and panjabi was the attire of the Bengali everyman was important; for, like the "cultivated Englishman," Leonard Woolf, it made the bhadralok at once invisible and newly visible. The worldwide history this person belonged to was a history of the modern, certainly, but it was also a history of the different; it was a narrative of "high" culture as well as being a narrative of otherness. That narrative, as was to be expected, had a limited life; the figure in the dhuti and panjabi has all but disappeared. This makes it possible to consider afresh the contraries that were visible but never fully declared in its appearance.

The Origins of Dislike

2010, talk at the South Asia Initiative, Harvard University

After our marriage, my wife discovered it was risky accompanying me to art galleries. In the Louvre, in 1996, I kept up a relentless commentary as we passed from one room of great Western art to another, registering, in various degrees, my intolerance (unless we entered a non-Western room, or found we were among the post-Impressionists or the moderns). I wasn't playing the "postcolonial" card—why should I, with my wife? Besides, that would have been clear in the delight I took in the post-Impressionists; though, even here, I had to interject and point out I'd never cared for Monet's water lilies. No, I was expressing a deep, ingrained impatience—which is not to say that, simply because it was deep, it had no cultural context or historical ancestry—while taking advantage of the fact that my wife would be a cooperative victim or listener.

What was it about Western art that I recoiled from? In what capacity exactly had I generalised when I used the term "Western"? In many ways, all I abhorred was contained in arguably the most important rooms in the Louvre—the ones exhibiting Renaissance painting and Greek sculpture. In order to have a proper feeling for and understanding of Western art, you had to walk around these rooms with a proprietary ease—or at least ostensible respect. You didn't skulk in them in a state of antagonism. Try as I might, though, I couldn't open up to a Rembrandt.

Some part of me acknowledged this both as a deficiency on my part and as an unavoidable situation—that my upbringing may have ensured that I didn't have the intellectual background, or enough connectedness to that background, to prevent myself from seeing this tradition from the outside. The matter of being "inside" or "outside" a certain circle—let's call it the believers in and aficionados of the Renaissance for the moment—was subterranean but present; and, with it, the business of feeling included or excluded.

In the early years of the new millennium, I saw, in Amsterdam, paintings by contemporaries of Rembrandt that seemed to me more interesting than anything I'd encountered by the great man; they were portraits of burghers of the town. Each group portrait marked the emergence of both biographical narrative and the social as we've long understood them: that each life, in fruition of past achievements, and looking toward the future, came together in a static, rehearsed moment of sociability, in what D. H. Lawrence, in the more fluid context of the novel, had called "subtle human interrelationship." It was as a parameter for a certain kind of novel that I found these Dutch portraits remarkable. I was also aware, as I gazed upon these pictures, that I was constructing the prehistory of the kind of novel I didn't really care for.

•

Should I provide instances of things in the museum I couldn't bring myself to admire? A list of dislikes always seems more feral, and less related to a rational cause, than a list of things you approve of. Anyway, on my list were Titian and Rubens, varieties of Renaissance oil painting, and the very texture of Greek and Renaissance sculpture: the fold of a pleated gown, the crease between the eyebrows, the muscles impressed on a stomach all set my teeth on edge. All careful marks on stone, and to what purpose? To capture and replicate life? To demonstrate such replication was achievable? When Lawrence said of Cézanne's apples that they were "not true to life, but more true to life," he was speaking of an art that had escaped the Renaissance's bulging, three-dimensional quality. Yet this quality was, we'd been told when we were children, one of the pinnacles of Western art: the precision and individuality of the folds and pleats on a gown.

The moment we slipped into the rooms containing Mesopotamian sculpture, I experienced a sense of release—I was moved by this regal, alien notion of gracefulness. I was also reminded a bit of the Zoroastrian figures carved into the Parsi buildings in Bombay, which I'd noticed since I was a schoolboy, but never enquired after or properly understood. But subjective association couldn't fully explain my sense of recognition in the Mesopotamian room; because I'd never been properly aware that I *liked* the Zoroastrian figures. Then my wife and I went to the part of the gallery where the Russian art that preceded the Enlightenment was displayed; here, too, I felt I was in proximity to a world at once infinitely distant and known. Moving to the icons—those repetitive images of adoration—meant coming face to face with what I'd only encountered before in Tarkovsky's *Andrei Rublev*. Harold Bloom describes a condition, an anxiety, that the writer or artist is susceptible to, probably from Romanticism onward, and certainly until postmodernity, which he terms "belatedness": the writer's intuition (experienced as a crisis) that he—Bloom's examples are male—was born at the wrong moment in history, just after the masters who are formative to him, and in an environment in which he can't put his "natural" gifts to use. (Although "writing naturally," qua Keats, for whom poetry must come as "naturally as leaves to a tree or not at all," is considered part of the mythology of Romanticism, "belatedness" reminds us that the Romantic poet had also fallen irretrievably from nature.) The context of Bloom's discussion, as we know, is principally Milton and the English Romantics; but "belatedness" has many incarnations, some of them cultural rather than ontological. Seamus Heaney's crisis in the early eighties, when he seemed, in effect, to believe that the free world couldn't produce poets of the stature of Miroslav Holub because it lacked East Europe's repressive political history is an odd example of "belatedness." Adorno's commandment that writing poetry is impossible after Auschwitz is surely a species of belatedness, since it presumes there was a time, before that historical trauma occurred, when poetry was natural and spontaneously possible. In modern India, the conflation, from the nineteenth century onwards, of the use of the mother-tongue with creative authenticity is a version of belatedness; all would be well, according to this line of thought, with the canon of Indian Anglophone writing if only its practitioners returned to their own language. Some such yearning, and the awareness of being historical latecomers, must have informed the turn initiated by a few key writers in Bengal from the 1860s onward from English to Bengali. That this didn't banish belatedness becomes clear when we find the great poet of the age, Tagore, feeling as acutely belated as any writer previously had, and longing, despite himself, to be a contemporary of the 4th-century court poet Kalidasa.

Yet it wasn't belatedness I felt in the Louvre while confronting Titian on the one hand and the Russian icon on the other. It was the superannuation of certain civilisations, of certain forms of representation and viewing the world, that I found myself participating in, while rediscovering the extant reign and encompassing dominion of others. Closest to the inviolate hegemon were the rooms related to the Renaissance; while the Mesopotamian and Russian rooms gave us a chance to come into contact with styles and views that had, essentially, been vanquished or sidelined. And yet, making one's way to the civilisation that reigned, you felt an incongruous deadness, while among the superannuated worldviews there was a residue that corresponded to something still vital and alive in us. In such a way, imperceptible battle lines were drawn across the museum, and to move from one part of it to another was also to travel from an area of imprisonment to that of freedom, and then back again, through a doorway, to the imprisoning; the sense of alternating, neighbourly entrapment and escape was literal and real. The visits to these zones determined the nature of my commentary to my wife, which changed from angry, heretical, muttered invectives into sudden, easy paeans of worship, and then, in another room, in another dominion, reverted to resentful, libellous slanders.

•

That my dislike of the Renaissance wasn't a solitary failing, or an entirely personal eccentricity—that there were great Renaissance-haters before me, like John Ruskin—didn't become clear to me until later. And it took me a while to understand that uncovering the origins of dislike can be instructive—not therapeutic, in the way that discovering the root of a neurosis can cure it, but helpful in comprehending fidelities and affiliations, and especially why, often, one doesn't adhere to the expected affiliations—the expected "likes"—according to class, colour, education, and identity. How nice it would be to like the things one is supposed to; life would so much more comfortable, so much calmer! Dislike, then, is potentially more disruptive and disorienting than ideology or taste. Partly this might be because, for the artist or writer, it's related to an emotional state that's constantly, strategically, evolving, and this emotional state is inextricable from an intellectual position that may not have wholly been brought to light, while the intellectual position can't be seen divorced from the most important consideration of all for an artist—the question of survival. The artist argues for the survival not of a species, or a race, or a class, but of a particular practice and lineage, as well as a specific interpretation of that practice; in the interests of this mission—survival—she or he might, of course, appear, at times, to conveniently will the destruction of art itself. The polemic against art is just one of the numerous strategies with which the artist attempts to gain the upper hand in the interests of *his* brand of art. Survival and power govern the continuum of art, but not just in the institutional, socialised, and discursive sense in which Foucault and Bourdieu understood such decision-making or governance. Dislike is essential to the artist's art, and his task, of survival as a particular kind of artist.

•

To experience dislike is also to experience sudden isolation. In, and from, that isolation germinate the strategies of the artist or writer, and his or her business of forming, even fabricating, not friendships or coteries, but alliances. An alliance is an extension of an argument; it is, often, two persons united in a dislike; it's the first gesture towards inventing a tradition, or a climate, or a lineage—or, if you like, an anti-tradition or antilineage. The first time I properly realised that there was another who viewed the Renaissance with scepticism was when I read John Berger's Benjaminesque *Ways of Seeing*; although the section that I was most struck by, the section on oil painting, is too polemical to recall Benjamin. Berger begins with some extraordinarily categorical statements: "Oil paintings often depict things. Things which in reality are buyable. To have a thing painted and put on a canvas is not unlike buying it and putting it in your house." As Berger quickly points out, he's taking his cue from Claude Lévi-Strauss: "It is this avid and ambitious desire to take possession of the object for the benefit of the owner or even the spectator which seems to me to constitute one of the outstandingly original features of the art of Western civilisation." How straight-faced is that "outstandingly original"? At any rate, according to Berger, the urge to possess, to encompass, reaches its apogee with painting in oil. (The ambiguous literary term, "to capture," is surely related to but also subversive of the "avid and ambitious desire to take possession of the object," in that "to capture" or evoke a world, in a poem or story, is also to suggest the impossibility of regaining it except obliquely, and through memory.) In Chapter 5, Berger riffs on Lévi-

Strauss beautifully and abrasively: here he is, for instance, on three portraits of Mary Magdalene, from the sixteenth, seventeenth, and eighteenth centuries:

> The point of her story is that she so loved Christ that she repented of her past and came to accept the mortality of flesh and the immortality of the soul. Yet the way the pictures are painted contradicts the essence of this story. It is as though the transformation of her life brought about by her repentance has not taken place. The method of painting is incapable of making the renunciation she is meant to have made. She is painted as being, before she is anything else, a takeable and desirable woman.

Renunciation means withdrawal or abnegation, and Berger is using it here as an aesthetic term, to gesture to the painter's, or the painting's, inability to abnegate from, to renounce, the conventions of full-on, realist representation. Berger cites a couple of exceptions in the course of his demolition drive: William Blake and a good deal of landscape painting. His reason for this seems, in both cases, to have to do with tangibility. He praises Blake for doing "everything he could to make his figures lose substance . . . to be present but intangible, to glow without a definable surface . . ." Of landscape painting, he points out: "The sky has no surface and is intangible; the sky cannot be turned into a thing or given a quantity. And landscape painting begins with the problem of painting sky and distance." That is, both Blake and some of the landscape painters grapple with material resistant to being turned into (in the value-laden, pejorative meaning Berger accords to that word) objects. And so, what appears simple and buoyant (a painting by Corot) or idiosyncratic and miraculous (a scene from Blake) also, in a sense, becomes resistant and unyielding (Berger's euphemism is "intangible"); subtly, dislike transfers itself, and gives to luminosity in painting its moral, unassimilable quality. And just as rules are proven by exceptions, so too, apparently, is dislike shaped and defined by them. Even on the odd chance that you, like me, don't care for Renaissance art, there will always be one or two painters from that period you will admire. You might find yourself being drawn to Brueghel. You might consider the enigma of Vermeer, and why he appeals to you while Rembrandt doesn't—what it is that makes Vermeer escape the Renaissance ethos? You might covertly admire Giotto, because of the echo in his figures of a Byzantine formalism, and take to some of the early Renaissance and all of Fra Angelico for the same reason. In my case, the oil paintings that absorb me from the end of the period I've been referring to are from early nineteenth-century Bengal, the Chinsura oils depicting sacred and epic subjects painted by anonymous *patuas*. These works have little of the hyper-realism of a Titian or Rubens, a hyper-realism which tells us that the world is present for us in finite but irrefutable gradations of verisimilitude and colour. With the Chinsura oils, we have the paradox of attending to a created world that shines but is unfinished, is opulent but is in the process of being made. Some of these are owned today by Aveek Sarkar, but they are, metaphorically, on loan; their aesthetic and representational mode doesn't abide by the Renaissance principle of ownership, as defined by Lévi-Strauss and recited by Berger. When a writer such as myself, a disliker of oils, admits to *liking* a certain genre of oil painting from before the advent of impressionism, he's making a critical statement, and hinting not so much at an accommodation as to an adjustment that changes, imperceptibly, the outward reaches of what he stubbornly is.

•

The writer's life, or the artist's, is not only punctuated by epiphanies and visitations. It's constituted of moments of recognition that are directly related to one's own practice, to the kind of practitioner one is, to the sort of practice that's anathema to one's temperament, and, arising from this, of a series of decisions such as the Bourdieuan analysis seldom addresses, deeming those decisions to belong to the realm of literary mythology. When I say "temperament," I mean something different from both the old, now discredited, literary term "sensibility" and from the dreamy "artistic temperament"; I mean something that, at first at least, appears intractable and not entirely within the realm of the artist's conscious understanding or volition. After all, we can't be sure why certain artists or writers are drawn to miniaturism rather than to the epic, and why the latter upsets and agitates them; we don't know why certain writers tend toward historical narrative or fantasy rather than, say, realism. Temperament, which is not entirely governable, rather than sensibility, which can be cultivated, seems to hold the key; one can't help one's temperament, or shed it or acquire another one. The matter of temperament becomes crucial to understanding why one might be working in a style or mode that lacks prestige at a particular moment in literary history: for instance, one might be writing in the epic mode when the lyric is predominant, and the epic is out of favour. To write in the epic mode is, then, suicidal at that moment; yet what I've called "temperament" dictates that one undertake a suicidal activity. Yet writing, and the philosophy of writing, tend not toward self-destruction but self-perpetuation; so the artist's temperament attempts to ensure that temperament's survival through a number of means. A purely Bourdieuan, sociological view of the literary "field" would tell us that writers are drawn irresistibly to centres, publications, and genres of prestige; but this is not wholly true—indeed, much of literary history and debate comprises that "not wholly." There are writers who might actively, and perversely, dislike and militate against the genres of prestige of the day. How do we account for this antithetical, seemingly self-destructive urge? One explanation would be to invoke class, national, and political affiliations; that certain anomalous forms of narrative or representation are used by artists of a political minority or a colonised nationality in order to assail or overthrow forms predominantly used in the hegemony. This still doesn't tell us why many writers and artist distance themselves from forms and expressions that may be conflated at a certain point of history with their political, racial, or class identity, and cultivate forms that are, in these practitioners' own context, anomalous. Art and writing is, indeed, a field of battle, but battle is not really undertaken for the purposes of either identity or metropolitan prestige, but intentions that seem, on a first examination, unfathomable. Nevertheless, an inordinate amount of energy and strategy and a considerable marshalling of resources are devoted to this ongoing battle.

Strategic thinking for a writer articulates itself as dislike and as allegiance. So Philip Larkin, who began by being an apprentice to the style and language of W. B. Yeats, makes a conscious and exhibitionist disavowal of Yeats the moment he finds his voice, and turns with great fanfare instead to Thomas Hardy. Poor Yeats gets similar treatment later from Seamus Heaney, who chooses Patrick Kavanagh as his forebear. In this matter of artistic allegiance, the student chooses his teacher—conferring teacherhood on the earlier figure as a sort of calculated gift—rather than the other way round. The forebear may well be a relatively marginal figure, as Kavanagh was in Ireland; as Henry Green, John Updike's chosen precursor, was in England; as Hardy the poet was in comparison to Yeats—the marginality accentuating the seemingly arbitrary and temperamental nature of the allegiance, but gesturing toward and raising other questions to do with writerly intention. The allegiance may set aside nationality—Green was English, Updike American; Dante Italian, his disciple T. S. Eliot Anglo-American—in a way that's barely noticeable but again hints at argumentations and strategies of survival beyond the first impression of arbitrariness.

Tagore's case—his low tolerance of Shakespeare; his choice of the Sanskrit poet Kalidasa as precursor—might make more sense on postcolonial and racial grounds. But it doesn't really: for Tagore turns to Kalidasa not for his obviously Oriental or Indian qualities, but for being a protomodernist and realist, a poet of suggestion and of the concrete—all very modernist concerns—in a way that, he suggests, Shakespeare wasn't. In his simultaneous concern with the concrete, the momentary, and with tradition and strategic positioning (that is, *his* relationship to these things), Tagore emphatically becomes part of a larger fabric of modernist argumentation. Decades later, the Indian poet Arvind Krishna Mehrotra makes a similar move when, long after having read Pound, he observes that the poems he discovered in, and translated from, the ancient Prakrit, reminded him, in their economy, of Pound's Confucian analects. Mehrotra's not just making an analogy here, or tracing routes along an internationalist map of literature, but forging a rhetoric of survival, uncovering lines of contact to which he too is invisibly joined—escape routes, emergency pathways, often pursued or taken advantage of in the interests and compulsions of practice. In doing so, Mehrotra is also making adjustments to the linearity of history, to the familiar story of cause and effect, to the paths and routes via which we're supposed to arrive at the contemporary.

Sometimes, a writer might identify a single precursor with disparagement on the one hand, and an acknowledgement of partnership on the other. This might well have to do with the writer's own troubled and contradictory position in relation to a tradition or practice he represents, and may even have helped shape. I have in mind Pound's dislike and adoration of Whitman: "I have detested you long enough . . ." he begins in "A Pact," concluding a few lines later, ". . . we have one sap and one root." Whitman might well be Anglophone modernist poetry's great secret, testing its limits in his open display of carnality and joie de vivre and his blithe lack of belatedness. There's a metaphysical, hieratic, ironic side to Pound that "detests" the older poet; there's a physical, worldly, and exhibitionistic side that sees him as a partner. Pound's turbulent relationship with Whitman reminds us of the former's peculiar, contradictory location in modernism: as on one of its high priests, but also as one of its delighters, a propagator of the image, and, via the image, an advocate of the worldly and the luminous. "Those who know aren't up to those who love; nor those who love, to those who delight in," he remarks, translating Confucius. But it's a conviction he derives, I think, from Whitman, and it introduces an all-important element of spaciousness to modernism's apparent existential despondency. All these modulations are the compulsions of temperament, and they create literary culture as we know it.

Another instance occurs to me, this time of an unexpected case of liking rather than disliking: F. R. Leavis's odd championing of D. H. Lawrence. What compulsion draws an exemplar of the literary like Leavis toward a dishabille outsider (and admirer of Whitman) like Lawrence? It's an intriguing move, and forces us to rethink how we often make synonymous, disdainfully, a certain idea of Leavis and a certain idea of literature. It's intriguing, too, that Leavis should identify (correctly) the significance of one of Lawrence's most revealing, and on the whole forgotten, expressions of dislike—his review of Thomas Mann's *Death in Venice*. For Lawrence, writing in 1918, Mann is the "last sick progeny of Flaubert," and his novella an incarnation of "Flaubertian control" and "will-to-power." Leavis's crucial defence and reconstruction of this increasingly angular, antiliterary Lawrence points to a surprising complexity in his missionary, "high" literary Englishness.

The examples I've cited are meant only as a reminder that an artist has no innocent likes or dislikes; that his or her decisions and choices regarding the dead and living are governed by the question of self-interest and self-preservation, where the self and its well-being and life are inextricable from a particular interpretation of a craft, and, crucially, vice versa. What's at stake is not just Bourdieuan metropolitan prestige or Foucauldian power, but a network of escape routes that are often taken advantage of in the interests of the perpetuation of a lineage or, in Berger's words, "ways of seeing." The poem is a provisional space, like the room of Mesopotamian sculpture in the Louvre, where some lines of contacts and affinities converge while others are left behind. These cat and mouse feints, these moments of recognition, these peripatetic wandering movements from room to room can't be contained or traced in linear, or canonical, or national histories; these connections are made laterally, or sideways, often with no regard for what came first and what later, for what's native and what foreign. To the person gripped by strategic likes and dislikes, the Russian icon might seem new, the Titian old-fashioned, just as Pound's Confucian analects and the Prakrit love poems might appear contemporaneous.

•

This brings me back to where I started, to the Renaissance painting. "Avid" and "ambitious" are the adjectives Lévi-Strauss uses in relation to Western art, and to its "desire to take possession of the object for the benefit of the owner or even the spectator." While talking about a kind of art, he's gesturing, coterminously, toward a particular narrative of history that Walter Benjamin named "historicism": a linear account of development, of the "onward march of progress," so definitive to Western man from the Renaissance and certainly the nineteenth century onward. The Renaissance painting—which, admittedly, I'm using as much as a generalised bogey as Berger did—is a virtuoso performance: it possesses, replicates, manufactures, and perfects reality. In playing this bravura role, it presupposes a story of progress, by making possible what was previously impossible: the perfect reproduction of reality. In this feat, and in its historicist assumption—that the closer you get to reproducing reality, the more "advanced" you are—it's the moral precursor of cloning. The so-called "developed societies" are close to the Renaissance painting in another way: they not only perfect reality, they possess and embody it. Other societies are not only less "developed"; they're also, consequently, somehow less real. The whole business of "possessing," in Renaissance art, has not just to do with acquisition and desire, but perfectability or development, using what the twentieth century called "technology"—a secret, albeit transferable, instrument essential to this miracle: development; reproducing the real. The "real," especially as "realism," is a key feature of the modern, the developed; it's a crucial component in progress. The arrival of perspective in Western art—the opening up not of space but of a new means of capturing and mimicking it—is a significant ingredient in the historicist story, and spoken of as a great stride forward in the story of art. So is, more recently—though we may scorn it—a technological advance like 3D, which takes the Renaissance image literally one step further, or outward. This is true, too, of "special effects," which has been bringing, for several decades now, imagined universes to our doorstep, replete with historicism, presenting us not only with extraordinary futures, but a well-rounded simulacrum. At the heart of historicism lies our approach to the "real"—the real being marked by completeness and, tautologically, by veracity. As Berger points out, the things in Renaissance painting—even, or perhaps especially, in the mythological scenes—look very real, and they do so by being ripe and heavy. The same's true of "special effects"; that, paradoxically, objects appear more real in entirely fantastic and futuristic domains. Completeness and veracity are the end of development; memory may be smudged and unclear, but objects situated in the future of historicist time must especially draw attention to their lifelike qualities.

This species of historicism not only pervades the Renaissance and the visual field, but informs literary and generic considerations. Reality, in the realist novel or film, is an accumulation, an addition, of pertinent fact, information, and detail; the novel, as a genre, most symbolises this accumulation, completeness, and development. The short story, in Anglophone culture, and certainly in British culture today, is described in historicist terms, as a backward version of, and a stepping-stone to graduating toward, the novel. I'm not sure how this relates to non-Anglophone cultures of the written word. One can only throw up possibilities. Would Colette have been the national treasure she is in France had she been an English writer living in England? To an observer on the outside, Junichiro Tanizaki's short tales don't appear to carry less weight, metaphorically, in Japan than does his compendious novel, *The Makioka Sisters*. In an Anglophone literary culture, Tanizaki's novella, "Portrait of Shunkin," would automatically be considered a minor achievement, and *The Makioka Sisters* his major work. "Major" and "minor" are historicist terms in Anglophone literary criticism, inadvertent euphemisms for developed and less developed. On first thought, I find it hard to arrive at words that have exactly the same meaning in Bengali literary language, where importance might be identified not only with achievement, but with amplification and completeness. Does this influential version of historicism, then, have less of an absolute hold on the world of the modern Indian languages, in, say, Kannada or Urdu, just as it may exercise less authority in Japanese or French? Would it be rash to suggest that an absence, in these cases, of a hierarchy between longer and shorter forms seems to have created, in the late nineteenth and twentieth centuries, literatures that had an ambiguous relationship with the ethos of nationalism?

•

Modernism has a curious relationship to historicism. On the one hand, by cherishing the fragment, by refuting totality, it dismantles the presuppositions of development. In doing so, it doesn't, crucially, look with nostalgia, at least in its aesthetic, to a past that's lost but organically whole—a sort of inversion of historicism. In its fascination with ruins and derelict objects, it makes the past constitute the present with an incongruous immediacy, the immediacy of decay; it robs linearity of its momentum. Modernism's relationship to the real—contained in a language of images and fragments—is idiosyncratic and fundamental, but not cumulative; as a consequence, it's the opposite of developmental. As a part of Western literary history, though, modernism is triumphantly appropriated by the historicism that its aesthetic rejects: it's viewed exclusively by its propagandists in terms of newness, vanguardism, and breakthroughs. There's hardly a popular critical language of modernism that emerges from the antihistoricism its artistic departures embrace.

Two critical interjections, one from within the heart of modernism, the other from the cusp of a succeeding epoch, are worth mentioning very briefly here. The first comes from Virginia Woolf's essay, "Mr. Bennett and Mrs. Brown." Alongside her famously exasperated observation about "this appalling narrative business of the realist: getting on from lunch to dinner," this essay attacks the cumulative and enumerative in the novels of Arnold Bennett and much realist writing, rejecting it as a means of arriving at the "truth" about character and setting. Her piece itself is about sitting in a train compartment with a lady she names "Mrs. Brown," about whom she realises that no amount of information provided about Mrs. Brown's life and milieu is going to enable Woolf to imaginatively create her character. As an essay, Woolf's piece perfectly exemplifies modernism's vocabulary of a thrilled historicism— it begins with the remark, "On or about December 1910 human character changed"—as well as its deep antihistoricist, antidevelopmental agitation, its revolt against the sort of attempts to possess reality that, for her, Bennett's work represents, attempts that are among the Renaissance's legacies.

The other interjection I'm referring to is from Roland Barthes's *Writing Degree Zero*. Barthes reminds us, as he reflects on the genre of the novel, of its use of the *passé simple*, or the simple past tense or preterite: "Its function is no longer that of a tense. The part it plays is to reduce reality to a point of time, and to abstract, from the depth of a multiplicity of experiences, a pure verbal act..." In other words, the simple past tense achieves in narrative what the representation of a scene does in Renaissance painting: an apogee or culmination, a transcendence of process. "This is why," says Barthes, "it [the simple past tense] is the ideal instrument for every construction of a world; it is the unreal time of cosmogonies, myths, History and Novels." Barthes's "unreal time of... History and Novels" echoes Benjamin's "homogeneous, empty time of history," in which the onward march of progress occurs, which we now see is also the time of the novel. "When the historian," says Barthes, "states that the duc de Guise died on December 23rd, 1588, or when the novelist relates that the Marchioness went out at five o' clock, such actions emerge from a past without substance; purged of the uncertainty of existence . . ." The other way of purging time, space, and history of that "uncertainty" is, as in the Renaissance artwork, to replace time and space with finished objects you can literally possess in lieu of reality. In both cases—the simple past tense and the oil painting—we're talking of a mode of development that completes historical time.

•

It's possible that my feelings of dislike in the Louvre have something to do with an inchoate prejudice against historicism. It's historicism, with its message of progress and perfection, that I perhaps secretly feel I confront when I view the pleated garment in sculpture; and escape it when I move towards the stately Mesopotamian figures. Understanding the origin doesn't cure the dislike; it just brings it out into the open.

There are many reasons why a writer might make one kind of allegiance, or experience a particular sort of dislike, rather than another; however, in this context, I'm mainly interested, as I've already stated, in the artist's relationship with, and understanding of, the historical. Again, there could plausibly be several reasons as to why artists or writers treat the business of historical representation in different ways; for my purposes, I'm going to throw up some notions regarding this question that have to do with a cultural milieu's relationship with its historical inheritance.

Here, I'll take the liberty of moving into a series of speculations. It appears to me that the world of the Anglophone middle class, the Indian middle class included, is particularly informed by historicism in the way it relates to, and imagines, the past. Let me, after having made this vast generalisation, mention two writers in passing. The first, William Dalrymple, is a product of British society while at once being an honorary Indian, or at the very least an honorary Delhiite. I much admire his writing for its elegance, shrewdness of judgement, and humour; still, I'm also interested in some of the narrative devices he uses when writing popular history, a genre of which he's a robust proponent. Occasionally, you notice Dalrymple catch the mood of historicism, which is so seductively present in both the British and Indian view of the past, and which has had a resurgence in narrative histories and Anglophone historical novels. In *The Last Mughal*, Dalrymple comes up repeatedly, deliberately, with the simple past tense (interspersed, in a way that doesn't disrupt his aims, with the past imperfect) in a crucial chapter, when he's describing the coming of dawn on the day of the Sepoy Mutiny. So, "The British were the first up: in the cantonments to the north of the Delhi Civil Lines, the bugle sounded at 3.30 am etc."; also, "Two hours later, by the time the sun was beginning to rise over the Yamuna, and the poets, the courtesans, and the patrons were all heading back to bed"; and again, "As the cantonment memsahibs awaited the return of their menfolk from the parade ground . . ."; moreover, "As the sun rose, and as the British were returning from their morning rides and preparing for breakfast . . ."; finally, "At the Raj Ghat Gate, the earlier-rising Hindu faithful . . ." Did all this happen that day in 1857? Dalrymple would claim it's in the archive, and that, through his labours and his imagination, he's pieced together the doomed picture like a jigsaw puzzle. Yet what gives the account its air of having happened is the preterite, which locks the past as history. The past tense also gives to the chapter its fictionality, its air of inhabiting what Barthes called the "unreal time of cosmogonies, myths, History and Novels," of narratives that suppress the "uncertainty of existence" by beginning with statements like "The Marchioness went out at five o' clock." Dalrymple, even while using this tested method, tries to undermine that unreality through calculated repetition and incantation, whereby he senses, perhaps, that the simple past tense will lose its reliability. And yet the past tense can't help but imply: "This is what happened"; and, moreover, "The past is out there to be pieced together again." This is what another writer, the novelist Amitav Ghosh, also assumes when he reveals to us how he researches every aspect of his historical novels: of how he will climb aboard the actual counterpart of a ship he's writing about, or put together, through his research, piece by piece, a horse-drawn carriage from the nineteenth century. It's as if the past is not only an entity that can be revisited, but, with adequate groundwork, possessed.

This leads me to dwell on a particular interpretation, and the recent prestige, of the word "research" in India. Its significance in the domain of science is well known, as is the narrative it plays a role in: a scientist amasses material, hypotheses, and evidence to do with immunology or malaria, and comes up with findings. This, at least, is the lay understanding of scientific research, one that scientists haven't done much to dispute. Since the context and infrastructure for such output needs constant abetment and funding, it's right that, say, organisations like the Infosys foundation, with its grants and prizes, should be involved in funding and encouragement. Not long ago, the foundation introduced prizes for the social sciences (though it had no separate prize for history till 2012). After all, the social sciences are an important body of knowledge, and they emerge from research: archival material; fieldwork. Of course, the social sciences and history are generally—but especially in India—seen not only to be dependent on research, but legitimised by it. In this, we are children of the European Renaissance—research verifies and reproduces reality; "thinking" is an imponderable, and in some ways closer to the "imagination." For instance, I once noticed that some readers view Dipesh Chakrabarty's *Provincializing Europe* with wariness, as it explores a thought-process instead of bearing the unmistakable imprimatur of archival labour. Which brings me to fiction. With the conflation, in some circles, of the Indian novel in

English with a particular sort of historical novel, it isn't unusual to encounter Indian readers who praise such-and-such novelist because they "do a lot of research." The remark expresses a familiar sense of relief, as well as the triumphal faith our educated Anglophone classes have in the rationally verifiable. Research authenticates the novel's putative ambition of representing reality—of embodying the evolution from archival forays to fictionalisation, which sometimes becomes indistinguishable from reconstruction. Indians who clearly haven't read my work sometimes ask me (as I'm a novelist): "You must do a lot of research." I've pondered on this query, and what I've begun to say to them is this: that I "do research" all the time, but not for specific books or projects. That is, the imagination—at least my imagination—doesn't seem to follow the model of scientific work, from premise to fieldwork to hypothesis to published findings.

What makes one believe that the past is out there, waiting to be joined together in its various elements? Partly, it's do with a vantage point which allows one to look back on history from a distance, as a spectator. To be such a spectator, one must be on the right side of history, and have moved on from the past one is looking at, sharing little complicity with it. The past doesn't, in other words, impinge on the historicist imagination through shame or guilt; and this lack of impingement is essential to viewing the past clearly, and putting it together into a whole. Indian middle-class self-consciousness (although, or perhaps because, it makes much of colonisation, subjecthood, and indigenous elites) is, I sense, relatively free of guilt about history. It won't address complicity or aesthetic self-contradiction: that, for example, it may be drawn to something on a sensory or imaginative level which it morally disapproves of entirely. One reason for this may be (and, again, I freely speculate) that the Indian liberal bourgeoisie in India made a clean break with *sati*, making it, thankfully, an intellectual and emotional taboo that couldn't be engaged with on any level, but also, as a consequence, distancing itself from its own "otherness." *Sati* belongs to the past—a disgraceful past, no doubt, but one that has no power to impinge any more on the historicist consciousness of the Indian liberal. I might hazard a guess and say the same might be true of our relationship with the caste system: that it may well be a burdensome, even traumatic, political reality, but (to use a catchword reclaimed by Žižek) our superego has thoroughly (and correctly) disowned it; it's an inadmissible, if terrible, aspect of our tradition. And so, I think, the past fails to really encroach upon, to compromise, or to taint the liberal bourgeoisie in India, because it is behind us—especially the Anglophone bourgeoisie, for whom the break is most effective and clear-cut. In spite of having once been colonised, despite living in a context of profound inequity, and despite violence in Kashmir and Gujarat, the liberal Anglophone Indian feels relatively little anxiety about being on the wrong side of history. He or she might feel exercised, angry, or outraged about various things, but always from the distance that historicism provides, which allows these problems to exist outside oneself without in any way entering or issuing from the self that is outraged. When representing these problems in narrative or visual terms, in fiction or cinema, the lack of implicatedness allows the creators of those novels and films to stand back and view, or reconstruct, the landscape or event in its fullness. And while historicism gives the viewer a kind of distance, it also gives her or him a sense of ownership: that the past can be not only reconstructed, but laid claim to, as "our" heritage or tradition. *Sati* and its defeat at the hands of the nationalist reformers is an episode in the history we own. Historicism ensures that an unbroken line leads up from the past to ourselves; history isn't foreign—it is, in a sense (like the objects or figures in the Renaissance painting were for the man who owned it), our property.

•

I've always been moved by the historical imagination in artists who represent an aberration rather than the norm. I'm thinking of the Russian filmmaker Andrei Tarkovsky, as well as a few twentieth-century Japanese writers and filmmakers. I'm no expert on film, Russia, or Japan, but I'm going to pursue this curious feeling of affinity a bit longer.

Tarkovsky is extraordinary in his distinctive approach to Russian history. This is in evidence in almost all his films, particularly in *Andrei Rublev*, his reimagining of the eponymous fourteenth-century icon-maker's life and times. The film is divided into black and white sections. There's a hint of colour at the beginning, and there are several minutes of colour at the very end, when we're shown the actual icons by the painter—strange pictures, if we're judging them through conventions of classic Western paintings; as strange, in their way, as the Russia depicted in the film. In the course of the film's considerable duration, we realise that Rublev's Russia isn't quite Europe; its religion is partly witchcraft and mystic superstition; its politics is barbaric conquest; and it is within this context that its Christianity exists. However, this landscape is not a less evolved and, therefore, recognisable stage in the European telos; its violence and magic aren't those depicted in films like *Troy*, where the action is detailed in a burnished way, in a manner that permits us to spectate on those cruelties and heroic feats from this side of history. Tarkovsky's Russia is essentially foreign, foreign even to the notion of the historical, more "third world" than "Europe," and will not be contained by soothing terms like "early modern," "medieval," or "historical"; Tarkovsky might study it, but, crucially, he can't lay claim to it. When I think of the Russia in *Andrei Rublev*, I'm reminded of what the East German playwright Heiner Mueller once said in an interview: "We in the Eastern Bloc have a great Third World in our midst."

It's clear to anyone who knows Tarkovsky's oeuvre that he believed himself to be an inheritor of "high" European culture. His films are populated with references to Western painting, and these references surface in the unlikeliest of locations—in a spaceship in *Solaris*, in an apartment in *Mirror*, the reproduction of the painting glimpsed briefly within the covers of a book. Tarkovsky's younger contemporary Aleksandr Sokurov's *Russian Ark* (filmed in a single shot in the Winter Palace of the State Hermitage Museum in St. Petersburg) is a record of some of the great treasures of Western art while also incorporating enactments of scenes from Russian political history; yet *Russian Ark* could also be seen as a homage to the European metier of Tarkovsky's work. For all that, I think that Tarkovsky, upon encountering Rublev's icons—sacred pictures with repetitive outlines and stylised expressions, remarkable for their abstention from inwardness (which suffuses paintings after the Renaissance like water does wet cloth)—I believe that, on studying these icons, Tarkovsky was faced with a dilemma. He'd have been made aware that to be a Russian and to be a European are not coterminous. There's no easy passage or bridge connecting the icon to Renaissance "high" art; even to move from one room to the other in the Louvre is to traverse a great change. To be Russian, *Andrei Rublev* instructs us, is to be "other": a source, perhaps, of both shame and wonder. And, we realise, there's no unbroken line from medieval Russia to the Renaissance to the present historical moment which Tarkovsky occupies doubly as a great Russian and European artist; the disjunction represented by those strange icons can't be soothingly transformed into an inheritance. Tarkovsky himself responds, in the film, disjunctively, angularly, very differently from how a Renaissance painter would. Of course, the moment I've just described, of Tarkovsky confronting the icons, of coming to terms with the fact that the historical past isn't out there to be accessed in a straightforward fashion, is pure speculation, even fiction.

Perhaps I've taken the liberty of making up this piece of fiction about Tarkovsky because of an experience I had a few years ago near Bhubaneswar, when I went, accompanied by my wife and daughter, to the Sun Temple at Konark, once in ruins and then resurrected by native and colonial archaeologists. A prurient guide, ignoring my family, showed me the multiplicity of erotic sculpture occupying almost every inch of the temples, on ground level and at impossible heights—of couples copulating, and participating in an unbelievably fecund array of positions. I was filled with wonder—at the exuberance of these figures, yes, but, even more powerfully, at a culture and tradition that was fundamentally foreign. I realised I didn't know my ancestors, and also that they *weren't*, in a sense, my ancestors; and I thought I understood what Tarkovsky had felt upon viewing those icons. The wonder I felt, then, was quite different from the excitement of the popular historian or historical novelist as they piece together the past. Who were these people, having sex indefatigably, carved into stone? Were they my heritage? They seemed to be telling me something. It was a time when the Hindu right wing was vandalising contemporary works of art that depicted religious figures in an erotic way; M. F. Husain was under attack. The liberal intelligentsia, as a result, was invoking the sexually liberated, even profligate, antiquity of Hinduism as its inheritance, as if an unbroken path stretched from the past to the present. In Konark, though, I experienced not recognition but strangeness. Whatever the sculptures were telling me couldn't be translated into a past-to-present-to-future story.

•

What could the sculptures or icons be saying? Tagore, too, had trouble with decipherment. Obsessed with Kaildasa and the fourth century CE, he, in a poem called "Dream," speaks of himself as one who "once went to find / my first love / from a previous life" in a "dream-world, in the city of Ujjain, by the River Shipra." Finding her leads to a breakdown in communication: "I looked at her face, / tried to speak, / but found no words. / That language was lost to me..." Of course, Tagore was especially interested, for reasons of affinity, and from visceral biases and prejudices to do with survival strategy, in claiming Kalidasa as both his precursor and his contemporary—rejecting, in the process, his immediate predecessor, Madhusudan Dutt, and the earlier Bengali poets, Chandidas and Vidyapati, of whose work he'd composed an enthusiastic pastiche when he was sixteen. But reading Kalidasa also tells Tagore that Kalidasa can't be possessed; that's why "Meghdut," Tagore's poem about Kaidasa's long poem-sequence *Meghadutam*, describes a world coming to life as he reads—"In a gloomy room I sit alone / And read the *Meghadūta* . . . / There is the Amrakuta Mountain, / There is the clear and slender Reva river, / Tumbling over stones in the Vindhya foothills . . ."—and also notes, by the time he's finished both poems (the one he's reading and the one he's writing), that history will not become full and present, but will diminish and withdraw: "The vision goes . . . I watch / the rain again / Pouring steadily all around." Tagore's affinities with Kalidasa's craft makes him approach him in a way that's recuperative and proprietary; but he's aware that Kalidasa resists being appropriated—in his essay on the court poet, he points out that "we are banished from that India," from the "slow, measured mandrakanta metre of the *Meghadutam*," "not just during the rains but for all time." Nothing as reassuring as colonisation creates this disjunction. Tagore knows it comes from his contradictory instincts as a modern as he views the physical object (the Amrakuta and Ramagiri mountains) or Kalidasa; it is, in a way, similar to Woolf's anxiety as she faces Mrs. Brown in the train compartment—that details and traits taken incrementally won't add up to a time or "character." Tagore's poem is probably the first literary work anywhere that expresses an aesthetic of the historical imagination that states history can be felt most powerfully only in its resistance to appropriation. In this, it's different from the narrative histories in verse written in Bengal in the nineteenth century—indeed, from his own verse narratives about history—and from romantic assessments of the ruins of the past, such as Derozio's; distinct, too, from earlier poems by Hölderlin about the departure of the gods, or from Matthew Arnold's "Stanzas from the

Grande Chartreuse," about travelling between two worlds. Tagore's temperament sees to it that the tone of the Bengal Renaissance is—not in a nationalistic or postcolonial way, but in a manner that articulates itself through dislike—counter to the ethos of the Italian Renaissance, with its hyper-production of the real and its great monuments. It's no paradox that, within the counter-naturalistic mood of this later renaissance, one of its principal artists, Binode Behari Mukherkjee, should paint in a state of semi-blindness or blindness, and go to Indian history taking not the European Renaissance's art as his model, but, among his various sources, images that were already irretrievably fading: the frescoes of Ajanta. As for Tagore, his unease with aesthetic appropriation, as expressed in his writings on Kalidasa, must explain in part his disquiet with and strategic disavowals and, indeed, dislike of nationalism from the 1890s onward. This incongruous dislike put him, Tagore would have known, on the wrong side of history.

•

Being on the wrong side of history is what gives to certain Japanese writers and filmmakers their anomalous aesthetic—an aesthetic of prevarication, and one that brings together pastiche and the poetic image. The Anglophone historical novel, emerging from traditions that have a more robust investment in development, is, in contrast, a different sort of beast. The reasons, in twentieth-century Japan, for national embarrassment were clear. Firstly, in the context of growing modernity and so-called Westernisation in the early twentieth century, there was the imaginative ambivalence towards the samurai code and the scandal of ritual suicide—represented in films and books as tragic and heroic, but with a suggestive light and shade that's unknown to the historicist imagination, and the way in which it burnishes the past as it represents it. Again, in keeping with the speculative manner of the rest of this talk, I speculate here and guess that there was no clean break in Japan in relation to its samurai code as there was in India with regard to *sati*. The other reason has to do, of course, with the worldview that led to the Second World War, and subsequent defeat. Both facts may be pertinent to a literature and an art that lack, in their versions of history or myth, the gleaming objects viewed from a historicist distance, as well as the "unreal time" established by the simple past tense. Kurosawa's *Rashomon*, for example, is a story from the past narrated from three perspectives that, like the icons in Tarkovsky's film, confront us but won't address us directly, coming to us, instead, from multiple, confusing directions. The frame, in the film, is not just the narrative voice, but rain—it's raining as the story is told three times. The viewer of the film, as at the end of Tagore's "Meghdut," watches, at the close of each episode, "the rain again / Pouring steadily all around." Rain is the element into which the narrative's historicity vanishes. Each time we return to the present, when it's raining, we see that no one version has veracity, and that we've been impeded from possessing the past.

Examples must abound in Japanese writing of this aesthetic—where history becomes palpable only in its resistance—but I'm particularly struck by three. Two of these are stories by Junichiro Tanizaki. "Portrait of Shunkin" is, as the title indicates, a portrait, though hardly a Renaissance-type one, of an imperious and cruel musician from the end of the Meiji era in the late nineteenth century. The narrator's sources are a bland guidebook-like biography—a pastiche—and a possibly apocryphal and unreliable piecing together of the story of Shunkin's principal student, Sasuke, who also, later, became her husband. Sasuke's devotion to his teacher-wife extends to the fact that he evidently blinds himself after *she* goes blind from an infection. The narrative is light and dark; the one remaining visual representation of Shunkin is a faded, indiscernible photo. Some kind of shame or disgrace is being concealed by the narrator's evasive account of things, his bogus allusions to the biography, and his anxiousness to appease. All the while, an impulse opposite to the possessive urge of the Renaissance painting as described by Berger is at work here; indeed, it's a destructive urge, as exemplified, in the arts, by the fragment, but, here, not only narrated but, in the act of self-blinding, disturbingly reified.

Tanizaki's "Bridge of Dreams" is a tale told by a young man who's having an incestuous relationship with his stepmother, whom his father married after the young man's mother died. The relationship began alarmingly early; at the teat, as it were. At times, the narrator can't recall at which point the stepmother entered the family and merged with his true mother. The era the story is set in is invoked by judicious allusions to poems, to the crafts of the time, and calligraphy. But neither the narrator, nor the foundation of his existence, the mother-figure, will speak to us plainly about what's happening. With two mothers, one adored but dimly remembered, the other desired but enigmatic, the narrator loses his ability to lay claim to where he emerges from: it's impossible for him to own his origins. It's in this impossibility that the troubled past pulsates most in Tanizaki's story. Meanwhile, a source of shame (probably incest) is being constantly hinted at and elegantly glossed over. This source, like the proximity of the stepmother's body, actively impinges upon the narrative distance essential to historicism's clear view of heritage.

My final example comes not from Japan, but from a British writer of Japanese origin, Kazuo Ishiguro. In his second novel, and his best one, *An Artist of the Floating World*, Ishiguro is still dealing with Japanese subject matter, and, while doing so, undermining the reassurance of the preterite, and bringing a rare note of uncertainty to the English "period" novel. The novel assumes the form of a memoir; yet it's the perfect example of the novel of prevarication. The novel of prevarication (Richard Ford's *The Sportswriter* is another example) is different from the novel of irony: the ironicist says one thing and believes another; the prevaricator not only wants you to believe his account is true, he's keen to believe in its truth himself. Partly this is because the prevaricator wishes to *forget* the real truth, whatever that may be. The ironicist is economical, because he or she is out to imply a great deal; the prevaricator is loquacious, because he has much to conceal. The prevaricator is on the wrong side of history; no comfortingly unbroken line stretches back from him and his utterances to his cultural past or identity. History, because of the narrator's complicity in its shame, can't be viewed, in the narrative of prevarication, from a distance, in cumulative detail—in Ishiguro's novel, the evasive narrator, an old man, was a famous artist favoured by the emperor before the War. Now, after the war, we learn—from unintended slips in his story—that he's in disgrace, and lives in relative isolation, except when he's being an indulgent grandfather. He's mainly unwanted by his former students, who sometimes pretend not to see him when they pass him on the street. Ishiguro's first-person narrative's primary fictions are self-belief and bogus cheerfulness, both of which—self-belief and cheerfulness—the narrator lacks. In order to conceal complicity, a new sort of space and movement come into play, circular, prevaricatory, which is not available to the historicist novel, with its onward movement and its conviction that history is always "out there" in the archive, waiting to be reclaimed. The novel starts, "If on a sunny day you climb up the steep path leading up from the little wooden bridge still referred to around here as 'the Bridge of Hesitation,' you will not have to walk long before the roof of my house becomes visible between the top of two ginkgo trees." The future conditional tense plunges the reader into a hypothetical situation far from the "unreal time" of the preterite—and it ramifies, in the novel, into an account that's disquietingly puzzling.

Poetry as Polemic

2011, introduction to *The Essential Tagore* (Harvard University Press)

Whatever the unborn and the dead may know, they cannot know the beauty, the marvel of being alive in the flesh.

—D. H. Lawrence, *Apocalypse*

I began to feel put off by Tagore in my late teens, around the time I discovered Indian classical music, the devotional songs of Meerabai, Tulsidas, and Kabir, not to speak of the work of the modernists. I was also—to place the moment further in context—reading contemporary European poetry in translation, in the tremendous series edited by Al Alvarez, the *Penguin Modern European Poets*. My father knew of my promiscuous adventurousness when it came to poetry, and, in tender deference to this, he (a corporate man) would buy these books from bookshops in the five-star hotels he frequented, such as the mythic Nalanda at the Taj. Among the poets I discovered through this route of privilege was the Israeli Dan Pagis, of whom the blurb stated: "A survivor of a concentration camp, Dan Pagis possesses a vision which is essentially tragic." I don't recall how my seventeen-year-old self responded to Pagis, but I do remember the poem he is most famous for, "Written in Pencil in the Sealed Railway-Car." Here it is in its entirety:

> here in this carload
> i am eve
> with abel my son
> if you see my other son

cain son of man
tell him i

The resonance of the poem escaped me at the time: this history was not mine. What struck me were the qualities I found most attractive when I was seventeen—metaphysical despair; deliberate irresolution. I mention the poem because I think it figured as a subtext to a difference of opinion I had with my uncle when my parents and I visited him in London in 1979. My uncle, a bachelor and an executive in shipping, was the most shameless propagandist for Tagore I have ever met, and his enthusiasm only furthered my dislike for the Bengali poet. Walking around Belsize Park, he would tell me that Tagore was the greatest poet the world had ever seen, surpassing everybody, including "the poets of the *Bhagavad Gita*." (Homer and Shakespeare didn't even merit a mention.) I countered with the name of my favourite poet, T. S. Eliot, flag-bearer of a certain kind of twentieth-century despondency especially attractive to teenagers, and spoke too of Meera's devotionals, saying I preferred the latter to Tagore's lyrics. "You somehow feel," I said, "that there's a real urgency and immediacy about her songs. They could have been scribbled upon a prison wall." I was probably invoking Pagis here, and also having a go at Tagore's premeditated and loving craftsmanship. Many poets—besides, of course, philosophers—have insisted that there are things that are more important than poetry, especially in the face of trauma; for poets, this disavowal is, in fact, a respectable literary strategy. Even an adolescent detractor could tell that, to Tagore, nothing was as important as poetry.

My uncle attempted to indoctrinate me each time I went to London in the 1970s. In his eyes, Tagore was an amazingly contradictory agglomeration of virtues and characteristics. "If Tolstoy was a sage whose heart bled for mankind," said my uncle, "then Rabi Thakur was a greater sage. No one has felt more pity for man's sorrows." He spoke of him in the semi-familiar, affectionate way of the Bengali *bhadralok*, as if Tagore were a cherished acquaintance—"Rabi Thakur"—and not hieratically, as "Gurudev," the appellation Gandhi had conferred on him (as, in turn, Tagore had reportedly conferred "Mahatma" on Gandhi). He sometimes hummed Tagore's more popular and plangent lines ("My days wouldn't remain in the golden cage / those many-coloured days of mine" and "I know, I know that the prayers that went / unanswered in life haven't been lost") mainly to express his sadness: for he was a man who loved company, and family, but had oddly chosen to be alone, and an expatriate. Then, the mood would change abruptly. Tagore, according to my uncle, was a "tennis player"—this odd metaphor was deployed to suggest, I think, a series of departures: the breaking away of Tagore's family, starting with his great-grandfather Nilmoni Tagore, from its conservative Brahminical roots; Tagore's own breaking out from his "aristocratic," landed past into modernity, art, individualism, and, of course, glamorous mystique. The latter, presumably, is what Tagore, the celebrity poet, and the tennis player had in common—besides finesse and control.

My uncle was as much in awe of Tagore's looks as he was of his work—both were, in fact, impossible to disentangle from one another. Despite his immemorial, world-denying air from his forties onward, Tagore and everything associated with him—his handwriting; the interiors he inhabited, with their new "ethnic" design; the habitations he constructed for himself in Santiniketan; the paintings created out of manuscript corrections—had an air of provisionality and experiment. They emanated from a man taking his cue from, or experiencing resonances with, a number of sources and excitements—tribal arts and crafts; the devotional-mystic music of Bengal; the dance traditions of neighbouring regions, like Manipur; Shelley; the Upanishads; Paul Klee. All this translated, in the public domain, into the personality and the appearance themselves—the commanding but ineffable, and somehow wholly contemporary, presence of the "world poet." It was this image that held my uncle in thrall. "'People who compare me with

Shakespeare should realise that I had to make a leap of five hundred years to write as I do,' said Rabindranath," reported my uncle calmly. There was a remonstrative edge to his words, though, for his identification with Tagore was fierce. "All men who repeat one line of Shakespeare are William Shakespeare," said Jorge Luis Borges; all Bengalis of a certain generation were, at one point or another, Tagore. And, of course, there are many Tagores, as anyone becoming acquainted with him will discover. The phrase "Renaissance man" does not capture the restless energy and vitality with which he—a colonial subject—journeyed toward different genres in the manner of one learning, mastering, and finally altering new languages. He undertook each genre as an exploration: the revealing (in all kinds of ways) letter-writing of the young man; the shadowy microcosm contained in the plays; the great novels and stories; the often deeply original but underrated essays; the paintings that emerged almost by accident—from manuscript corrections—when he was a much older man. The act of journeying and the element of chance were (as I discovered later) both crucial to Tagore.

For the versatility I've just mentioned, Tagore is occasionally compared to Goethe. I see him as being closer to another German, Josef Beuys, as someone who wants not only to address or to influence the world around him, but to rearrange and reorder it—creatively, radically, sometimes physically. As a consequence, Tagore was interested not only in literature but in book design, apparel, and the decorative and cultural aspects of our drawing rooms. Indeed, Buddhadeva Bose, writing about a visit to the Tagore household, mentions how subtly innovative and experimental (and finely judged) both the food and the decor were. Tagore's urge to experiment was relentless; and we can't really pretend that what he did within the covers of a book and what he did outside it emerge from two wholly divergent impulses. Beuys refuses to distinguish between the text and the world that is his immediate material and, in many ways, dissolves the frame around the artwork; Tagore, too, frequently refuses to make the same distinction. No volume or compilation of Tagore's songs, poems, stories, extracts from his novels, reflections on literature and politics and on his frequent and exhausting travels, and even instances of his sui generis humour should be read as his "writings" alone, but seen in conjunction with his larger interest—evident in almost all he did—in intervening in and reshaping his surroundings. His school, Santiniketan, served as a hothouse and a laboratory for this creative experiment. In important ways, Santiniketan—indeed, the many-pronged, all-embracing Tagorean project—was a precursor to Beuys's vision of "total art" and "social sculpture," and a successor to the Wagnerian *Gesamtkunstwerk*, the art performance in which every form of art is incorporated. Yet Tagore's impulse needs to be distinguished from Wagner's messianic vision. Tagore was absorbed in the everyday, the domestic, and his love of the momentary.

Naturally, my uncle had a view on Tagore's metamorphic effect: "Let's say you were to set a murder mystery in the early twentieth century, and the murder had been committed by someone who grew up before Tagore became famous. Let's say a manuscript page was the single available clue. You'd catch the murderer just by looking at the handwriting, because Bengali handwriting changed forever after Tagore." Moreover, "Words like Keatsian and Wordsworthian describe a literary style associated with that particular poet," he pointed out, for he had read a great deal. "Only Rabindrik" —the Bengali adjective derived from Tagore's first name—"encompasses an entire generation, an outlook, that came into being with the poet's work." For my uncle, this was a matter of intransigent pride. For the very original poets who followed Tagore in the Bengali language, the legacy was a mixed one. "It was impossible to write like Rabindranath, and it was impossible not to write like Rabindranath," said Buddhadeva Bose. When, in fact, I quoted and cited the great post-Tagorean poets I particularly loved, like Jibanananda Das or Bose, to my uncle, he was completely immune to their music: "I've heard it all before. Don't you see none of this would be possible without Rabindranath?" Thus my uncle, an idiosyncratic but sensitive reader, deliberately echoed a vulgar undertone of a particular form of Bengali romanticism—that Tagore was a historical pinnacle, after which everything was a kind of decline, and every writer a latecomer. This view precluded any further fruitful discussion between my uncle and myself, though that didn't stop either of us.

There was another dimension to these conversations in London. My uncle knew, as I think I must have, that the dismantling of Tagore's reputation as a serious poet had started early—soon after the Nobel Prize in 1913—and that, by the seventies, very little survived of that reputation in the West, or, for that matter, anywhere outside the cocoon of Bengal. The rise itself had been at once astonishing and suspect, impossible without the interconnectedness of the world from the nineteenth century onward, and points to the dangers and benefits of the sort of global fame we've now become familiar with. In my introduction to the *Picador / Vintage Book of Modern Indian Literature*, I'd said that Tagore was probably the world's "first international literary celebrity"; an Indian reviewer, who must have immediately concluded I was celebrating the fact, said my claim was "risible." An English poet who taught at Oxford said the dubious honour might belong to Byron. People have forgotten how startling Tagore's incursion was into the various languages of the twentieth century. Martin Kaempchen points out that he was Germany's first best-seller; Jiménez's translations made him a cult in the Spanish-speaking world; this is not to invoke his renown in China, Japan, Russia, Eastern Europe, and the United States. This fame was a product, largely, of Tagore's English-language, Nobel Prize–winning *Gitanjali*; the English *Gitanjali* is perhaps one of the earliest examples of how capitalism fetishises the book. To use the word celebrity, then (rather than terms like "high critical standing"), isn't inappropriate, as Tagore's presence was felt so predominantly outside the field of literature, as it still is—except in the forgotten sphere of Bengali literature. And to recover Tagore today as a poet and writer must entail some sense of the Bengali language becoming a realm of literary possibility.

•

Looking back today to the middle of the nineteenth century, we feel compelled to admit that something exceptional occurred with the emergence of Bengali as a literary language. Disturbingly, we still know very little of this moment, partly because an easeful way of looking at colonial history (according to which modernity comes from elsewhere, bringing with it certain genres and practices) has saved us from engaging too strenuously with the question of how and why things changed when they did. For instance, I don't think we still have a proper genealogy of the word *sahitya*, which we've been using for more than a century to mean "literature" and "literary tradition" in the modern, secular sense, and not to mean, as it once did in the Indian languages, "literary content" or "literary meaning." Tagore's own etymological gloss on the word asks us to look at its root, *sahit* ("to be with"), thereby turning literature into a social, companionable thing. It is fairly certain, though, that *sahitya*, as we understand it, is not a timeless Indian verity (for that, we should perhaps look up the word *kavya*) but a contingent, humanist construct, just as "Indianness" and the modern Bengali language are. It is also certain that the emergence of Bengali encompassed more than nationalism. It became—in lieu of English—a respectable vehicle for cosmopolitan self-expression by the 1860s. It is the latter development that failed in Ireland and Wales with regard to Gaelic and Welsh, and nationalism alone (of which there was no shortage in Ireland) didn't succeed in turning those languages into viable literatures or prevent them from becoming, essentially, curios. In Ireland, it is the English language that became the medium through which the modern formulated his or her ambivalence and self-division, so giving Irish literature and diction its shifting registers in English. Gaelic, largely associated with identity and nation, became, with a few striking exceptions, an unusable artefact. Something quite different and exceptional happened in Bengali colonial modernity. The Bengali language emerged from not only a conviction about identity but an intimation of distance, from not just the wellspring of race but disjunction and severance. These essentially cosmopolitan tensions always animate Tagore's language.

I used the word "curio" deliberately, in order to recall Buddhadeva Bose's unfair but revealing attack on Indian poets writing in English in the 1960s, in which he accused them of producing, by choosing not to write in the mother tongue, not poems but "curios." In one sense, Bose is right. It is the English language that has risked becoming, over and over, a sort of Gaelic in India: not because, as Bose would have it, it was a foreign or colonial tongue, but because, like Gaelic, it bore too notionally the burden of identity and nationality. The relative and paradoxical freedom from this burden in the emergence of modern Bengali gave it its special air of play and potential. In other, fundamental ways, Bose was wrong. The poets he attacked had based their achievement on a cunning with which they had sabotaged and complicated the possibility of a pan-Indian tradition; they too were writing, in their way, in a vernacular. In fact, it was the long poem that Bose held up as the great exemplary Indian English poem, "Savitri" by Sri Aurobindo, that the shrewd Nissim Ezekiel pointed out as the actual curio for, presumably, its faux high cultural atmosphere of the Orient as well as its emulation of the English canon (it was composed in iambs). It should be pointed out that Tagore's English translation of *Gitanjali* would be—for Indian poets writing in English like Ezekiel, A. K. Ramanujan, Arvind Krishna Mehrotra—yet another Gaelic artefact to bypass or circumvent. In his brief memoir "Partial Recall," Mehrotra quotes, with little indulgence toward his youthful self, from the ambitious and sonorous pastiche of that *Gitanjali* which he produced as a teenager.

•

The fact that literature—specifically English literature—was a university discipline first invented for the colonies has been in circulation for a while. In the 1880s, English literature became an object of study leading to a degree at the University of Calcutta, well before any such development had taken place elsewhere, let alone Oxford or Cambridge. But the incursion of English and European literary texts into Bengal had begun a century earlier. The study of literature cannot be seen simply as an instrument of imperialist pedagogy from 1820s onward (when it first surfaces as a taught discipline-in-germination in Calcutta). By the early nineteenth century, Bengalis, especially when naming literary and cultural societies, were reflecting on what literature, or, in Bengali, *sahitya*, might be—great texts of all kinds, or a different way of approaching and valuing texts? A significant historical narrative is contained in the evolution of the word *sahitya* into its present-day meaning. What seems pretty sure is that it was not a word just lying around, ready to slip into its contemporary, secular role. Nor is it a simple translation of the word literature, though it means much the same thing from the middle of the nineteenth century onward. That is, it is neither a purely Indian (whatever that may be) nor colonial term, but one that keeps abreast of these dichotomies until they start to waver. Tagore, in his first essay on the subject in 1889, defines it in negatives: "The essence of literature does not allow itself to be trapped within a definition. It is like the essence of life: we know what it cannot exist without, but what it is we do not know." These are the words of a poet who has come into his own at a cusp in history. Perhaps the specificity of Tagore's problem, and the duress of the historical moment he's speaking in and of, would become clearer if the key word were left untranslated: "The essence of *sahitya* does not allow itself to be trapped," and so on. But the translator, Sukanta Chaudhuri, doesn't do so because he presumes Tagore has already leaped toward the sense in which that word operates today; and, in part, he's right. By 1889, Tagore's readers have definitely begun to recognise the literary, in spite of the strangeness of the sentences I have quoted. Yet one must keep in mind the strangeness of the time. Tagore's complex and difficult position as a modern Indian, a colonial subject, an elite cosmopolitan, an inheritor and inventor of Eastern civilisational values, and a progeny of the Enlightenment allows him to partake of the exclusive secular ethos of literature but also to view it from the outside, as a process. You feel more than once as you gaze back on that crucial period that you are over-familiar with its outlines, and also that you are only on the verge of understanding it.

•

Tagore has been such a fountainhead of nationalist pride, such a static emblem ever since one can remember that we forget that he was clearly aware, as a writer, of living in a unique and transformative time. There is, in Tagore, a constant acknowledgment of the power of the past, and of the canonical riches of Indian tradition, and constant inquiry about the terms in which these are available to us. In this, he is different from either the Hindu reformers or the Indian nationalists, for whom tradition has an integrity and wholeness, and is a given to be improved upon or invoked in the services of politics and identity. For Tagore, tradition is at once contemporary and immediate, and inaccessible and disjunctive. As a result, contrary emotions permeate his great essay on the fourth-century Kalidasa's poem on the rainy season, *Meghadutam* ("The Cloud-Messenger"):

> From Ramgiri to the Himalayas ran a long stretch of ancient India over which life used to flow to the slow, measured *mandrakanta* metre of the *Meghadutam*. We are banished from that India, not just during the rains but for all time. Gone is Dasharna with its groves hedged with *ketaki* plants where, before the onset of the rains, the birds among the roadside trees fed on household scraps and busily built their nests, while in the *jaam* copse on the outskirts of the village, the fruit ripened to a colour dark as the clouds.

The intimation of contemporaneity here is astonishingly suburban; it has to do with nature, yes, but nature viewed from the point of view of the town and the ebb and flow of domesticity: the "household scraps" the birds feed on, the ripening jaam that will be collected and brought home to the family. Kalidasa is not a naïve poet; he is a court sophisticate, an urban sensibility, already viewing the natural at one remove. The loss experienced here, then—"We are banished from that India, not just during the rains but for all time"—is a double, even a multiple, one. From which India, exactly, are we banished? This paradox—to do with immediacy, recognisability, and absolute inaccessibility—is also the subject of Tagore's own poem, "Meghdut," which records the experience of rereading Kalidasa's eponymous poem. Tagore's poem, filled with images of human activity and habitation, describes how the reader comes to inhabit Kalidasa's world as he reads and becomes an exile from it once the poem is over.

Tagore's fascination and absorption in heritage could have made him an elegist, or a poet who turned from the physical life of the present to contemplate the ruins of the past. This trajectory was, to a certain extent, T. S. Eliot's. But, oddly, this is not the case. Tagore's way of suggesting that he lives in a unique moment in history is to embrace change as a fundamental constituent of existence—indeed, as a crucial constituent of diction, imagination, and craft. "In order to find you anew, I lose you every moment / O beloved treasure." In this line from a song and others like it, Tagore embraces accident. He weds contingency to the modernist's love of the moment, the here and now. The latter—as in the Joycean epiphany—heightens the quotidian: Tagore's welcoming of contingency introduces an element of risk to the epiphany and the image. He introduces the possibility of any imaginable consequence, including an intuition of the divine. Tagore's apotheosis of his historical moment, his here and now, is not a surreptitious celebration of the colonial history into which he was born, but a recognition of the fact that no historical period can be contained within its canonical definition. Accident and chance ensure that its outcomes are unpredictable and life-transforming.

This embrace of life, of chance, of play, makes Tagore stand out in the intellectual and moral ethos of late Romanticism and modernism—an ethos with which Tagore shares several obsessions (time, memory, the moment, the nature of reality, poetic form), but whose metaphysics he constantly refutes. By *metaphysics* I mean a system whereby value and meaning have their source elsewhere, somewhere beyond the experienced world—whether it is European civilisation, antiquity, the Celtic twilight, or some other lost world. The present, severed from its organic resources in that past, becomes degraded and splintered, and yet continues to be haunted, even burnished, by what it has lost. I think Tagore is deeply interested in this metaphysics in the context of Bengal, and it runs through his songs, with their momentary scenes, encounters, and revelations, where any hint of transcendence is qualified by the temporal and the fragmentary. This metaphysics is partly invoked as incantation in the refrain from the poem "Balaka," or "The Wild Geese": "*Hethha noi, hethha noi, onno konokhane!*" ("Not here, not here—elsewhere!") But there is also—in the same oeuvre, often in the very same songs and poems—the Tagore of whom I have become more and more aware, the near-contemporary of Nietzsche's, who, like the latter, makes a break with that "elsewhere" and constructs a sustained argument against it in song, and in the terms that life and desire give him: "I've become infinite: / such is the consequence of your play. / Pouring me out, you fill me / with new life once again." This, in many ways, is an astonishing and audacious assertion, all the more striking for being entirely self-aware about its audacity (this is a tonal characteristic Tagore shares with Nietzsche). The oeuvre is full of such assertions, running counter to both Romanticism's backward glance and his own "Not here, not here" refrain. It marks him out, like D. H. Lawrence, as a writer embodying a radical historical break. The lines I have tried to reproduce in English are among the most difficult to translate from the work of this largely untranslatable poet. They (in Tagore's own English) are also among his most famous, being the opening lines of the first song in the English *Gitanjali*. In Tagore's English prose-poem version: "Thou hast made me endless, such is thy pleasure." All sorts of echoes adorn the next two lines in Tagore's English—"This frail vessel thou emptiest again and again . . ." and "This little flute of a reed thou hast carried over hills and dales"—placing the song now in the context of a psalmlike, New Testament sweetness ("this frail vessel") and now in an English arcadia ("little flute of a reed . . . hills and dales"). The words are removed, in effect, from the radical moment they inhabit in the Bengali. The original—"Amare tumi ashesh korechho / emoni leela taba"—is remarkable, as I've said, on many levels. The word *leela* can be translated as divine play: Hindu philosophy sees divine play as childlike and solipsistic, and the creation and destruction of the universe, and of man, among its various corollaries. Tagore translates the word as "pleasure," to denote the primacy of delight and desire, rather than moral design, in divine creation. Among the unintended, almost inadvertent, results of that play, the song has it, is man's immortality, or "infinity" (my word), or "endlessness" (Tagore's). And so the centrality of the human is bestowed upon her or him by divinity, certainly, but not by design or according to a legible purpose. In this way, Tagore introduces the notion of chance and coincidence into the story of man's emergence, and removes the human narrative from its familiar logical movement (an ascent or a decline) from the past to the present, from tradition to modernity.

Radical claims abound in the songs and poems. Also in the *Gitanjali* is the song beginning (in my translation): "To the festival of creation I have had an invitation: / Blessed, blessed is human life!" In Tagore's English prose-poem, though, the song's declaration is more modest: "I have had my invitation to this world's festival, and thus my life has been blessed." This is almost Christian, a muttering of grace. The Bengali is far more unsettling: it has "human life" (*manab jiban*) instead of the prayerful "my life." It is more triumphal. Again, alongside the celebration of the occurrence of life and consciousness is the deliberate celebration of contingency. An invitation is always a bonus and a gift; you can't really expect it or plan for it or demand it. And, once more, the two lines, with their narrative of cause and effect, are structured at once to invoke logic and to mock it. In the earlier song, Tagore writes as if he knows that the self's infinity or endlessness should be a natural consequence of divine play, while also knowing very well there is absolutely no logical reason for the one to lead to the other. In the second song, the progression, from discovering the invitation to the festival of existence to the assertion that human life is "blessed" (*dhanya*), is presented seamlessly, although we know there is actually no good reason why the second should follow from the first. (In the English version, which adds a "thus" that is absent in the Bengali, the progression in the first line is far more acceptable.) But why should divine play lead to the speaker's belief in his own infinitude? Why should his being invited to earthly existence be a cause of joy for all human life? There's a logical structure to the way these statements develop, but it is a structure that conceals a deep arbitrariness. The second song strongly implies, in its movement from the first line to the second in Bengali, a "thus" or "therefore" or "tai," without being able to quite justify or explain that powerful implication. The English translation, by adding a "thus" and substituting "human life" with "my life," simply dispenses with that mysterious tension and diminishes the audacity of the opening. We, as listeners of the Bengali song, are moved and unsettled, but we ask, in the end, for no justification: it is almost as if we know that, in Tagore's world, anything is possible.

Much of Tagore's work, then, is preoccupied with—indeed, mesmerised by—coincidence and possibility. It is a preoccupation that seems to go against the closure and yearning of "Not here, not here, elsewhere," because one can never predict when or where that moment of possibility will occur. One of the songs I have translated for this volume, "The sky full of the sun and stars, the world full of life, / in the midst of this, I find myself— / so, surprised, my song awakens," is, again, a paean to coincidence. It is also a refutation of metaphysics, of a higher purpose (whatever that might be), according to whose design existence or consciousness might find its proper meaning and arrangement. I have translated Tagore's word *bismaye* as "surprised," though it could plausibly be rendered as "in wonder." The role of the naïve or nature poet, or even a certain kind of romantic, is to wonder at the real, at the universe, but the speaker in the song is not just transfixed by the beauty of the universe but by the happenstance that's brought him to it: "in the midst of this, I find myself." This is what gives to the poet-mystic's bismay (his sense of wonder) the element of the unexpected, of surprise—the surprise of the time traveller (expressed in the poem "Meghdut") moving between worlds and phases of history. Tagore's peculiar lyric voice, with its curiously urgent apotheosis of the world, its constant note of arrival, can be partly understood through the trope of science fiction (one of whose recurrent themes is the sudden advent into new universes), or through the notion of rebirth and return, or both. This is an odd but powerful, and revealing, characteristic in the foremost artist to have emerged from a background of Brahmo reformism and the Bengali Enlightenment.

•

Tagore's recurrent metaphors of time travel, return, and arrival, and the fact that the great protagonist of his songs and poems is a figure determinedly committed to journeying toward life and birth, were picked up by two great Bengali artists who came after him: the poet Jibanananda Das and the filmmaker Ritwik Ghatak. Das (1899–1954), who, after his untimely death in an accident with a tram, has come to be seen as the outstanding Bengali poet after Tagore, and whose personality—solitary, disturbed—is the antithesis of the older poet's, sensed that

Tagore was the principal writer of his time of the will to, and desire for, life. Without remarking upon this in so many words, he took on this mantle himself, but expressed himself far more equivocally, if no less forcefully. Das's time traveller, in his poem "Banalata Sen," moves through epochs and civilisations, arriving at last in a modern drawing room in Bengal, in a journey during which both mythic and ordinary place names are made strange:

> For thousands of years I roamed the paths of this earth,
> From waters round Ceylon in dead of night to Malayan seas.
> Much have I wandered. I was there in the grey world of Asoka
> And Bimbisara, pressed on through darkness to the city of Vidarbha.
> I am a weary heart surrounded by life's frothy ocean.
> To me she gave a moment's peace—Banalata Sen from Natore.
>
> (translated by Clinton B. Seely)

The irrepressible Tagorean energy, the irresistible will to arrive—"in the midst of this, I find myself— / so, surprised, my song awakens"—has faded here but not vanished. Das gets his habit of repeating ancient place names from Tagore as one of the ways in which the traveller orders his journey while commemorating past arrivals; here is Tagore in his eponymous essay on Kalidasa's poem, the *Meghadutam*: "Avanti, Vidisha, Ujjayini, Vindhya, Kailas, Devagiri, the Reva, the Shipra, the Vetravati." But Das's speaker experiences a fatigue that the radical Tagorean protagonist didn't know. Das's hero, or antihero, must press on, despite his "weary heart": he has inherited, perplexingly, the same life-urge. Das too is a great poet of the will to live—precisely because his view of it is darker, and far more qualified. His protagonist desires to be born despite being conscious that birth is not an unmixed blessing. This is Das's troubling modulation upon the Tagorean idea of the "invitation" to earthly existence, as a result of which "human life" is "blessed":

> Drawn to the Earth's ground, to the house of human birth
> I have come, and I feel, better not to have been born—
> yet having come all this I see as a deeper gain
> when I touch a body of dew in an incandescent dawn.
>
> ("Suchetana," translated by Joe Winter)

In the first two lines of this famous stanza, Das has a familiar Sophoclean moment; but, in the third and fourth lines, he's come round to the Tagorean belief that arrival and return create their own article of faith; the body becomes an incarnation of the will ("I touch a body of dew"); in Tagore's words, "I've pressed upon each blade of grass on my way to the forest." Again and again, Das will be of two minds about this matter, about withdrawing from the cycle of life or, taking his cue from his great precursor, returning to it:

> When once I leave this body
> Shall I come back to the world?
> If only I might return
> On a winter's evening
> Taking on the compassionate flesh of a cold tangerine
> At the bedside of some dying acquaintance.
>
> ("Tangerine," translated by Clinton B. Seely)

For Tagore, withdrawal was out of the question. "In the midst of this, I find myself," he'd said in the song. In the poem "Liberation" ("Mukti"), he put it elegantly but with directness: "Liberation through renunciation—that's not for me"; and, later, "To shut / in penance, the senses' doorway—that's not for me." We can connect this to the Buddhist thought that deeply attracted Tagore; but if we place it in the context of his oeuvre, of the modernity he lived in, and the modernism he was always ambivalent about, we must put him in the lineage of

Nietzsche, Whitman, Lawrence, and others who made a similar rebuttal of negation. Actually, looking again at the poem "Balaka" ("The Wild Geese"), in which the admonitory refrain "Not here, not here, elsewhere" occurs, I find it lit not so much by a desire for "elsewhere" (the foundational desire of metaphysics) but, again, by the subversive urge for life itself. The poet is standing after sunset before a landscape of hills and deodar trees, near the river Jhelum, when, unexpectedly, the sudden transit of a flock of geese flying transmogrifies the observer and his vision of nature. The Tagorean landscape is often orchestral, participatory, musical, synchronic, but not Wordsworthian, with the "still, sad music of humanity"; it is alive, but not in an anthropomorphic sense. In another, early poem, "*Jete nahi dibo*" ("I Won't Let You Go!"), all of nature, as the speaker departs from home and family on a long absence involving work, echoes his daughter's final words to him in an actively participatory way, in what can only be called an orchestral threnody:

> What immense sadness has engulfed
> The entire sky and the whole world!
> The farther I go the more clearly I hear
> Those poignant words, "Won't let you go!"
> From world's end to the blue dome of the sky
> Echoes the eternal cry: "Won't let you go!"
> Everything cries, "I won't let you go!"
> Mother Earth too cries out to the tiny grass
> It hugs on its bosom, "I won't let you go!"
>
> (translated by Fakrul Alam)

This is not anthropomorphism; it is the landscape agitated by the life urge, and making a vocal, direct intervention. In "The Wild Geese," Tagore revisits and revises his vision:

It seemed that those wings
Bore away tidings
Of stillness thrilled in its innermost being
By the intensity of motion . . .

And again:

. . . The grass fluttering its wings
On the earth that is its air—
Underneath the darkness of the soil
Millions of seeds sprouting wings
I see today

(translated by Fakrul Alam)

From Tagore, the filmmaker Ritwik Ghatak (1925–1976) got his sense of the landscape being not just a serene, indifferent, permanent background to human endeavour, as in the Brueghel painting of Icarus's fall described wryly by W. H. Auden in his "Musée des Beaux Arts," but as a multivocal, orchestral entity actively involved in the desire for existence. So, at different points of time in Ghatak's films, the landscape appears to move and listen; it is aware of the protagonist, just as the protagonist is partly conscious of it being conscious of him. Ghatak's great modulation upon "The Wild Geese" and its cry—as well as the cry "I won't let you go"—occurs toward the end of *Meghe Dhaka Tara* (*The Cloud-Covered Star*), his most fraught and painful film. Nita, once the breadwinner of a family of East Bengali refugees displaced by migration, is now terminally ill with tuberculosis. She has been transferred by her brother, Shankar, from their house in Calcutta to a sanatorium in the hill-station, Shillong. Anil, now a successful singer, comes to visit her; the two figures are surrounded by an astonishing panorama. As she listens to him talk about their younger sister's mischievous child, Nita bursts out without warning, "Dada, I *did* want to live!" Crushed, attempting to placate and silence her, Anil responds with "Idiot!" (Indeed, there is something comic, even imbecilic, about the life-urge and its insistent simplicity; which is why we, on occasion, shake our heads in consternation at Tagore and Whitman and Lawrence and Ghatak—all very different kinds of artists, admittedly.) In a series of rapid frames, we witness the landscape congregating from various angles and echoing her words, "I so love life, dada! I *will* live!" This is the primordial Tagorean "message" ("I felt the message of those beating wings") of a near-heretical faith; ironicised by Ghatak, seen unflinchingly for its heresy, but not made meaningless. This faith contains an acknowledgment of death and "elsewhere," but also an answer and a refutation.

•

Death and life share the quality of being contingent, accidental: we don't know when and how they will happen, or even, really, why they do. (This would have been pretty clear to Tagore, who lost his muse and sister-in-law Kadambari Devi when he was twenty-two—she had died by her own hand—and then, over the years, his wife and two of his children.) Tagore's work is less about universals, absolutes, and unities (though it is also about these) than about the role of chance governing the shape of the universe and of the work itself, taking the form of a sustained meditation: "In order to find you anew, I lose you every moment / O beloved treasure." Contingency preoccupied him all his life. In 1930, when he had a couple of meetings with Albert Einstein, he opened the dialogue enthusiastically with, "I was discussing with Dr. Mendel today the new mathematical discoveries which tell us that in the realm of infinitesimal atoms chance has its play; the drama of existence is not absolutely predestined in character." Einstein replies with a dampener: "The facts that make science tend toward this view do not say goodbye to causality." This famous, overpublicised conversation can be read in a number of ways. Einstein clearly sees Tagore as a "poet" in the "high" cultural western sense, but still more as an eastern sage, and is dry and cautious as a result. He—not Tagore—keeps bringing up the word *religion* in a mildly defensive, mildly accusatory manner. Einstein, responsible for a shatteringly disorienting theory that would forever change philosophy and the humanities, not to speak of the sciences, forecloses, in response to Tagore, that strand of insight, and becomes a conventional scientist-empiricist: for "that," he says, "is my religion." Tagore, in the course of the two slightly anxious, circular conversations, appears in various fluid incarnations: as a romantic poet, talking about beauty and truth; as a transcendentalist; a believer in the absolute; a propagandist for universal man. We have dealt with him in these guises in the last one hundred years of discussions about Tagore; no doubt we will again, 150 years after his birth. But Tagore's secret concern with life, play, and contingency keeps resurfacing in his part of the dialogue; he might well have believed that this powerful undercurrent would provide common ground with the German. Einstein, though, pushes the interaction toward a more conservative dichotomy: that of the romantic, the man of religion, or the metaphysician with his purely subjective response to the universe, on the one hand, and the scientist with his empirical and objective vantage point, on the other.

•

For me, there are two great lineages in poetry from the upheavals of the nineteenth century onward: the metaphysical, or the poetry of the beautiful (sometimes anguished) fragment made radiant by the light of the vanished old world and of bygone value; and the polemical, sounding the note of constant, occasionally arbitrary, arrival and return, disrupting not just linearity, as the former does, but causality. I think Tagore belongs deeply, if only partially, to the first category, and I have written before of his songs in this light. But, increasingly, I believe his great power derives from being essentially in the second camp, from denying, like Whitman and Lawrence, that there is any need to apologise for life and its accidental provenance. One characteristic of the writers in the first camp is how they practice their art and their criticism in distinct domains, and, in a sense, detach themselves from the "meaning" of their artistic work, like Joyce's fingernail-paring author-god, or James's evolving "figure in the carpet," upon which the narrator will deliberately not elaborate. The polemicists, on the other hand, not only immerse themselves in the thrust of their work with every fibre of their being—"a man in his wholeness wholly attending," as Lawrence said of poetry—but in every sphere of activity they undertake, as Tagore did. This is why they seem open to deciphering and are more vulnerable to misunderstanding.

I had begun by mentioning my adolescent impatience with Tagore and my enthusiasm for Dan Pagis's poem about the Holocaust. I still admire that poem—in fact, more than I did when I was seventeen—for its craft, tragic exactness, and its shrinking shape informed by Adorno's stark dictum that poetry is no longer tenable after Auschwitz. Adorno's admonition, however, has a history older than the horrors of the twentieth century: it comes from a metaphysical belief that, on many levels, life (and, as a result, its chief expression, language) is too fragile to wholly justify itself. Tagore is still the great poet in our age of life's inherent and inexhaustible justification—this is what he is actually conveying to Einstein—but his argument is plainest in the songs and poems. Accustomed as we are to the luminosity of elsewhere, to the backward glance, to action and outcome with a cause, and less accustomed to the joy of unforeseen arrival (which, after all, rapidly wanes into alienation), encountering Tagore has to be an unsettling experience—but one through which we also come to recognise our deepest unspoken urges and beliefs incarnated in the most surprising and incomparable language.

On the *Gita*
Krishna as Poetic Language

2012, introduction to the Folio Society edition

The Bhagavad Gita begins at a moment of crisis—not just a crisis of the community and the nation, as it certainly is, but one of a personal and (to use a relatively contemporary term) existential nature. When the influential Kannada novelist U. R. Ananthamurthy published his first novel, *Samskara*, about a Brahmin who deliberately chooses to estrange and isolate himself from other Brahmin priests, it invited the thought, even from its translator A. K. Ramanujan, that Ananthamurthy might have made his protagonist more of an existentialist than his Brahminical identity could credibly allow for. But Arjuna, in the *Gita* (of course, he's a Kshatriya, a warrior, not a Brahmin), reveals that anguished choice-making in relation to the world—the characteristic preoccupation and mood of existentialism—is hardly new to India; that, at least in cultural antecedents, Ananthamurthy's Praneshacharya is not alone.

What kind of crisis, exactly? The *Gita* is an episode—a slightly anomalous, somewhat unassimilable episode, but an episode nevertheless—in the epic the *Mahabharata*. The epic (composed roughly between 400 BCE and 400 CE) is the story of two warring clans of cousins, the Pandavas and the Kauravas. The Pandavas, the family to which the great warrior Arjuna and his four brothers belong, are the "good guys." In other words, Vyasa, the author of the epic, means us to see the action through the Pandavas' eyes, from (to use an ugly piece of creative writing school jargon) their "point of view." The Kauravas are treacherous; they inveigle the Pandavas into a game of dice and rob them of their kingdom, even attempting to disrobe Draupadi, the Pandava brothers' wife (how Draupadi came simultaneously to marry five men is another story).

The Pandavas go into exile for the mandatory mythic period of thirteen years or thereabouts (the *Ramayana* has Rama banished for fourteen). The deal at the close of the game of dice was that they would resume their reign once that period was over. Returning, they discover the Kauravas have no intention of letting that happen. The two clans are now formally at war. There's a crucial scene before the actual conflict begins on the battle-field of Kurukshetra (which, in the course of the rest of the epic, will become a site that, in scale and destruction, out-Guernicas any imaginable Guernica). Both clans have gathered before Krishna, like bidders at a Premier League auction, to petition him for his support and also for his powerful army. Krishna says that each clan can have one or the other; that he will provide advice to the clan that chooses him over his army, but will abstain from fighting himself. The Kauravas decide they want Krishna's army; Arjuna elects to have Krishna as his charioteer.

Krishna is God incarnate; charming, beautiful, he is in other respects inexplicably volatile, unpredictable, and transmogrifying. In other words, being divine, in Krishna's case, is to be surprising to the point of being alienating: not burdened by a human code of conduct, Krishna can resort, occasionally, to all kinds of duplicity to further his team's interests. His amorality is quite different from the Kauravas' tragic treacherousness or the sleights-of-hand that the Pandavas indulge in; it leads us towards the abyss of meaning, or meaninglessness, from which the *Mahabharata*'s great power emerges. As a consequence, what's destroyed in the *Mahabharata* is not just a great deal of human life, but a stable "point of view" that might give rise to a clear sense of good and bad characters, of virtuous and evil action. The great and perennial casualty of the *Mahabharata* is the stability of value; its excitement and animation lies in its constant shifting of the centre.

•

The *Bhagavad Gita* is a conversation between Arjuna and his charioteer Krishna which takes place just before the Battle of Kurukshetra is to begin. Both armies are on the battle-field: in the opposing camp, Arjuna can see kinsmen he's known since childhood, "teachers, fathers and sons; grandsons, grandfathers, wives' brothers; mothers' brothers and fathers of wives." On the eve of battle, then, he's agonised, full of doubt: "These I do not wish to slay, even if I myself am slain." It's now up to Krishna to exhort and rouse him to action. This exhortation, briefly, is the gist of the *Gita*.

By the time we arrive at this point in the *Mahabharata*, we already know Arjuna as flamboyant and heroic, possessed of unsurpassed skills in the art of war, and, most importantly, as one of the privileged (despite his travails, and in contrast to his gifted but unfortunate half-brother Karna)—that is, as someone whom both the narrator and the gods smile upon. To see him now changed into an overwrought, Hamlet-like ditherer is intriguing. But Hamlet is no existentialist; he's disturbed, and part of the source of his disturbance is derived from his new-found disgust at his mother's sexual availability. Although, vacillating between "being" and "not being," Hamlet asks some of the same questions as Arjuna, Shakespeare allows us to view him from the outside, enmeshed in his own moment of theatre. A small but stubborn question mark hangs over him, both in our minds and inside the play, as to whether he's making too much of nothing (as T. S. Eliot accused Shakespeare of doing with the play itself). This distance opens up the character and his agonies to a latent comedy, which spoof-makers have tapped into in various parodies of the tortured prince. No such distance qualifies

Arjuna, and, as a result, it's more difficult to parody his anguish. We don't, here, view Arjuna as a dramatic character with motives and a psychology, although we don't necessarily think he lacks these things. Nor is he a cipher, a mouthpiece, for a set of questions. In the *Gita*, Arjuna is inseparable from human language, a language alive with disquiet, prescience, and yearning.

Krishna, too, is a different Krishna in the *Gita*. In the rest of the epic, and even outside it, in songs and in folklore, Krishna is Ovidian. I use the word to hint at Krishna's self-transforming and metamorphic nature—an errant and greedy child in the *Bhagavata Purana* and in folklore; a lover of numberless women; in the epic, too, a politician, an inscrutable trickster and strategist; and, all the while, in various manifestations, divine. He is Ovidian because his transformations, or personalities, are, in a sense, material: a dazzling array of registers in the world we experience. Like the metamorphoses that Ovid ebulliently records, Krishna is a reminder that play and creation are synonymous and inexhaustible. Of all the gods, it's Krishna who's identified with *leela*, or the infinitely tantalising play, chicanery, and light and shade of the created universe. This uncontainable Ovidian mood is particularly true of the folksy cowherd Krishna of the *Bhagavata Purana*, beloved of the devotional Bhakti poets; but we also encounter it in the *Mahabharata*, where Krishna, at once Machiavellian, merciful, and estranging, engages in war as a very serious kind of game, or play.

In the *Gita*, we encounter a Krishna we can find absolutely nowhere else. This Krishna tells Arjuna that it's he who is the source of everything; and yet he's "invisible." This paradox demands a different response, a different order of recognition, a different sort of suspended disbelief, from the Krishna who performs astounding feats and multiplies through stories. What could run through the visible universe, but not be seen itself? We're not being asked to believe in the sort of astonishing event that epic, myth, or fiction often offer us, but in a paradox that's peculiar to the poetic: "I am not bound by this vast work of creation," says Krishna. "I am and I watch the drama of works." What *is* he, then? Clearly something even more difficult to understand by a concatenation of logical thinking than the Krishna of the *Mahabharata* or the *Bhagavata* tradition is. Not only does Krishna at once situate himself in creation and distance himself from it ("I am not bound by this vast work of creation"); he appears to be distancing himself from the epic mode that the *Gita* and he are presently embedded in: "I watch the drama of works." On one revolutionary level, then, the *Gita* is a critique of the epic narrative that it finds itself in, of its outwardly endless range and its momentary way of making meaning: "When one sees Eternity in things that pass away and Infinity in finite things, then one has pure knowledge. / But if one merely sees the diversity of things, with their divisions and limitations, then one has impure knowledge." Instead, the *Gita* signals its own radical shift in register by suggesting the power of something that's contradictory, something that inheres at once in the visible universe and in darkness, in abstraction and in language:

> a sense sublime
> ...Whose dwelling is the light of setting suns,
> And the round ocean, and the living air,
> And the blue sky, and in the mind of man;
> A motion and a spirit, that impels
> All thinking things, all objects of all thought...

Of course, this is not from the *Gita*, but from Wordsworth's "Tintern Abbey." But the lines (Wordsworth would have known the *Gita* in Charles Wilkins's translation, and probably through August Wilhelm Schlegel) gesture towards the oddness of poetic meaning as a special meaning: something simultaneously animate and still, impelling and concealed. This note of eloquent, visionary special pleading for a meaning that contradicts itself constantly in order to generate itself, and which has no discernible justification, rationale, manifestation, or cause, comes from the *Gita*'s Krishna: "That splendour of light that comes from the sun and which illumines the whole universe, the soft light of the moon, the brightness of fire—know that they all come from me." Again and again, in Krishna's most famous maxims concerning "action" to Arjuna, it's the strange, contradictory nature of true meaning that's being explored and fortified. "Arise and fight!" he exhorts the warrior, but asks him to do so without thought of the "fruit of one's actions." Meaning comes into being, then, only when there's no thought of, or desire for, the outcome. This difficult concept is what Arjuna gets, instead of a clear and practical manual of dos and don'ts, or an exhortation to selfless love and compassion, as in the Gospels. Where does that idiosyncratic idea of meaning, and the power of meaning, operate but in poetry itself? In the *Gita*, Krishna becomes poetic language.

•

This is not to say that there is a complete discontinuity between the *Mahabharata*'s analysis of the world as a place of politics, of actions governed by power, and the moment the *Gita* inhabits.

There are instances when Krishna's role in the *Gita* is at once historical, admonitory, and cathartic: "When righteousness is weak and faints and unrighteousness exults in pride, then my Spirit arises on earth." At such points in the *Gita*, the world already seems very old, its conventions and pieties tested and turned inside out, as it does often in the rest of the *Mahabharata*, whose author manages the astonishing feat of being simultaneously disabused and wonderstruck. Certainly, neither the epic nor the song (for that's what *gita* means) has the auspicious, inaugural air of the early *Upanishads*, or the pastoral freshness of the *Bhagavata* tradition. Instead they possess (in the case of the epic, almost completely) a quality of lateness and intransigence ("I am time, destroyer of men") that's combined, in the epic narrative, with an amazing sense of fecundity. It's the *Gita*'s belated, backward look, glancing at the residues of texts and ages it's emerged from, that prompted J. Robert Oppenheimer to quote it when witnessing the first atomic explosion in New Mexico: "I am become death."

And although the *Gita* isn't, in a strict sense, mythopoeic, its central image—of Arjuna, unable to act in a battle-field full of kinsmen, turning to Krishna—is mythic. It is where, in India, history and myth, reality and the ideal, rulers and the notion of Man, converge repeatedly, in the series of tragic episodes and subsequent attempts at self-renewal of which this civilisation is composed. The emperor Ashoka's massacre of innocents at Kalinga, and his later passionate turn towards non-violence and Buddhism; Gandhi and Nehru's terrible dilemma upon Partition—these, after the fact, set up a surreptitious confluence, in the Indian experience, between history and theatre, civilisation and allegory.

•

The earliest mention of the *Gita* in an extant text occurs in the work of the philosopher Shankaracharya (c. 788–820 CE), the first and most important theorist of *advaita vedanta*, or nondualism. (For some of the facts in this section, I'm indebted to Professor Sibaji Bandyopadhyay.) Shankaracharya chooses three canonical texts to advance his argument: the *Bhramasutra* (a work whose centrality has receded entirely), the *Upanishads*, and the *Gita*. In relation to the first two, the *Gita* occupies, in Shankaracharya's argument and scheme, a relatively minor, supplementary position. It isn't known if prior commentaries on the *Gita* existed and are now lost. Shankaracharya's text is structured as a dialogue, where an interlocutor states a position regarding the *Gita*, and the author answers or refutes him. This could point to earlier positions, earlier commentaries; on the other hand, it might not, for, as Professor Bandyopadhyay tells me, this form of dialogue, at the time, was an accepted convention for presenting an argument.

The *Gita*'s next significant appearance in the chain of Indian thinking is when the anti-Shankaracharya philosopher, the dualist Ramanuj (traditionally c.1017–1137 CE), uses the same three works to advance *his* cause. That texts may yield a multiplicity of meaning to readers and commentators of different ages is clear when we glance at the *Gita*'s history; but the idea of multiple interpretations is a New Critical, literary one, and it's rarely an advertisement for the *Gita*, though it embodies it well.

What's striking about the *Gita*, and what's been noted about it more than once, is the constant cautionary note it sounds about the principal precursor scriptures, the *Vedas*. It's not enough to follow the word of the scriptures, and to undertake the various sacrifices and rituals they enjoin you to do: the *Vedas* provide no guarantee against darkness and unknowing, the *Gita* reminds us. Moreover, that kind of religious literalism is anathema to the man seeking knowledge and a detached, "impersonal" (I use Eliot's now dated buzzword) state of illumination. Bankimchandra Chatterjee, the first major Bengali novelist, writing the earliest modern commentary on the *Gita* (published posthumously as a book in 1902), remarks on this rebuttal of the *Vedas* as evidence of the *Gita*'s subversiveness. But Professor Bandyopadhyay believes that, if the *Gita* was composed after the advent of Buddhism (as he thinks it was), it simply represents Brahminical thought's robust ability to appropriate critiques directed at it: for an antagonism towards the *Vedas*, emanating from Buddhist sources, was then very much in the air.

Whatever the truth, it's clear that the rejection of mere Vedic or scriptural observance is not just a strategic interpolation or an add-on that belongs to the time, but is contributory to the *Gita*'s peculiar tenor, and its oddly "timeless" polemic. The study of the Vedas, we're made to understand, is instrumental; because it involves ritual and instruction, it belongs to the domain of the visible. The *Gita* distrusts the visible, and conflates it with instrumentality. Most interestingly, in criticising the *Vedas*, the *Gita* is also criticising the primacy of the textual, the verbal; in other words, the *Gita* is not only in a state of tension with the epic, narrative material it's inserted into (the *Mahabharata*), it's also, being a text, at odds with itself. It views the word suspiciously, as if the word were always in danger of becoming institutional. It's a pronouncement that's implicitly, and sometimes explicitly, against pronouncement. In this, it represents a Protestant moment (albeit several centuries before the European Reformation) that exceeds and complicates Protestantism. For the latter refuted the Church in the interests of the possibility of grace—but not the Bible. The *Gita*, in rebutting mere textuality, is rejecting the form in which it's available to us. In this capacity to be, in a sense, at war with itself, it constitutes a certain definition of poetry.

•

Charles Wilkins, a servant of the East India Company, was introduced to the *Mahabharata* by Brahmins, and undertook a translation into English. The *Gita* especially caught his and other Englishmen's attention, among them, Warren Hastings (then Governor-General of British India). It was published on the latter's encouragement and with the letter of support he'd written for it serving as a kind of foreword. In it, Hastings predicted that the *Gita* would outlast the British Empire. His enthusiasm, like that of other English readers, derived from the echoes he caught in this Hindu text of certain strands of Christian theology, particularly Unitarianism. Wilkins's translation was published in 1785, and was probably read by most of the Romantic poets. They would also have possibly been acquainted, later, with August Wilhelm Schlegel's edition of the Latin translation of the *Gita* in 1823, and the excitement with which this was received in Europe. Indian antiquity was, by the late eighteenth and early nineteenth centuries, directly informing the European idea of humanism. By the late nineteenth century, the *Gita* had become not only a property of Indian nationalists, but a resource for secular modernity in India. That is, it was being approached by Indian moderns not just as a sacred text, but as a literary one—in other words, the type of chosen work that modernity deems, for a number of reasons, quasi-sacred. Gandhi, for instance, reads the *Gita* as "allegory"—by which he means, I suppose, a work whose meaning must be created by the reader, a work that belongs neither to the old, exclusive world of Hindu conventions, nor to the realm of literal veracity in which history, the sciences, and even the Semitic religions exist (Christ *was* crucified; He *was* resurrected—these are not figurative events). By gradually turning the *Gita* into allegory and poetry, secular modernity in India responds in its own way to its call that veracity and truth are never visible or obvious. The *Gita*'s contribution to secular modernity in Europe too is, I think, immense, particularly the role it plays in the formation of the "literary" in England. The reason this remains largely unacknowledged may have partly to do with the negative reception the *Gita*'s philosophy received in 1827 from Hegel, after which it slowly slipped from the canonical shelf of high "Western" culture.

*

How does the *Gita* signal to us that it's a poetic text, which asks to be read differently from the way either the epic is, or a sacred text of practical and moral dos and don'ts, or a sruti text like the *Vedas*, whose message comes from high above, or indeed a purely philosophical work?

Firstly, the epic or fictional narrative may begin *in medias res*; but the poem or poetic text is an interruption. It's a hiatus, a diversion, in some sort of meaning-producing business or activity—a larger narrative or story, say, or even life itself. Within the space of that interruption, it either offers a different order or scheme of imagined events, as is the case when Dante momentarily finds himself lost in "life's dark wood," or a different order of meaning, as with a Romantic or modernist poem. With the *Gita*, we're moving into the second kind of terrain, partly because some of us have been trained by the Romantic poem to read in a particular way, and partly because the Romantic poem, early in its career, might itself have received the *Gita*'s training. At any rate, the *Gita* constitutes not just an interpolation in the *Mahabharata*, an insertion by a later writer, but, on a more complex and generic level, a discontinuity in the narrative, a hiatus that's paradoxical, because it's surprisingly full.

The second difference concerns what happens to us, as readers, in the course of a poem. A narrative might unfold in a linear fashion, or in a manifold and multipronged way, as the *Mahabharata* does. It involves and engages us. It satisfies a particular appetite—to do with our curiosity regarding its characters and world they live in—and, once it's done, that appetite is sated; we don't need to return to the narrative for a while. The poetic text transforms us; that is, we know something has been changed by the time we finish it, though we aren't sure what new piece of information we've *learnt* that we didn't have before we began reading the poem. The effect is very different from finishing a narrative, or coming to the end of a story. Once we've read a poem, we can reread it immediately, and, as it were, relive that transformation. Our repeated experience of this transformation takes place regardless of whether we've "understood" the text completely; in this, too, the poem's impact differs from that of the narrative. We don't necessarily seem to have moved greatly from one point to another by the time we come to the end of a poem; but the poem *has* moved, achieving its transformative intention by a mixture of inner shifts and repetitions. This is how the *Gita* works: there are no plot developments, but there are movements—from Arjuna's despair to Krishna's advice on the nature of action, to the sections in which Krishna begins to divulge his own divinity, to where he "appears" in his true form to Arjuna, to the mysterious verses on the Asvattha tree, to the closing section about the "surrender of the reward of all work." This final section is, in a sense, a rehearsal of the beginning; there is, in the *Gita*, constant repetition and cross-referencing. By the time we finish reading it, we are changed without necessarily having progressed a great deal. Arjuna is now convinced and ready to take up arms; not only will the battle begin, but we're about to witness the resumption of the epic mode. When Sanjaya, the reporter of this conversation, says, "Thus I heard these words of glory between Arjuna and the God of all, and they fill my soul with awe and wonder," we know we're bidding farewell to the domain of the poem.

•

A curious stasis, then, lies at the heart of poetry, and this contradictory stillness also defines the *Gita*. Krishna articulates it in various ways. In the second chapter, he tells Arjuna, "Even as all waters flow into the ocean, but the ocean never overflows, even so the sage feels desires, but he is ever one in his infinite peace." In the third chapter: "I have no work to do in all the worlds, Arjuna—for these are mine. I have nothing to obtain, because I have all. And yet I work." In the fourth: "Although I am unborn, everlasting . . . through my wondrous power I am born." Here, whether we're conscious of it or not, we're awestruck by the *Gita*'s self-reflexivity. In giving such insistent value to the surplus, the superfluous ("I have no work to do . . . and yet I work"), the *Gita* defines an expression that's sui generis and ahistorical. It's related to the *Mahabharata*, too, as a text that's in surplus, that has no clear function. And it's precisely because it represents a break in the action that its effect and role are epiphanic rather than didactic; like the true knowledge and action described in it, it has no quantifiable outcome. The *Gita* is embedded in the *itihasa* (the historical narrative) of the *Mahabharata* more or less as the universal is putatively embedded, in literature, in the particular: as a superfluous emanation that, for some reason, we cherish. The *Gita* proposes an aesthetic rather than just a tenet: to live your life by it would be exceedingly difficult—"Let thy actions then be pure, free from the bonds of desire"—except in the special, fictitious realm of the literary.

•

What the contribution of the *Gita* is to the category of the "literary" that emerged in the nineteenth and twentieth centuries—a category attacked and almost rendered defunct in the second half of the twentieth century—is a matter of speculation. A nonauthoritative glance tells me that the *Gita*'s notion of the surplus—the idea that meaning lies not in consequence or outcome but elsewhere, in a simultaneous investment in and detachment from action—circulated in Europe in the late eighteenth and nineteenth centuries, and informed certain people's view of the creative and critical act; indeed, of culture itself. The domain of culture is a superfluous domain; the creative act is a surplus without outcome. This is a familiar position; so is the interpretative move through which things once outside that domain are annexed to it—thus, Matthew Arnold's proclamation that the Bible is "literature." No doubt Arnold was making that judgement from the vantage point of what he called "disinterestedness," a critical mood that's akin not so much to tolerance or even objectivity, but to what Arnold's successor and rival T. S. Eliot called "impersonality," or, an "escape from personality"—the upsurge of the surplus that has no worldly consequence. Eliot is proposing a paradigm for the creative act, Arnold for the critical one; the notion of the surplus runs like a thread through both, and fashions a definitive reciprocity between creative and critical actions. Arnold, who read Wilkins's translation of the *Gita* in 1845, makes a case for criticism nineteen years later, in 1864:

"It will be said that it is a very subtle and indirect action which I am thus prescribing for criticism, and that, by embracing in this manner the Indian virtue of detachment and abandoning the sphere of practical life, it condemns itself to a slow and obscure work. Slow and obscure it may be, but it is the only proper work of criticism." "Slowness" is stasis: Arnold is, via the *Gita*, blurring the boundary between criticism and poetry, and setting up, again, a reciprocity between the two that's crucial to secular modernity. For the poem, by having no clear outcome, by being "a very subtle and indirect action," is also a critical act; and criticism, in being neither story nor history, is a narrative without an outcome. This takes us back to why the *Gita* itself is a critical work; why its "slow and obscure" quality, its stasis, its lack of "determinateness," its "stupefaction," its *Insichsein* or quality of "nothingness" (all Hegel's words), would so annoy the German historicist. And the *Gita*'s blurring of boundaries, such as Arnold implicitly encourages while defining the function of criticism, also unsettles Hegel: "There is no distinction [in it] between religion and philosophy."

"Slow and obscure," says Arnold of the work of criticism: "slow" invoking stasis, and "obscure" the near-invisible. "Beyond my visible nature is my invisible Spirit," says Krishna. "This is the fountain of life whereby this universe has its being." Further, "I am the taste of living waters and the light of the sun and the moon." Wordsworth picks up on this when writing his "Tintern Abbey"; and Coleridge converts the notion of invisibility, of a hidden surplus, into an immanent trope for both reading and writing: "Our genuine admiration of a great poet is a continuous *undercurrent* of feeling; it is everywhere present, but seldom anywhere as a separate excitement." This echo of the *Gita* is itself echoed by Flaubert, who was deeply immersed in Indian texts, and who was trying to push prose towards a region where it would be read not for narrative consequence, but with the same sort of attention devoted to poetry: "The author, like God in the universe, is everywhere present but nowhere visible in his work." Here's the irritating, contradictory "remoteness" of temperament that provokes Hegel's disdain for the *Gita*; James Joyce, Flaubert's disciple, presents and parodies it in Stephen Dedalus's words at the end of *A Portrait of the Artist as a Young Man*: "The artist, like the God of creation, remains within or behind or beyond or above his handiwork, invisible, refined out of existence, indifferent, paring his fingernails." This is the *Gita* again, resurfacing. But Stephen is double-edged ("refined out of existence") and may also be alluding to Hegel, who, in his "On the Episode of the Mahabharata Known as the Bhagavad Gita by Wilhelm von Humboldt," describes sardonically the "Yogi sitting there mentally and physically unmoved, staring at the tip of his nose."

By the middle of the twentieth century, the legacy of Coleridge, Arnold, Flaubert, Eliot and Joyce had complicated the "literary" to the point that it defied easy generic categorisation. It became an act whose outcome might be argued over, but never entirely known. Flaubert, and the modernists who were indebted to him, pushed prose into an area that lay beyond the rewards of narrative, into a domain that Roland Barthes calls, retrospectively, in *Writing Degree Zero* in 1953, "poetry." In the classical period, says Barthes, poetry was simply prose dressed up with outward signs of difference: metre, ornament, rhyme. In modernity, he says, those visible signs vanish, and poetry becomes an ethos: "It is a quality *sui generis* and without antecedents. It is no longer an attribute but a substance, and therefore it can very well renounce signs, since it carries its own nature within itself, and does not need to signal its identity outwardly..."

How did this change take place? The query is similar to the question we ask ourselves upon being transformed after reading a poem. It's a singular way of viewing writing that lasted roughly two hundred years, and began to end about fifteen years after Barthes wrote those words. How is the *Gita* woven into that relatively brief history? My intention is not to prove its influence, but to review our experience of reading in the receding, but not yet vanished, secular world. Clearly, it's not just tolerance and multiplicity that define the secular, but some acknowledgement of the importance of the surplus: that which is valuable beyond the approbation of authority, whether of the *Vedas*, of an ideology, or even of "literature." It's the realm of the aesthetic that responds strongly to the *Gita*'s strange exhortation to ignore the visible. Secularism is a religion like any other, and its sacred texts are literary works. At some crucial point in history, in the late eighteenth century (around the time of the *Gita*'s worldwide dissemination), some sacred texts also began to *become* its literary works. The reason you hold this book in your hand today is the outcome of that legacy.

The Piazza and the Car Park

2014, *n+1*

IT WAS 1989. I was a graduate student at Oxford. I had made little progress with my doctoral dissertation and I had written a novel that had almost, but not quite, found a publisher. One of the routes that had taken me, in my fiction, towards Calcutta was Irish literature—its provincialism and cosmopolitanism, its eccentricity and refinement. So I was pleased when I heard that Seamus Heaney was the likeliest candidate to win the elections for the Oxford Professorship of Poetry. Paul Muldoon's anthology, *The Faber Book of Contemporary Irish Poetry*, had reintroduced Heaney to me: the magical early poems about the transformative odd-jobs men of a prehistoric economy—"diviners" and "thatchers"; the features of that economy: wells and anvils; the Dantesque political cosmology (Heaney's overt response to the "troubles") of *Station Island*.

A diversion was caused by the nomination of the Rastafarian performance and dub poet Benjamin Zephaniah. It was a strategically absurd nomination, made in the political tradition that periodically produces a fringe contender from the Monster Raving Loony Party to clear the air. Meanwhile, Heaney himself had begun subtly to remake himself as a postcolonial poet since *Wintering Out* and particularly *North*. By "postcolonial" I mean a particular allegorical aesthetic to do with power, Empire, violence, and empowerment: an allegory that, in

Heaney's case, had seen him scrutinising, since 1971, Iron Age John Does buried for centuries in the peat and Tollund men who had once been the victims of state violence; it now also involved the glamour his words imparted to bottomless bogs and to Celtic orality. There was a hint of magic realism to *North*'s politics and poetics. In retrospect, I realise this reinvention on Heaney's part was making me uneasy.

Naturally, Heaney won by a wide margin. The poet's lectures were thronged with students and Heaney's performances often had the dazzling quality of brilliant undergraduate papers. There was another narrative unfolding in these lectures, though, which would become clearer when they were collected in *The Redress of Poetry*, some of these thoughts having already been rehearsed in *The Government of the Tongue*. It was to do with Heaney's exploration of artistic delight alongside his increasing disquiet about, and premonition of, the emptiness of the poet's life in liberal democracies. Against this he had begun to counterpoise, more and more, the exemplary pressure that East European poets experienced under punitive, totalitarian regimes. Those regimes seemed to become a kind of inverse pastoral for Heaney: enclosed, isolated, and capable, paradoxically, of producing the great artists that the West no longer did. Was Heaney at a dead end? Had he been made less creative somehow, or less powerful—not only by success, but by the collapse of those regimes that had unwittingly legitimised what for him was the only great poetry being written at that time: regimes that, one by one, began to fall almost immediately after he took up the Professorship?

A decade is a long time in the life of a culture, and much changed during the 1980s. But arguably far more changed—unthinkably—between 1989 and 1993. The American writer Benjamin Kunkel said in an interview published in 2014:

> . . . I'm now old enough to remember when the Cold War just seemed like a permanent geological feature of the world. And then it just vanished.

> Then people would talk about how Japan was going to be a wealthier economy than the United States in 10 years. It would have seemed totally insane that there was going to be a black president and that gay people were going to get married...

Kunkel is telling us how difficult it was, and always is, to predict the outcomes that we now take so for granted that we no longer think about them; no longer, experientially, perceive a discontinuity. But perhaps he's also telling us how hard it is to remember—actually to feel the veracity of a time when it would have seemed "insane" to make those predictions. The imminence of a changed world order and the ignorance of that imminence are only two features of that world to which Kunkel is referring—for that world also had an infinity of other features whose reality it is now almost impossible to recollect. In order to remember, we need to rely on a species of voluntary memory, that is, a willed remembering whose consequences are largely predetermined by the conceptual structures of the present; so we are led to recall large categories, but not what it would have meant to inhabit them. Kunkel is trying to imply the lived immediacy of inhabiting a moral order by one of the strategies through which we can move beyond voluntary memory—by gesturing towards the unthinkable: "It would have seemed totally insane..." In this business of recollecting the world before the free market, before globalisation, voluntary memory misleads, and the flicker of involuntary memory throws up an array of sensations, but doesn't, in itself, instruct us in the ethics of the vanished order, an ethics we have critiqued but whose proximity we no longer sense. So it is almost impossible now to remember—as it was impossible then to predict the fall of the Berlin Wall and the advent of President Obama—that poetry was the literary genre to which the greatest prestige accrued until the mid-1980s; that one might have spent an afternoon talking with an acquaintance about the rhythm of a writer's sentences (in my specific instance, the novelist was James Kelman, the acquaintance an English graduate student in Oxford whose name I have now forgotten). In the same way, it's hard to recall that we didn't think of success in writing mainly in relation to the market, and in relation to a particular genre, the novel, and to a specific incarnation of that genre, the first novel, possibly until 1993, when *A Suitable Boy* was published, or a year earlier, when Donna Tartt's *The Secret History* appeared. It is now difficult to understand these examples as watershed occurrences in an emerging order, and difficult to experience again the moral implications of living—as I lived then, and maybe Benjamin Kunkel, who's much younger than I am, did too—in an order that was superseded.

This might be because the brain or mind or whatever you call it—our emotional and psychological make-up—is geared to cope with death, not just our own, but especially of our loved ones, with whom we identify the founding phases in our lives. Upon a significant death, we mourn the irrevocable closure of that phase; then, pretty consistently, we find it almost impossible to comprehend what it means for that person not to be alive.

This mechanism constantly translates into our experience of the everyday. In Oxford, I recall a dimly lit car park next to the cinema on George Street that was finally turned into a fake piazza in which a market now congregates on Wednesdays. I find it difficult to recall the car park except theoretically. I know very well that it was there. I have to rely on a moral variant of voluntary memory, on a willed excavation, to bring it back. This excavation—this ethical variation of voluntary memory—is increasingly important to those of us who have lived through a bygone epoch into this one. Without it, we accept the timelessness, the givenness, of whatever is equivalent to the piazza in our present-day existence. In other words, voluntary memory—or that form of excavation—must take us towards what from our point of view is plausible, but essentially unthinkable: not just the past's ignorance of its own future, as in Kunkel's anecdote about a world presided upon by the Cold War and unable to conceive of its own contingency, but the past studied from the vantage point of a present in which we know the Cold War to be a historical fact, but unthinkable. To truly attest today to the existence of the car park, or our habits of reading before the free market, is, to use Kunkel's word, "insane": or uncanny. We presume, immediately upon taking on new habits, that those habits are inborn reflexes. We are shocked to hear that poets were central to the culture; that writers once deliberately distanced themselves from material success. The past, as we reacquaint ourselves with these unthinkable facts, begins to look like that rare thing: compelling science fiction—utterly new, and unsettling. Our excavation is perhaps all the more important because we have been inhabiting, for twenty-five years, an epoch in which there has been really no contesting order, no alternative economic or political model. Only through a moral variant of voluntary memory might we, who belong to a particular generation, intuit a different order and logic which isn't really recoverable, and which challenges the present one—the piazza—simply by exposing its contingency, its constructedness.

What are the features, since the 1990s, of the piazza that have almost obliterated our memory of the car park, making us doubt it existed? Let's enumerate, quickly and crassly, some of the obvious developments in literary culture, focussing on publishing and dissemination, and the ways in which they converged with a rewriting of the literary. Let me restrict myself to Britain, my primary location during that time, taking the developments there to be in some senses paradigmatic. For one thing, most British publishing houses, as we know, were acquired by three or four German and French conglomerates, leading to a version, in publishing, of the Blairite consensus: a sort of faithful mimicking of the absence of true oppositionality in British politics following the creation of New Labour in the image of the Thatcherite Tory party. Bookshop chains such as Dillons and Waterstone's emerged, at first heterogeneous in terms of their individual outlets, then becoming merged and centralised. As many of us also know, the Net Book Agreement collapsed—that is, the agreement that had protected books from being sold under an agreed minimum price. Offers and price reductions not only became possible, they became the context for what determined shelf space and, thus, what was read. The books on price reductions and three-for-the-price-of-two offers were those that had been deemed commercial by marketing executives—the new, unacknowledged bosses of the editors and publishers—and bookshop chains, the new, unacknowledged bosses of the marketing executives.

What we were presented with, then, was a stylised hierarchy in which the author, at its bottom, was, like a monarch in a parliamentary democracy, celebrated or reviled—because, as with the monarchy, there was no agreement on whether the author was really *necessary*—and in which even publishers and agents played stellar roles only within accommodations determined by marketing men and bookshop-chain bureaucrats. This is not to say that agents or publishers didn't *believe* in unlikely books. The shift lay here: they believed in them in the cause of their untapped market potential. However, with the creation of a new marketing category, "literary fiction," market potential would *only* be expressed in terms of aesthetic excellence. No publisher would claim, in their press release: "We believe this novel is going to sell tens of thousands of copies." They would say, instead: "We believe this novel puts the writer in the ranks of V. S. Naipaul and Salman Rushdie." Belief is a sacred constituent of radical departures in literature and publishing: so it appeared, by a slight adjustment of language, as if the literary were being invested in.

Here was a commercial strategy that would not speak its name except in the context of literary populism: "More and more people are reading books." At the top of the hierarchy was the figure the marketing men scrambled to obey: the reader. The word "reader" possessed a mix of registers: it evoked the old world of humanistic individualism that had ensconced the act of reading, while, at once, it embraced the new, transformative populism. This populism worked so well in culture precisely because it didn't dispense with the language of the old humanism even though it rejected almost everything it had stood for; it simply embraced that language and used it *on its own terms*.

Who was the "reader"? He or she was an average person, put together by marketing with basic techniques of realist writing (in the way Arnold Bennett, according to Woolf, created characters by making them an agglomeration of characteristics). The reader was, according to marketing, unburdened by intelligence; easily challenged by expressions of the intellect; easily diverted by a story, an adventure, a foreign place or fairy tale, or an issue or theme of importance. This reader was transparent, democratic, and resistant only to resistance, occlusion, and difficulty. Writing must assume the characteristics of the "reader": the term for this process, in which literature took on a desirable human quality, was "accessibility." In order to placate the "reader," who, despite being invented by marketing staff, disappointed them constantly, jacket designs had to be adjusted, and literariness programmatically marginalised. But, crucially, the notion of the "reader" made it possible to claim that literature was thriving, so it wouldn't seem that its humanistic context had been made defunct, but, instead, renewed. There were more and more readers. New literatures were coming of age: "like a continent finding its voice," the *New York Times* had said of *Midnight's Children* more than a decade previously, though the pronouncement still seemed recent in the mid-nineties. Abundance was curiously repressive. Here, via the later incarnations of Waterstone's and the Booker Prize, with their ambition to capture readers, were early instances of what would become a typical convergence between the vocabulary used canonically, and retrospectively, to describe a renaissance with the ethos and vocabulary of boom-time.

What was the academy doing at this point? By the late 1980s, critical theory and its mutations—including postcolonial theory, which would take on the responsibility of defining and discussing the increasingly important literature of Empire—had begun to make incursions into Oxbridge and other universities. The departments of English, by now, looked with some prejudice upon value and the symbols of value, such as the canon; problematised or disowned terms such as "classic" and "masterpiece"; often ascribed a positive political value to orality, which it conflated with non-Western culture, and a negative one to inscription or "good writing," which it identified with the European Enlightenment. Some of this was overdue and necessary.

Meanwhile, publishers robustly adopted the language of value—to do with the "masterpiece" and "classic" and "great writer"—that had fallen out of use in its old location, fashioning it in *their own terms*. And these were terms that academics essentially accepted. They critiqued literary value in their own domain, but they were unopposed to it when it was transferred to the marketplace. Part of the reason for this was the language of the market and the language of the publishing industry were (like the language of New Labour) populist during a time of anti-elitism. Part of this had to do with the fact that publishers adopted complex semantic registers. For example: from the 1990s onwards, publishers insisted there was no reason that literary novels couldn't sell. This was an irrefutable populist message disguising a significant commercial development. What publishers meant was that, in the new mainstream category of "literary fiction," only literary novels that sold well would be deemed valid literary novels. Academics neither exposed this semantic conflict nor challenged the way literary value had been reconfigured. When, in response to political changes in the intellectual landscape, they extended the old canon and began to teach contemporary writers, or novelists from the former colonies, they largely chose as their texts novels whose position had been already decided by the market and its instruments, such as certain literary prizes.

Experts, critics, and academics took on, then, the role of service providers in the public sphere. This dawned on me in 2005, when I was spending a couple of months with my family in Cambridge. Watching TV in the evening, possibly Channel 4, we chanced upon a programme on "The 10 best British film directors"; the list had been created on the basis of votes from viewers. As with all such exercises, it was an odd compilation, displaying the blithe disregard for history so essential to the market's radicalism. Chaplin had either been left out or occupied a pretty low rung; Kenneth Branagh might have been at the top. Each choice was discussed by a group of film critics and experts (such as Derek Malcolm) who, in another age, would have had the final say. Here, they neither interrogated the choices nor the legitimacy of the list; they solemnly weighed the results. Respect and a species of survival skills were their hallmark. If Channel 4 viewers had come up with a completely different list, it would have been accorded the same seriousness by the experts. They were here to perform a specific function. The programme made me realise that it's not that the market *doesn't* want the expert or the intellectual; it simply wants them *on its own terms*. The arbiter of taste and culture and the expert—whether they're a film critic, or a celebrity chef, or a professor of English judging the Booker Prize—is a service provider. The circumstances—such as the "public" vote that had gone towards the list, or the six months in which the Booker judge reads 150 novels (two novels nominated by each publishing house) in order to choose the best literary novel of the year—will invariably be absurd from one point of view, and revolutionary and renovating from the point of view of the market. The expert, in a limited and predetermined way, is a requisite for this renovation. The genius of market activism lies in the fact that, unlike critical theory, it doesn't reject the terminology of literary value; it disinherits and revivifies it, and uses it as a very particular and powerful code. This accounts for its resilience.

What's interesting in this scenario is how far the consensus about the logic of the market extends, encompassing what might seem to be rents in the fabric. Take, for example, the phenomenon of "pirated" books in urban India, more or less coterminous with the emergence of the mainstream "literary novel" in the nineties. "Pirated" books are cheap copies, illegally reproduced and sold at traffic lights and on pavements. Confronting them, you have the same sense of disapproval and curiosity that you might towards contraband. In other words, the sight of "pirated" books provokes an excitement and unease in the middle-class person that recalls, from another age, a response to the avant-garde, the out-of-the-way; the word "pirated" adds to the aura of illegality. Only when you scrutinise the titles do you realise that pirated books are no alternative to the bookshop chain. The selection represents the most conservative bourgeois taste; popular fiction, horoscopes, best-selling nonfiction (*Mein Kampf* is perennially available), and Booker Prize winners are arrayed side by side.

Any notion of "literary activism" positions itself not against the market, but the sense of continuity it creates. For instance, literary activism needs to proclaim its solidarity with, as well as distance itself from, the old processes of "championing" and reassessment. Distance itself because, in the age of the market, publishers and marketing institutions such as the Booker Prize themselves became champions. Their aim was to enlist notional "readers" in greater numbers. In one of the many semantic convergences of the period, the language of championing, so fundamental to criticism and its influence, flowed, with the Booker Prize and publishing houses in the nineties, into the market's upbeat terminology of "bullishness." (It would be worth knowing when betting was introduced in the run-up to the Booker results. Ladbrokes seems to have been operating in the Booker arena from 2004.)

The Booker Prize morphed from a prize judged by distinguished novelists into a device for "market activism" in the 1990s, with juries comprising politicians and comedians. The agitation caused by the Booker was, even by the late 1980s, not so much related to the excitement of the literary, which has to do with the strangeness of poetic language (or as Housman put it, "If a line of poetry strays into my memory, my skin bristles so that the razor ceases to act"), as it was an effect of a hyper-excited environment. The principal way in which the Booker achieved this was by confirming, and allowing itself to be informed by, the market's most value-generating characteristics: volatility and random rewards. The market never promised equitable gain and wealth for all; what it said was: "Anyone can get rich." The distance between equitable gain (the idea that everyone can be reasonably well-off) and the guarantee, "anyone can get rich," seems at first a matter of semantics, and nonexistent; but it is very real and is reproduced exactly by the distance between the reader in the 1970s and the "reader" in the time of market activism. In the age of full-blown capitalism, anyone *can* get rich through the market, and, also, anyone can get poor; and these occurrences are disconnected from anachronistic ideas of merit and justice. In this disconnection lies the magic of the free market, its ebullience and emancipation. So the Booker Prize implicitly proclaims: "Anyone can win." As long as the work in contention is a novel and is in English, both qualifications embedded in, and representing, the globalised world, we can peel away the superfluous dermatological layers of literariness by agreeing that the essay, the story, and poetry are ineligible and superfluous. "Anyone can win" suggests a revolutionary opening-up typical of the language of market activism. As the Booker's constituency—for some time now, a worldwide one—accepts the fact that anyone can win, there is, ritually, a degree of volatility about the construction, announcement, and reception of the short list—of late, even the long list—which captures the agitation that propels market activism. Famous writers and critically acclaimed books are often ignored; at least one unknown novelist is thrown into the limelight; one putatively mediocre novel is chosen. The book is severed from oeuvre and literary tradition, as if it existed only in the moment; the history and cross-referencing that create a literary work are correctively dispensed with.

Since the history of so-called "new literatures" such as the Indian novel in English is tied up (especially since *Midnight's Children*) with the Booker Prize and the manner in which it endorses novels, we subsist on a sense that the lineage of the Indian English novel is an exemplary anthology of single works, rather than a tradition of cross-referencing, borrowing, and interdependency. The random mix on the short list and the incursion of first-time novelists as short-listed authors, often even as winners, might echo the sort of championing that drew attention to new or marginal writing; while it is actually enlivened by the volatility of market activism. Each year there's the ritual outcry from critics and journalists that the judges have missed out on some meritorious works. This outcry is not a critique of the Booker; it's germane to its workings and an integral component of its activism. The culminatory outcry comes when the winner is announced; the result is occasionally shocking. Again, this phase, of disbelief and outrage, is an indispensable part of the Booker's celebration—its confirmation—of the market's metamorphic capacities; the prize would be diminished without it. This randomness should be distinguished from the perversity of the Nobel, where a little-known committee crowns a body of work generally marked by the old-fashioned quality of "greatness," or rewards a writer for what's construed to be political reasons. The Nobel's arbitrariness is bureaucratic, its randomness a reliable function of bureaucracy. (Recent evolution suggests that the Nobel may no longer be averse to a bit of market activism itself.)

Partly the Booker goes periodically to first novels because its form of activism dispenses with the body-of-work narratives that conventionally define literary histories and prizes such as the Nobel; it responds to the market's shrinking of time, its jettisoning of pedigree in favour of an open-ended moment: the "now" of the market, in which anything can happen, and everything is changing. The fact that Indian writing in English since *Midnight's Children* has been handcuffed to the Booker means that it exists in this perpetual now, that its history is periodically obliterated and recreated each time an Indian gets the prize, leading

Indian newspapers to proclaim every few years: "Indian writing has come of age." The first novel, since the early 1990s, came to embody this compressed time frame in which speculation occurs, fortunes are lost and made, radical transformation effected. Publishers who contributed significantly to market activism appropriated this sub-genre and, by often calling books that were yet to be published "masterpieces" (the publisher Philip Gwyn Jones's prepublication statement about *The God of Small Things*, "a masterpiece fallen out of the sky fully formed," comes to mind), made pronouncements in terms of the market's shrinking of time, its subtle reframing of context and linearity, its insistence on the miraculous. The word "masterpiece" itself became a predictive category, connected to the market's bullishness and optimism, rather than a retrospective endorsement. When a publisher proclaims today: "The new novel we're publishing in the autumn is a masterpiece," they mean: "We think it will sell fifty thousand copies." No novel that's expected to sell five hundred copies is deemed a "masterpiece" by a mainstream publisher. Gwyn Jones's statement about Arundhati Roy's first novel needs, then, to be read as a prediction rather than an assessment, and a prediction made in the domain of a bullish marketplace. On the other hand, the Booker's retrospective accolades—"Which book would have won in 1939?"—again disrupt conventional histories and aim to bring past texts into the "now" of the market's activism.

The most striking instance of a publishing house and author inhabiting this "now" through a literary concept that once represented historical time is the publication of the musician Morrissey's first book, *Autobiography*, in 2013 as a Penguin Classic, the rubric evidently an authorial prerequisite. In 1992, Vikram Seth undertook a pioneering form of market activism by interviewing literary agents in order to decide who would be best equipped to auction *A Suitable Boy* to UK publishers. Notwithstanding Seth's commercial and critical success with *The Golden Gate*, he had only written his first (prose) novel. Meetings between authors and agents usually take place on fairly equal footing, with the weight of authority slightly on the side of the more powerful party. Seth's unprecedented style shifted the balance in the interests of the novel's commercial success and the sort of advance on royalties he thought it deserved. Morrissey's prepublication mindset, two decades later, represents an evolution. No overt mention is made of figures or of the advance; it's the standard of the "classic" that's at stake. It's as if Morrissey grasps the reification of literary concepts in the "now" of the marketplace. Once, critics spoke ironically of the "stocks and shares" in a writer's books being high or low with reference to their critical reputation; today, the same statement is made without irony and with a straightforward literalism. As part of this reification, however, certain words—such as "classic"—become ironical, and come close to signifying a guarantee that needs to be fiercely bargained for. That Morrissey's hunch was right was proved by *Autobiography* climbing to number one on the best sellers' chart upon publication. It would surely be the one Penguin "classic" to have had such an entry.

•

This, then, is what the piazza began to look like by the mid-1990s. We may have been bemused by what was unfolding in the first two years, but by the third year we believed it had always been like this. We had no memory of the car park. This no doubt had to do with the way the mind converts the dead into a fact: the dead are incontrovertible, but we don't know who they are. But partly it was the effect of the compressed time and space of globalisation, of inhabiting an epoch in which materiality was shrinking and our principal devices could be fitted into the palm of a hand, and periodically replaced. Personal memory, cultural institutions, and popular culture responded to this shrinkage, this ethos of recurring disposability, variously, for distinct but contiguous reasons. While literary language was acquired by publishers for the purposes of marketing, literary departments reneged, as I've said, on any discussion that connected value to the passage of time: they disavowed the "masterpiece," "canon," and "classic." Popular culture not only annexed these concepts, it produced its own terminology of eternity: for instance, the word "all-time," as in "all-time favourite guitarist" or "all-time great movie director." "All-time," it soon became evident, covered a span of five, maybe ten, years; that is, the time of deregulated globalisation—"all-time" was a means of managing the classic. In consonance with the eternity conjured up by "all-time," popular culture—and even the so-called "serious" media—abounds with lists: "10 favourite movies"; "100 great novels"; and so on. Lists both mimic and annihilate the historicity of the canon; they reduce time, making it seemingly comprehensible; they exude volatility and are meaningless because the market is energised by the meaningless. Given the pervasiveness of the "all-time," it wasn't surprising that it was difficult to give credence to the car park.

But other things were happening in the 1990s that didn't quite fit in. I was rereading, and often discovering for the first time, the modernism of Indian literatures as I prepared to compile the *Picador Book of Modern Indian Literature*. In 1992, I'd also turned my attention to Arvind Krishna Mehrotra, whose poetry I'd read on and off since the late 1970s and whose anthology, *The Oxford India Anthology of Twelve Modern Indian Poets*, published that year, made an intervention on behalf of a discredited tradition, contemporary Indian poetry in English, without having recourse to the new interpretative apparatus. His primary intervention was the making of the anthology itself, where he brought poets and their work together in a way that redefined their relationship to each other without either explicitly rejecting or taking for granted the notion of a preexisting canon. This was a way of looking at literary history that neither fitted in entirely with the humanist procedures of valuation (Indian poetry in English had never anyway really been a legitimate subject of such authoritative procedures) nor subscribed to the prevalent methods connected to the postcolonial, the hybrid, or even to list-making, since Mehrotra's juxtapositions seemed to be exploring and arguing for a particular experience of the literary.

I recalled, as I was thinking of essays to include in the Picador anthology, a long, polemical critical article that Mehrotra had published in 1980 in a little magazine out of Cuttack called *Chandrabhaga* and edited by the poet Jayanta Mahapatra. The essay was "The Emperor Has No Clothes," and I was eighteen when it came out, but I still had a sense of its central tenet: simply put, the Indian poem in English has no obvious markers of "Indianness." Similarly, the poem produced by the multilingual imagination has no visible hierarchy in, or signs of, the manner in which a multiplicity of languages inhabits it. With hindsight (and upon rediscovery of that issue after a strenuous search), this argument read like a prescient rebuttal of precisely one of the sacred dogmas that came into play from the 1980s onwards: that, in the case of the multicultural literary work, the admixture and its proportions were immediately noticeable, and it was therefore possible to applaud and celebrate them, rather than necessarily the work, accordingly.

When the idea came to me of getting Mehrotra nominated for the Oxford Professorship of Poetry, I can't recall, but it was obviously post-1989, with the Benjamin Zephaniah nomination pointing towards a course of action. Not that I was thinking of Mehrotra in terms of his potential comic disruptiveness; but *some* sort of unsettlement was going to be welcome. Besides, I felt Mehrotra would make for a genuinely interesting lecturer, and his self-aware position as an Indian modern made him, for me, a far better choice for the Professorship than the sort of "great" poet who'd lost his tenancy in the emptiness of evangelical liberal democracy during globalisation.

The Picador anthology came out in 2001. The director of British Council India, in a moment of generosity, commissioned a poster exhibition as a response to it. I asked Naveen Kishore, publisher of Seagull Books, an imprint known for the beauty of its jacket designs, whether he'd take on the brief of producing the posters. Naveen created an elegant series using black-and-white photographs he'd taken himself, playing with typeface and selecting one randomly chosen quotation from pieces in the anthology per poster. One poster bore a line from Michael Madhusudan Dutt; one a remark from a letter Tagore had written; another a quote from "The Emperor Has No Clothes"; another simply displayed the title of an A. K. Ramanujan essay, "Is there an Indian way of thinking?" Peter D. McDonald, who teaches English at Oxford and saw some of the posters I'd taken there with me, was struck especially by the Mehrotra quote that Naveen had used, a slightly edited version of this long sentence: "Between Nabokov's English and Russian, between Borges's Spanish and English, between Ramanujan's English and Tamil-Kannada, between the pan-Indian Sanskritic tradition and folk material, and between the Bharhut Stupa and Gond carvings many cycles of give-and-take are set in motion."

The sentence is doing something that isn't obvious at first. The back and forth, or the "give-and-take... motion," between "Ramanujan's English and Tamil-Kannada, between the pan-Indian Sanskritic tradition and folk material" et cetera, isn't an unexpected sort of movement—between the "high," and the "low" or "popular." It's the transverse movement *across* the sentence, connecting Nabokov, Borges, Ramanujan, the pan-Indian Sanskritic tradition and the Bharhut Stupa to each other—characterising another kind of "give and take" that enables these very analogies—that constitutes its departure. It signals Mehrotra's unwillingness to be constrained by conventional histories of cultural interaction or influence across the "East" and the "West"—so that he slyly sidesteps them or appears inadvertently to ignore them. There's a transaction between the high, the sacred, with the vernacular and the profane, the sentence claims; this much is conventional wisdom. But the sentence also claims that such a transaction characterises every culture, in ways that puts cultures in conversation with each other. These conversations between cultures aren't to do with "difference" (in which, say, the East might play the role of the irrational, the West of Enlightenment humanism); nor do they represent a conciliatory humanism, in which East and West seek versions of themselves in each other. Instead, Mehrotra behaves as if each pairing represents comparable literary trajectories that echo and illuminate each other; one of the things that the sentence declares is that the colonial encounter is hardly the only way of interpreting the contiguity between the West and the East, or even the "high" to the "vernacular." The echoes that comprise the conversation ("Borges's Spanish and English . . . Ramanujan's English and Tamil-Kannada . . . the pan-Indian Sanskritic tradition and folk material") exist independently of each other, but their overlaps aren't entirely coincidental. They can only be noticed and connected in a head such as Mehrotra's, in whom, in some way not entirely explained by colonialism and Empire, with their restrictive itineraries, these histories (catalogued in the sentence) come together. The echoes, overheard by Mehrotra, signal a liberation from those clearly demarcated histories of cultural interchange.

It was around that time that I asked Peter to read "The Emperor Has No Clothes" in the Picador anthology, and also to consider the thought that Mehrotra be nominated for the Oxford Poetry Professorship. I hoped that Peter would be drawn to Mehrotra's larger statement, indeed to his work. This did become the case; so I'm not surprised to find an email query in my "sent" inbox, addressed to Peter on 23 January 2009, when the opportune moment had clearly arisen:

> Dear Peter,
>
> I notice they're looking for a new Professor of Poetry to dawdle beneath the dreaming spires. Should we conspire to get Arvind Krishna Mehrotra nominated?

Peter replied an hour later, saying he was going to try to enlist colleagues in the department and then proceed with the nomination, for which ten "members of congregation and convocation," or fully paid-up

Oxford University employees and / or degree-holders, were required. I alerted the Irish poet-critic Tom Paulin, who was out of sorts but still teaching at Hertford. Peter photocopied "The Emperor Has No Clothes" from the Picador anthology, I poems from *Middle Earth: New and Selected Poems* and *The Transfiguring Places* (the books, like those of most Indian English poets, were out of print) at a shop in Gariahat in Calcutta, and scanned and sent them to Peter, for circulation, and also to Tom, who said he would decide after he had investigated further.

Who is Arvind Krishna Mehrotra? No full account could be given to people—and I include, here, some of the nominators—who knew little of him and his work. All that could be done was to put samples, the essay, and a short biography out there and hope that this would open up a conversation that would introduce, in the lead-up to the elections, a new set of terms. Some might have noticed that Mehrotra, born in 1947, was a "midnight's child," but that neither his work nor life carried any news of the nation as we'd come to understand it. The middle-class suburb figured in the most characteristic poems—but not the state. He was born in Lahore. He grew up in a small town, Allahabad, and was educated there and in another one, Bhilai, and was later a graduate student in Bombay. Still later, he'd spend two years in Iowa, homesick for India, but there was no whiff, until the 2009 campaign, of Oxbridge about him. Allahabad was an intellectual centre that was moving unobtrusively, by the time Mehrotra was seventeen and already entertaining ambitions of being a poet, toward decline. And yet Allahabad is where he discovered Ezra Pound and the Beat poets, and, with a friend, brought into existence a short-lived little magazine, *damn you / a magazine of the arts*, echoing Ed Sanders's New York periodical from the early 1960s, *Fuck You: A Magazine of the Arts*. The publication's name, it seems to me, is intent on turning Sanders's challenge into a Poundian imprecation, from one who clearly shared with the narrator of "Hugh Selwyn Mauberley" a combative impatience about being "born / In a half savage country, out of date; / Bent resolutely on wringing lilies from the acorn." What sorts of lilies? At nineteen, he was a youthful and exasperated satirist in vers libre, in a declamatory mode borrowed from Ginsberg, opening his long poem to the nation, *Bharatmata: A Prayer*, with: "india / my beloved country, ah my motherland / you are, in the world's slum / the lavatory." It was 1966, two years after Nehru's death, a time in which the late prime minister's projects of industrialisation and austerity continued doggedly to be pursued. Then, around 1969–70, something magical happens, and, in rhythms and imagery that glance knowingly both at French surrealism and American poetry, Mehrotra begins to produce his first mature poems, which are often parables of Allahabad's neighbourhoods:

> This is about the green miraculous trees,
> And old clocks on stone towers,
> And playgrounds full of light
> And dark blue uniforms.
> At eight I'm a Boy Scout and make a tent
> By stretching a bed-sheet over parallel bars . . .
>
> ("Continuities")

At least two things strike us as we acquaint ourselves with Mehrotra's life and oeuvre. The first has to do with movement. How does a person who has moved relatively little encounter and even anticipate the contemporary world of ideas and letters—in an age without the fax and internet, in which the speediest epistolary communication is the telegram? It's a mystery that has no adequate explanation. Yet scratch the surface of the life and the history that produced it, and you find that Mehrotra exemplifies not an aberration but a pattern. It's a pattern that defines both India and much of literary modernity, and Mehrotra embodies it in the singular way in which he traverses the provincial and the cosmopolitan. This would have always made it difficult to present him in the campaign as a postcolonial who—like Derek Walcott, according to his supporters—had somehow transcended his identity into the realm of universality. ("With Walcott, you need only to remember the name," an English professor had said dreamily to students.) Mehrotra, like Allahabad, was an anomaly, and modernity was local and anomalous. The second thing that becomes clear quickly is Mehrotra's indifference to creating an authentic "Indian" idiom in English. Instead, like the speaker of a later poem, "Borges," he seems content to let "the borrowed voice / [set] the true one free." In an email to me he once admitted that, as a young man, he'd turned to French surrealism because he wanted to escape "the language of nightingales and skylarks." The same could presumably be said of his lifelong preoccupation, as both a poet and translator, with Pound, William Carlos Williams, and the emphatic dialogue of American cartoons. What's notable is the historical and creative intelligence latent in this statement: the notion that neither the English language nor Western culture is a continuous and unbroken entity, that each is heterogeneous and will contain *within* itself breaks and departures (such as French surrealism and the diction of Pound). No break need be made from it, because that's probably impossible; instead, a break might be effected *through* it by deliberately choosing one register or history over another. Modernism and Pound's poetry, then, aren't absolutes for Mehrotra; they comprise, instead, a breakdown in "the language of skylarks and nightingales." This breakdown will resonate very differently for an Indian—for whom "Western culture" is an ambivalent but real inheritance—from the way it will for a European to whom that inheritance is a given. It also means that the Indian poet in English will be less of a creator busy originating an authentic tongue, and more like a jazz musician, listening acutely to the conflicting tonality—nightingales, skylarks, the Beat poets, Pound—of what surrounds and precedes him. Out of this curious tradition (which in no way precludes Indian writing: Mehrotra's translations include versions of Prakrit love poetry, of Kabir, and of the contemporary Hindi poet Vinod Kumar Shukla, and it's often at the moment of translation that the registers I've mentioned are counterintuitively adopted), he must make something of his "own."

The enervating, bewildering, and thrilling elements of the Mehrotra campaign are too many in number to enumerate here. Let me recount a few points, some of which are already familiar to those who kept track of the event. We ended up recruiting a mix of well-wishers and personal contacts, all of them distinguished in their fields, as supporters, some of them already admirers of Mehrotra. Among the latter were the novelists Geoff Dyer and Toby Litt and the Romanticist Jon Mee. Tariq Ali was made to reacquaint himself with the work and became one of the most vocal supporters of the candidacy; Tom Paulin joined the campaign once his investigations confirmed the value of the candidate; Wendy Doniger and the philosopher Charles Taylor discovered Mehrotra for the first time and came on board; Homi Bhabha pledged support and mysteriously vanished; old friends and recent acquaintances including the scientists Sunetra Gupta and Rohit Manchanda, the historians Shahid Amin and Ananya Vajpeyi, the political thinker Pratap Bhanu Mehta, and the literary scholars Rajeswari Sunder Rajan, Swapan Chakravorty, Uttara Natarajan, Rosinka Chaudhuri and Subha Mukherjee—all "members of convocation"—put in their signatures. A lot of leg-work was put in by Dr. Sally Bayley, then a part-time lecturer at Balliol College, and she didn't seem to mind offending the faculty's inner circle, comprising, among others, Hermione Lee and my excellent former supervisor Jon Stallworthy. I was thinking of approaching another literary friend, the poet Ruth Padel, for a signature, when, curiously, she announced her candidacy and approached me for mine. Ruth is charming, and a good poet and speaker, but her hands-on approach to her own nomination *was* unprecedented; nominees are historically aloof from electioneering. Whether her style was an appropriation of the methods of market activism, to which the author's cooperation in, and production of, PR is oxygen, I can't decide; some form of activism it certainly was. Later, after the whole abortive 2009 elections were over, Tariq Ali, in a fit of anger, would, in an email to me, call Padel's a "New Labour-style campaign," a style manufactured in the 1990s and discomfiting to the old Left.

Still in the early days of the lead-up to the elections, I wrote a sonorous paragraph that was only slightly tweaked by Peter: "Arvind Krishna Mehrotra is one of the leading Indian poets in the English language, and one of the finest poets working in any language. Influential anthologist, translator, and commentator, he is a poet-critic of an exceptionally high order. Mehrotra has much to say of value—of urgency—on the matter of multilingualism, creative practice, and translation (in both its literal and figurative sense), issues that are pressingly important in today's world. He is not an easy 'postcolonial' choice, for he emerges from a rich and occasionally fraught world history of cosmopolitanism; but he is proof—as critic and artist—that cosmopolitanism is not only about European eclecticism, but about a wider, more complex network of languages and histories. For these reasons he would make an excellent, and timely, Professor of Poetry at Oxford." This was circulated widely and put in the flyer; Peter sent it out along with the poems and the essay into the English faculty. By now, the official candidate, Derek Walcott, was in place. Poems by the three contenders appeared in the *Oxford Magazine*, chosen by Bernard O'Donoghue of the "official" camp, but enough of a devotee of poetry (and a gentleman) to convey his admiration for Mehrotra's verse to Peter.

One thing Mehrotra had on his side as a writer was age—he was sixty-two. In the time of Romanticism and in the modernist twentieth century, early death or suicide was the writer's sole means of unfettering themselves of conventional valuation and breaking through instantaneously. In the shrunken time of globalisation, in the eternity of the piazza, when the constant cycles of boom and bust that governed the market ensured that many economic and cultural lifetimes could occur in a decade, the writer needed to simply survive, to grow old, so that he might outlive those cycles, the piazza's eternity, into a mini-epoch (maybe a period of bust) when the literary is again visible. This crucial task, of growing old, Mehrotra had performed perfectly. Just as the market had triumphantly annexed and put to use the language of literary valuation disposed of by literature departments, the literary activist after the nineties must ideally study the patterns of the free market, its repetition of boom and bust, its unravelling, to employ those rhythms on behalf of the literary. In the (often self-destructive) unpredictability of globalisation, the literary writer's function is to wait; and not die.

The story of the 2009 elections threatened to become sordid in the contemporary manner reserved for celebrity when the *Independent*, and consequently the *Sunday Times* and other papers, carried a report about how a dossier had begun to be circulated about Walcott's past misdemeanours: in particular, his alleged sexual harassment of two students, one at Harvard University and the other at Boston, in 1982 and 1996 respectively. These instances, however, were no secret. Before very long, Walcott withdrew from the race, with Padel earning great resentment from the "official" camp as she was accused of first alerting the press to Walcott's undeniable history—a charge she strenuously denied. Many in the "inner circle" pointed out that the only honourable course of action for the two remaining candidates now was to withdraw. Among those who advocated this course of action was a different Peter McDonald: the Irish poet and Christ Church lecturer. (I've always believed that Oxford is a place of doppelgängers.) All this time, another upheaval was taking place, unreported: various faculty members were discovering, via the emailed scans, a compelling poet and essayist in Mehrotra. So much so that Mehrotra became the first contender who, as a losing outsider, gained as many as 129 votes. Padel won handsomely with 297 votes on 16 May and in so doing became the first woman to be elected to the post in 301 years. She resigned nine days later, admitting, after her involvement in the matter became undeniable: "I did not engage in a smear campaign against [Walcott], but, as a result of student concern, I naively—and with hindsight unwisely—passed on to two journalists, whom I believed to be covering the whole election responsibly, information that was already in the public domain." Tariq Ali and others wondered why Mehrotra wasn't made Professor by default, as did a *New York Times* editorial on 26 May, which pointed out: "The only person who comes out well in all of this is . . . Mehrotra . . . Oxford would do well to confirm him and allow everyone to move along until the next election, five years hence." But Oxford declared the elections invalid, so paving the way for Geoffrey Hill's uncontested appointment to the post the next year: another "great" poet hobbled in some ways by the political order under liberal democracy, envious, occasionally, of the authoritative suffering caused by a now-historic totalitarianism.

What the 2009 elections are largely remembered for is Padel's radical, discredited, sui generis style, leading at first to success and then disgrace, but which widened the arcane sphere of the professorship into the logic of the epoch: the activism of the marketplace, where volatility now takes on the incarnation of literary value, now of justice, but remains otherwise irreducible. It is remembered for those regal, glacial categories or objects, such as Walcott's reputation, and, on closer examination, the undemocratic "inner circle," that transcended the workings of the market, but were vulnerable for precisely this reason and in a way appropriated. As for the Mehrotra campaign, which approached the press only on behalf of a poetic and critical practice and not ethnicity or identity, and which fell on neither side of the dichotomy, its fate, despite its impact, was to be not properly noticed and remembered. Perhaps it's integral to literary activism that it not be properly remembered or noticed, but experienced, uncovered, excavated, and read?

I should mention, before I conclude by reflecting on our adventure, that there was an attempt to push Mehrotra's candidacy into a postcolonial rubric, and then also to claim that he threatened to split the valuable "postcolonial" vote. That his candidacy was deliberately distanced from such a positioning—echoing Mehrotra's own description of the Indian multilingual poem as something that possesses no reliable signs of identity—should be something we consider when we account for what the aims of literary activism are. The official Oxford dispensation didn't know what to make of Mehrotra, as he didn't come with mainstream markers of literary pedigree; nor was he a hero of the new peripheries; nor did he embody market style. His behaviour as a candidate was impeccable, but the nature of his candidacy was on more than one level resistant. If resistance, or difficulty, enlarges our notion of literature, then the inner circle was, in turn, resistant to such an enlargement. After Walcott's withdrawal, it instructed its members and students—despite the fact that many of them were increasingly aware and appreciative of Mehrotra's merits—to abstain from voting: otherwise, there was every chance that Mehrotra would have won.

Our intention—the pronoun includes Peter D. McDonald, myself, and Mehrotra, who had graciously accepted our proposal in the first place—was, I venture, never to win. This doesn't mean that the campaign pursued a romantic courtship of failure; not at all. Rather, our marshalling of people and resources was worldly and political but being liberated from the thought of victory meant our activities could take on dimensions that would otherwise have been proscribed to it; it allowed Mehrotra to plot and devise his lectures in the way we had plotted the campaign, as a deliberate long shot that *should* succeed. To the literary pages of the *Hindu* Mehrotra proclaimed that he would "broaden the scope" of what had been a "Eurocentric" (an unusual word-choice for Mehrotra) job, and that he wasn't losing sleep over the imminent results. As it happens, Mehrotra and I had a long-distance phone conversation not long before the voting, and he said to me that he'd had a sleepless night at the not-wholly-improbable prospect of winning. It would have been a disaster—for him. In his way, Mehrotra was miming the elusiveness and difficulty of the literary as Padel had the methods of the market. This threw a kind of light, for me, on the event.

Where Does the Time Go?
On Joni Mitchell

2015, *The Common*

My relationship with Joni Mitchell and her music moves through two stages. My early admiration for her—in the seventies—in some ways anticipated the zeitgeist. Then I stopped listening to her for about a quarter of a century. I began to rediscover Mitchell's work in the new millennium, when, by coincidence, so did the rest of the world.

I grew up in Bombay in privileged circumstances. But privilege didn't just have to do with money. Some people in the set I'm thinking of had less money; others had more. In fact, having too much money was looked down upon. The time of my growing up—the sixties and seventies—overlapped with and succeeded Nehru, and carried forward his fastidious, progressive legacy of socialism and the "mixed economy." A "mixed economy" meant that the market was controlled, and subject to any number of restrictions. So businessmen were often glorified traders: they made their money on the sly and contributed to the huge "black" economy. The privilege I'm talking about claimed to keep its distance from this world.

My father was a company executive. When I was growing up, he was in charge of finance; when I was nineteen, he took over the company. This sounds grand, and it is, but not as grand as you'd expect. Twice a week, he flew to Delhi to deal with government bureaucrats, given the restrictions on the private sector. He met Indira Gandhi twice. Indira

Gandhi, an autocrat susceptible to conspiracies and conspiracy theories, did a lot of irretrievable harm to Indian politics, but, early on, she also took some radical socialist measures. She went on a nationalisation spree (the company my father worked in wasn't among the ones nationalised); she stripped royalty of its titles and took away its allowances (the "privy purse")—unlike, say, the English, who robbed the maharajahs of their political power but fetishised their lineage. She set a ceiling on salaries for private-sector executives like my father (his salary never rose higher than seven thousand five hundred rupees), and then imposed a tax of eighty percent upon them. The main attraction of company life in Indira Gandhi's time wasn't the income but the perks—luxuriously furnished flats in prime locations, the membership of clubs, the chauffeur-driven car, the paid holidays within India. My parents knew well that, when my father retired, they wouldn't be able to afford the flats in which we were living. I was aware of it too. So I experienced privilege as something of a performance.

I knew that when I grew up I wouldn't be able to lead this life through inherited wealth—since there wasn't that much wealth to inherit. The only option was to become my father. It became clear early on that I wasn't going for that option—this, I suppose, was the greatest privilege available to me: one exercised by few in my class, but one that I chose. My father spotted my plans to make an exit from his world, and didn't intervene. Instead, he abetted my egress. Almost every other month, he bought me the latest in A. Alvarez's Penguin Modern European Poets series from the Nalanda bookshop at the Taj Mahal hotel.

The decade I'm describing is the long seventies, from 1970 to 1981, which I identify with the twelfth-storey flat we then lived in, looking out on the Marine Drive and the Arabian Sea. The flat was in a building called Il Palazzo on Malabar Hill. The performance of privilege on various levels—including those of resistance and rejection, of exploring philosophy and music, wearing torn kurtas and chappals and mimicking a sort of poverty—worked beautifully here. I began to listen to pop and rock music in 1970, when I was eight years old, removing it from its original context and freely making it integral to mine. I acquired and absorbed the Bee Gees; The Who; The Beatles; Creedence Clearwater Revival; Pink Floyd; the Carpenters; Neil Diamond; Crosby, Stills, Nash & Young; Simon & Garfunkel. All this was accessible locally, at Rhythm House (or Hiro Music House or Melody). Some records had become extinct—out of print in India—by the time I grew interested in them: *Sweet Baby James*, for instance. The more arcane contemporary stuff, like Jethro Tull, I asked my father to get for me from London. He'd begun to go there every few years because the company he worked for had a substantial British shareholding. These were business trips, but he found time to frequent Our Price shops and return to Bombay with the records on my list. Meanwhile, in 1974, I began to play the guitar. My mother and I accompanied my father on a couple of his London sojourns, and it was probably in 1977 that we—all three of us—explored Denmark Street, and my father bought me a sweet-sounding Yamaha acoustic.

By this time, one of the fantasies germinating in my head had to do with being a singer-songwriter. The fantasy had its physical outgrowths: I began to sport long hair, which got me into trouble at school, and which looked unpleasantly flat, because my hair was greasy and I seldom shampooed. It had dulcet effects: I loved the acoustic sound, the tones produced by strumming and plucking. I was mesmerised by "sustained" and "add ninth" chord formations. By 1978, I wanted more Bob Dylan, Neil Young, and Leonard Cohen from the Our Price shops. I also began to ask for Joni Mitchell. I can't remember what led me to ask my father for her records. She was famous, of course. I'd have seen her as part of the folk phenomenon, but I may not have distinguished her at first from the likes of Joan Baez. Here was another ethereal being who combed her straight hair with puritanical dutifulness, eschewed rock amplification, strummed, and sang heartfelt lyrics. That she was Canadian would hardly have registered with Indian listeners; politically, her country of origin was a place that Sikhs had migrated to, but otherwise had no existence—for Indians—independent of America. Nevertheless, her presence on my list must represent some sort of evolution, because I find the records in my possession belong mainly to the phase when she was on a cusp, between playing folk music and discovering jazz. In other words, I didn't have the early acoustic material that made Mitchell well-known. The albums I acquired between 1977 and 1981 (in 1979, I visited America, so I would have purchased a couple then) were *For the Roses*, *Miles of Aisles*, *Court and Spark*, T*he Hissing of Summer Lawns*, *Hejira*, *Don Juan's Reckless Daughter*, and *Mingus*. The last named I may well have bought on my American trip, as it came out the same year. The list is predominantly a seventies list; *The Hissing of Summer Lawn*s and *Hejira* were released in 1975 and 1976 respectively, and they would have reached me two years later.

By the standards of the speed at which "Western" ideas, books, and technologies arrived at Indian shores (or vice versa, for that matter), this relatively short time lag had, historically, been the norm for three hundred years. Hundreds of copies of Thomas Paine's *Rights of Man* had come on a ship to Calcutta in the 1820s, three decades after publication: not a great gap for the era. This gap decreased soon after. It seems very likely that Rabindranath Tagore read William James on "stream of consciousness" in *The Principles of Psychology* a year or two after it was published in 1890 (James probably borrowed the notion from Buddhism). Indeed, Tagore was the first writer anywhere to import James's concept into critical discourse, mentioning it in an 1894 essay on Bengali nursery rhymes. Here, Tagore uses the Bengali phrase *nityaprabahita chetanar majhe*: "in the midst of the constant flow of consciousness." As to vinyl—it had been India for a long time, as had HMV. (My mother, a singer of Tagore songs, had cut her first 78 rpm disc with HMV in 1965.) In the seventies, stacks of pop and rock records were available to browsers at Rhythm House in Kala Ghoda. Even those that were harder to come by, like *The Hissing of Summer Lawns*, would have made their way to India by one means or another—my own case was one example of how this happened.

I probably first heard Joni Mitchell's early songs on the radio, or in other people's homes—and in other people's versions. Mitchell's work was subject to its own time lag. She was a successful songwriter first, and slightly later a successful singer. Towards the beginning of her career, her work became iconic in renditions by established "artists." There was, for example, Judy Collins's "Both Sides, Now." I got to know Mitchell's "Woodstock" through Crosby, Stills, Nash & Young, who converted it into a pop tune you could hum along with. Those who expressed their admiration at Mitchell's later "covers" of her own songs in the albums *Both Sides Now* (2000) and *Travelogue* (2002)—both of which invite the listener to note how the orchestral arrangements and slow tempo make room for a voice transformed by age and smoking—forget that she began her career by covering her compositions. When she recorded "Both Sides, Now" in 2000, Mitchell commented that she'd hardly experienced, firsthand, any of the song's themes—love, life, and disillusionment—when she'd composed it in 1967. More than thirty years later, then, she could speak, or sing, about them from the vantage point that the song had long ago anticipated. But if you listen to Collins's 1967 interpretation, which made the song famous, and then Mitchell's own version in 1969, you feel a great deal of time has already elapsed between Collins's mellifluous, plangent rendering and Mitchell's light but ponderous guitar strokes and melodic, deadpan singing.

Mitchell performs a similar task with "Woodstock," a song that Crosby, Stills, & Nash and she recorded more or less simultaneously in 1970, but which she seemed to come to after CSN had acquired a sort of ownership of it in the popular imagination. CSN add rock guitar and tempo and turn the song into an anthem. This is the version I listened to in Bombay. I had bought the predominantly white-jacketed *Greatest Hits* from Rhythm House; its cover had a doodle of CSN, with their d'Artagnan, Neil Young, appearing on the right. I often played it on the hi-fi that had been placed in the unwieldy wall-unit in the drawing room. To my right was the balcony, at a lower level than the rest of the flat, two steps going down to where it hung like a promontory over a view of the Marine Drive. "Almost Cut My Hair" emerged from the crevasse, and "Wooden Ships," and "Teach Your Children," and "Woodstock." Mitchell's interpretation of her composition, which I heard years later, is quite different. It's as if she has no natural right to it, and needs to repossess the song. Her attempt at doing so is slow-paced and sparse, dominated by electric piano and her voice. The slower tempo means she can elaborate on the tension within the phrases that CSN swallow up or elide, and which allude to the appropriation, by the pop industry, of the impulses that Woodstock briefly celebrated: "We are stardust / Billion year old carbon / We are golden / Caught in the devil's bargain." Her auto-covers, right from the start, were a means to being obdurately opposed to such pop appropriation, and her versions of "Both Sides, Now" and "Woodstock" have that stripped-down, stubborn quality. They also bear the mark of lateness, of the performer having lighted upon something—her own songs, in this case—after the moment of superficial excitement has passed. This reminds us of Mitchell's great preoccupation (as a songwriter, certainly, but as a performer too): time—its unfolding and return, its destructive and renovating influences. Time makes Mitchell not only a composer who survived the originary moment in the late sixties that created her generation. More significantly, it makes her a curator of music: others' and her own.

Which brings me back to the zeitgeist. For some reason, the Mitchell album that had the deepest impact on me was *Hejira*. I recall that I grew convinced that it was her defining achievement—indeed, not only hers, but a pinnacle of songwriting, musical arrangement, and performance. Why I thought so isn't clear. I certainly didn't have the authority, at seventeen, to make such a judgement. The songs, anyway, were unconcerned with enticing the young listener. They had none of the features that a teenage pop aficionado depends on: hooks, choruses, bridges—

not even (and this is true of much of Mitchell's oeuvre) a recognisable exploration of the blues scale or a basic rock-and-roll structure. There were the tantalising, emotionally inconclusive jazz-fusion arrangements, of course (she was working with Jaco Pastorius, the bass guitarist who was embarking on his remarkable fusion experiments on the album *Heavy Weather* around the same time as *Hejira*); but, unlike in jazz, there was much repetition, and an almost obsessive return, at the end of each stanza, to either the tonic or the key—like a prolepsis of trance music. No wonder, then, that the album, despite being praised by critics, failed to find a large audience or get nominated for awards, and took roughly three decades to be acknowledged by some of Mitchell's supporters as her best work. In this way, my early bond with Mitchell through *Hejira* was out of sync with the time that she and I were living in.

To be so out of sync is—for listener and artist—to be surreptitiously connected. The two may not know of the connection, but it exists. Just as the listener feels that an album that has been generally overlooked is somehow significant, the artist too is aware—whatever its reception—of her album's importance. Its time is to come. This belief places both artist and listener in a tiny minority. The artist may not have an explanation for why she believes this: but this experience, of a writer or filmmaker or musician concluding that a work she feels close to has been bypassed, isn't uncommon. The work often represents a convergence of personal resonance with immense creative innovation. It's evident that Mitchell knew *Hejira* had a special quality; she's talked about how it came to her when she was travelling the American highway and was seized by "inspiration." She wrote up and recorded the songs very fast. It would then take years for *Hejira* to be properly discovered. While the process of valuation took place, there was the loneliness, for me, of holding in high esteem something that wasn't widely popular or even known, a loneliness that felt less like a privilege than an anomaly.

What could have drawn me to it? What, listening to it in Bombay, was I encountering that I hadn't before? If mere social identification accounts for my taste for Joni Mitchell, then *The Hissing of Summer Lawns*, with its brilliant, angular depictions of the sterility of the well-to-do, should have spoken to me directly. For I was unhappy in Bombay, miserable at the Cathedral School, safer at home in Malabar Hill but still in exile. I found the Gothic buildings within which I was educated intimidating, as I did the quasi-colonial regime in which sporting glory was everything. Home was simply too high up; too removed from the street, too nonphysical, for me to be entirely convinced it was home. When we moved, after my father became chief executive officer, across the Marine Drive and the inlet created by the Arabian Sea, to Cuffe Parade and into a twenty-fifth-storey apartment, I was unhappier still. Perhaps *The Hissing of Summer Lawns* was too close to me to make sense; or possibly I was too young to understand the source of my unhappiness. But evidently I was old enough to recognise something in *Hejira*. My experience of *Hejira* was primarily an aesthetic one, and it's the only creative work that I assigned a value to when I was seventeen or eighteen whose status hasn't changed for me over time. Otherwise, my responses then were awry and often intensely wrongheaded. In the late seventies I read *A Portrait of the Artist as a Young Man*, *Ulysses*, and *Malone Die*s, all of which I failed to get a handle on and dismissed. I'd need to reach the age of twenty-four and begin rereading the first two to understand their importance to me.

•

From *Hejira*, I'll dwell only on two songs. The first is "Song for Sharon," which opens the record's B side. At almost eight and a half minutes, it's unthinkably long for a pop song. Its chords avoid development, and their main action is to circle around the tonic and return hypnotically to the key, E-flat. Musically, both "Song for Sharon" and *Hejira* represent Mitchell's preoccupation with circularity ("And the seasons, they go round and round / And the painted ponies go up and down"); with whether repetition is necessarily entrapping, or if it renovates us spiritually.

"Song for Sharon" reintroduces us to what may be Joni Mitchell's greatest conceptual innovation: the interlocutor. Fundamentally, the interlocutor is music. The singer / songwriter has had a chance encounter with music in a way that's changed her life. But the interlocutor is invariably embodied: he or she is a person. Here, it is Sharon. And, even if Sharon isn't a straightforward symbol of music, she raises the question of its custodianship.

Ostensibly, the tension played out in the song has to do with marriage: Sharon is happily married; the singer who addresses her (and who yearns to possess the "long white dress of love") isn't. The singer is a disappointed romantic, not to mention an itinerant. "Song for Sharon" talks of other things besides the desire for a husband: the suicide of a friend, the wish to buy a mandolin, the exhortations of relatives ("Find yourself a charity / Help the needy"), sex ("all I really want to do right now / Is find another lover"). It concludes with a verse that I found extraordinary when I first heard the record:

> Sharon you've got a husband
> And a family and a farm
> I've got the apple of temptation
> And a diamond snake around my arm
> But you still have your music
> And I've still got my eyes on the land and the sky
> You sing for your friends and your family
> I'll walk green pastures by and by

"You still have your music"? So there's the paradox of Mitchell's songwriting: it's always someone else who's the singer, while the songwriter herself is unmoored, with her "eyes on the land and the sky." Who, then, is the custodian of the pop song, and the dreams it promises to fulfil? Is it the songwriter, or the addressee? It's a question that Mitchell had put to her audience before, when she conjured up the interlocutor in "The Last Time I Saw Richard" in *Blue*. There, the singer and her crusty old friend Richard are in a bar or café; Richard admonishes her for investing in the fantasies that pop music creates: "Go look at your eyes they're full of moon / You like roses and kisses and pretty men to tell you / All those pretty lies." Again, there's the encounter with music, and the matter of custodianship: Richard "put a quarter in the Wurlitzer and he pushed / Three buttons and the thing began to whirr." Richard (like Sharon—who is, however, more affectionately portrayed) gets married ("to a figure skater") and settles down ("he bought her a dishwasher and a coffee percolator"), while the singer continues to hover hopelessly on the outskirts of sociability.

But the singer, for Mitchell, occupies the outskirts in many ways. "Song for Sharon" underlines Mitchell's sense of lacking ownership—not just of a husband, a family, a percolator, not even of the song, but of the identity of being a "songwriter." She came upon the pop song by accident: it—like family and the accoutrements of domesticity—really belonged to someone else. She has told interviewers more than once that she wanted to be a painter, and isn't sure how she ended up a songwriter. In 1994, when she was (somewhat reluctantly) plugging the album *Turbulent Indigo* and playing its lead track, "Sex Kills," at various venues, she said on the BBC's Late Review that, if the pop industry annulled artists like her, as it had been doing for fifteen years, she would go back to painting. In a club in Toronto that year, the prefatory remarks she made to a terrific acoustic performance of "Sex Kills" are even more revealing. The song had been provoked, she said, by a personalised number plate Mitchell had spotted in Los Angeles on the last night of the riots in 1992: it said JUST ICE. This led Mitchell—given the context—to read up on a word (justice) from which she'd been duly estranged by that number plate. One of the books she read was Plato's *Republic*. "But [the Socratic just society] would have been unjust to the likes of me," she told the audience in the bar in Toronto, "because it's a society of specialists. You had to be a painter or a poet or a musician, but you couldn't tackle all three. So I would already be pinched in this society...." Mitchell's words, both in her songs and in her interviews, let slip the fact that she's uncomfortable with the idea that an artist's best-known work must encompass her.

•

Nearly every track on *Hejira* is exceptional. But the other song I was arrested by all those years ago was "Furry Sings the Blues," the third track on Side A. Again, it asks: Who owns this music? Again, the singer confronts, or is confronted by, her interlocutor—in this case, "Furry," based on the blues singer Furry Lewis, whom Joni Mitchell met in Memphis in 1976. Mitchell is empathetic ("there was one song he played / I could really feel"), but the two share only an uneasy understanding. On one level, Furry is like Richard; he's sceptical of the younger singer's motives. Music, however, has brought interlocutor and songwriter together again; it was the Wurlitzer in the café, and it's the blues on Memphis's Beale Street. But "I don't like you," says Furry; and here, Mitchell abandons melody to mimic the old man's voice. In live versions of "The Last Time I Saw Richard," too, she mimics the barmaid who warns them: "Drink up now it's getting on time to close." There's music; and there's the unadorned human voice, expressing urgent needs, prejudice, and resistance: "Furry sings the blues / Why should I expect that old guy to give it to me true."

The scene is firmly, powerfully, located, not only on Beale Street but in the damage caused by time: "Pawn shops glitter like gold tooth caps / In the grey decay / They chew the last few dollars off / Old Beale Street's carcass." Never before, it seemed to me, had the material context of music been captured with such immediacy. The deep visual impact of the song helped me understand the journeys Mitchell was making (to Beale Street; towards her own creative idiom) and sense her position as interloper in Furry's room. I myself was more than an eavesdropper. I was an interloper too.

•

Those years, when I was listening to *Hejira*—the late seventies to, say, 1981—were, for me, a time of change and unravelling. For one thing, I'd become interested, from 1978 onwards, in North Indian classical music. In 1979, I began to formally learn singing in that tradition. My apprenticeship was partly a response to my belated discovery of that tradition's incredible beauty, and partly a cultural turn that almost had the intensity of a religious conversion. This music is mine, I felt; it is my land's, and expresses its light and seasons more truthfully than Western pop music. (I conveniently ignored that what I peremptorily termed "Western" music was woven into Bombay's life, even into its film songs.) The raga introduced to my day a punishing regime of practice and preparation. It was one of the reasons I began to withdraw from the institution I'd been enrolled in as a high school student—Elphinstone College—where I would have continued as an undergraduate. Without formally dropping out of Elphinstone, I began to spend most of my time at home: practicing ragas, writing poetry. I never took my undergraduate exams. Instead, I began to prepare for GCSE A-Levels with the help of a correspondence course from Oxford, with an eye to going to England for my further studies and becoming a published poet. My father arranged for the correspondence course: he almost always backed my quixotic projects.

Another reason I'd withdrawn into myself was the increasing corporatization of Bombay. Economic deregulation—India's entry into the free market—was a little more than a decade away, but I could sense its imminence without having any idea of the specific changes at hand. The great classical singers who lived in and near Bombay then—Kishori

Amonkar, Pandit Jasraj, Kumar Gandharva, Bhimsen Joshi—were in peak form. Their music had reached my ears. It galvanised me. On the other hand, the victory of the free market in the West was pushing the singer-songwriter underground, or into oblivion. New forms of music heavily dependent on the synthesiser began to emerge. My turnaround was complete: I embraced Indian classical music and went off Western pop at about the same time.

By 1982, I didn't so much forget Joni Mitchell as believe, with a certain sadness, that the world had forgotten her and her ilk—as, indeed, it had. I shed my acoustic-guitar-playing songwriter self. That year, I cut my hair to a manageable length. In 1983, I went to London as an undergraduate to read English, lived in a studio flat on Warren Street, and threw myself into my tussle with Hindustani classical music. My neighbours and I were constantly at loggerheads. At home, my father retired eight years too early to benefit from the post-1991 boom. Privilege, in his life, had been performance. He and my mother moved quite happily in 1989 from Bombay to Calcutta, a once-great city I'd grown to love on my visits as a child to my uncle's house.

•

For about two decades I listened to no Western popular music. I became a published novelist in the UK in 1991, the year of my marriage, and I recorded my first album of North Indian classical music with HMV India in 1993. I returned officially to India (to Calcutta) from the UK in 1999. My father was seventy-seven, my mother seventy-five—I am an only child, and my parents were one of the reasons for my return. Another reason was my ten-month-old daughter; another was my ongoing relationship with Indian music; yet another was the intolerable ethos of Blairite Britain.

One of the first things I did on my return was get my hi-fi and record player fixed. The age of disco, glam rock, and chain-wearing singers—

once the eternal present of popular music—was finally over. Besides, the ferocity of the ideological turn that had informed my early immersion in Indian music had waned. Gingerly, I began to play one or two records from my collection again—restricting myself mainly to Jimi Hendrix. I went back to England a couple of times a year for short visits. There were no direct flights except the thrice-weekly British Airways plane to Heathrow: one of the many consequences of Calcutta's long decline. Bombay and Delhi had become India's major centres with globalisation; Calcutta occupied the periphery.

I think British Airways stopped flying out of Calcutta in 2009, around the time the Left Front government's attempts to reindustrialise West Bengal came to a sudden end with Tata aborting its Nano "small car" project outside Calcutta, in the face of a huge controversy to do with a government-led land grab. Whether the scrapping of the British Airways flights was in any way a response to the scuppering of the Nano factory is hard to know. In the absence of a direct connection to Heathrow, many travellers, including myself, went for the best new alternative: Emirates. You flew to Dubai on a functional aircraft with staff who were pleasant enough. Then you changed planes and got on to a huge, resplendent A380 to Heathrow, with astonishing in-flight entertainment for seven hours. It was during this leg of the journey, after turning at some point from movies to listening to music, that I became reacquainted with Joni Mitchell.

•

One of the options Emirates offers under "CDs" is "Essential Albums." Here, besides *Disraeli Gears*, *The Dark Side of the Moon*, *Are You Experienced*, and many other albums you'd have heard ages ago, is Joni Mitchell's *Blue*. On the flight from Dubai to Heathrow (and back), I began to investigate an album I'd heard only in bits and pieces when I lived on Malabar Hill, and never in its entirety. I was transfixed not only by the guitar-playing—or by the cascading piano-playing, for that matter—but by the bodiless daring of the voice, the way it rose, dipped, and wove waywardly, never deviating inadvertently from pitch. I'd forgotten what an astonishing singer she was. The unfettered, risk-taking vocalising, along with the complex harmonic context of the chords, created a sound richer, more produced, than the acoustic recordings of Dylan or Cohen, whose characteristic texture was raw. Mitchell had the temperament and capacities of a jazz soloist long before she'd made any gesture in that direction. No wonder I'd been listening attentively to her just as I'd segued into Indian classical music.

Emirates's "CDs" also has a section called "Playlists." It includes a Joni Mitchell playlist. I have, since 2009, listened to it many times. I've found on it songs I'd missed from the early years, like "The Gallery," an elegant but mischievous study of the connection between a man's sex addiction and his paintings. Here I discovered the magnificent auto-covers with strings recorded in the present millennium, from *Both Sides Now* and *Travelogue*; and "Sex Kills," from 1994, which dwarfs anything else in popular music from that decade: "And the gas leaks / And the oil spills / And sex sells everything / And sex kills." Half the tracks on the playlist I hadn't heard, because of my turn away from Western music in the eighties, or because Mitchell herself seemed to disappear at the end of the twentieth century. That she'd never gone silent was evident to me now. And that the world was acknowledging her was clear too: just as, in 1978, its general indifference to *Hejira* had been clear. The fact that Joni Mitchell's songs were part of the Emirates collection was no coincidence—it was tied to a wider, contemporary reassessment. In this way, my own relationship with Mitchell had come together with the zeitgeist, the mood of the time.

On that playlist I heard "Chinese Café / Unchained Melody," which I think is her greatest composition. It's available on *Wild Things Run Fast*, released in 1982—the year I snapped my ties with Western music. And there's the 2002 version (which Emirates had chosen) from

Travelogue, recorded with strings when Mitchell was fifty-nine. There she is in the café again, with her interlocutor and friend: "Caught in the middle / Carol we're middle class / We're middle aged / We were wild in the old days / Birth of rock 'n' roll days." Once more, the addressee has settled into a rhythm, while the singer's life has a certain lack of finality, creating a frisson, a striking asymmetry, essential to the songwriting: "Now your kids are coming up straight / And my child's a stranger / I bore her / But I could not raise her."

What's at the heart of the song? There's Carol, of course; and the glimpses of Mitchell's life, the reference to the child she gave up for adoption when she was twenty-two (she was reunited with her daughter only in 1997); and, in the context of the friendship between the two women, there's music: the pop song on the jukebox. "Down at the Chinese café / We'd be dreaming on our dimes / We'd be playing 'Oh my love, my darling' / One more time." The song the two women play repeatedly is "Unchained Melody," released in the fifties and further popularised by the Righteous Brothers in 1965. Mitchell weaves and incorporates the song into her composition; this constitutes a musical departure on many levels. Generally, when Mitchell pays homage to a pop music genre or style in her lyrics—as in the line "We were rolling, rolling, rock 'n' rolling" in "In France They Kiss on Main Street"—musically, the song itself is a million miles away from what's being paid homage to. "In France They Kiss on Main Street" has nothing of rock and roll in its music; its chords come from jazz; its melody is sui generis. The same could be said of "Furry Sings the Blues": the blues is the last thing you think of while listening to its tune. In "Chinese Café," the harmonic context for "birth of rock 'n' roll days" is the G major ninth chord: hardly rock and roll. In other words, classic popular music is an invisible—a near-inaudible—presence in Joni Mitchell's songs, her avowed love of the rock and roll genre expressing itself in her work through elision. This ties up with the invisible presences Mitchell is constantly working with. There's the presence of the songwriter: hidden, never fully inhabited. There's the invisibility of national identity: the Canadian working in the American idiom, seeming to become American ("I went to Staten Island, Sharon / To buy myself a mandolin"), but never wholly so. Mitchell, like Cohen and Neil Young, is what Deleuze and Guattari describe as a practitioner of "minor literature," a practitioner who writes her work in a major language which is not her mother tongue. Such a practitioner is necessarily political, say Guattari and Deleuze, but, in Mitchell's case, being a Canadian in America—and the practitioner of a "minor" mode—liberates her from being the sort of national spokesperson Dylan was. Then there's gender. Despite her many incomparable portraits of women, the fact that Mitchell is a female songwriter has seemed almost as contingent to her as being a musician. This has made her elect not to be a spokesperson for her sex; because, as she implied to the *Late Review* interviewer in 1994, her gender was never a given: "a gypsy... a Sikh" once told her that this, in fact, was her first incarnation as a woman. She'd been "an English gent" in her last life, and "an Arab rug merchant" in another one. Gender only appears to be central to the songs; it's like the deceptive references to the blues and rock and roll.

Which is why the incorporation—the audible presence—of "Unchained Melody" in "Chinese Café" is unusual. Mitchell brings the two sections together, but never irrevocably, allowing one to float on the other, like oil on water. They don't become inseparable, yet they fuse. It's an enactment of a coming-together and separation at once accidental and predetermined, like the loss of, and still-unforeseen reunion with, the daughter. Also woven in are the depredations of capitalism (described before in "Big Yellow Taxi" and in the description of Beale Street): "Uranium money / Is booming in the old home town now / It's putting up sleek concrete / Tearing the old landmarks down now." "Nothing lasts for long," goes the refrain, "nothing lasts for long." But, on the other hand, "Unchained Melody," which ends the song as a coda, says, "And time goes by so slowly / And time can do so much." The song hovers between the two poles—memory and hope, loss and replenishment, time as loss and as renovation and desire, "caught in the middle." Musically, the composition has two homes, beginning and ending on the tonic, D major, but straying, each time it visits "Unchained Melody," into C major, as if it were a remembered world.

•

Thousands of feet above the ground, you find life as you know it replicated, abbreviated, and changed: the alternation of darkness and light; the meals on trays; the movies on small, bright screens; the sight of people wrapped in blankets; the periodic visits to the toilet. In other ways, you're released from the deadlines of earthbound existence, to which you secretly long to return. Between watching movies and nodding off, you think of life as a spirit might, loosened from earthly ties. This transcendence is not a happy feeling; it's frustrating. On the journeys on the A380, the discrete currents of my existence became apparent to me: the irretrievable loss of my childhood, for instance, and of Bombay. But surely that should have been a cause for rejoicing? I'd never before mourned the end of my childhood—because I'd never been happy as a child, or growing up in that city. My father's dementia, first noticeable in 2008, presented itself—the spectre of a living person's shameful inaction and forgetfulness. Then, in 2013, the unthinkable—his death. For long stretches of time, the plane didn't seem to move; it was as if we were stationary, pinned to a solid foundation. Then we'd hit a bump, short-lived turbulence shaking the aircraft, and we'd know what we already knew but had forgotten: there was nothing beneath us. Once or twice, I wept upon leaving Calcutta, realising, as we cruised and found our altitude, that the journey couldn't be reversed. "Nothing lasts for long," said the voice in my ear. It was a voice the world had first heard in the Upanishads. It was also a familiar voice, known to me from my teenage years. I hadn't expected to hear it again.

On the Paragraph

2017, *Granta*

I DON'T SUBSCRIBE to the idea of the strong opening sentence. Since the novel isn't a sprint to a finishing line, the first sentence is not necessarily about making a "strong beginning" similar to the athlete responding with instinctive release to the pistol shot. At best, it might establish a kind of magic. But other sentences must do the same: no sentence, in this regard, is more equal than the other.

I should add that an early reader of *Friend of My Youth* in India sent me a text saying: "What a wonderful opening sentence! It gave me goose-bumps!" I thanked her, and pointed out that it was by Walter Benjamin. In the novel—unlike the extract in *Granta*—the first paragraph (the quotation from Benjamin's *One-Way Street*) appears without acknowledgement of source or author, though it's in quotation marks. The paragraph is meant to be incorporated in the main narrative, rather than serve as an epigraph. This means that we're not reading Benjamin's words as if they were informing the narrative from the outside, but as part of the author's recounting. The act of recounting really begins with the title, which is also borrowed (from a title from an Alice Munro story), and the borrowing only dwelt upon in the last third of the short novel. The narrator, at the start, is thinking of his friend, who is now in rehab in Alibag and absent from the Bombay he's visiting;

remembering is indistinguishable, at this point, from the memory of other people's words.

For me, though, the paragraph—the first one in particular—is the significant unit rather than the first sentence. How do you characterise the first paragraph? I would say that it's marked by a quality of "opening out" on to something—not to the story, necessarily, but our sense of existence, which the story can hint at but never represent, since our "sense of existence" is transient and without resolution. As stories never begin at the beginning, but in *medias res*, the first paragraph has not so much the fixity of being point A in a narrative, but the air of buoyancy that all initial utterances have, as well as the irresolution of moments in which many strands are hanging, when you still lack clarity about where you're headed. This absence of fixity is what I mean by "opening out." Occasionally this irresolution and its accompanying excitement characterises the first page of a novel, or even the first chapter. These first paragraphs, pages, or chapters often have little in terms of event, and may be a meditation on place, or space, or any category that exists in lieu of narrative or story. Then, in the novel, that sense of arrest is painstakingly removed, and the "opening out" is tamed, as it were, by the discipline of narrative. This taming is a skill peculiar to the novelist; she or he must put their intimation of abeyance in the first paragraph or page itself into abeyance, and attend to the exigency of telling us what happened next. The other reason for this taming is, of course, that it isn't easy—some would even say, desirable—to sustain the "opening out" over an entire novel.

For me, each paragraph is like a first paragraph. It's probably an impossible aim—to want the paragraph, because of its peculiar enchantment, to be the primary unit; to want it to stand alone, available, at any point, for rereading; to give individual paragraphs primacy over the superstructure of narrative itself; to view the novel as an assemblage of paragraphs and, in a sense, quotations.

I say "quotation" because the paragraph and the quote are to me almost interchangeable. I spent my years as a reader and apprentice writer devoted to poetry. I was first drawn to novels in the 1980s through quotations in critical essays. I remember encountering *A House for Mr. Biswas* in that way—as a paragraph in an essay describing Mr. Biswas's early days as a sign painter in Trinidad. Mr. Biswas can't decide which letter in the English language he adores more, the R or the S. I recall marvelling at the paragraph and reading it repeatedly. It seemed to contain the wonder and humour, the irresolution and opening out into existence, that I would from now take to be the paragraph's domain. I thought it was a shame that I would have to read the novel. The superstructure, the narrative and plot, were made almost redundant by comparison.

The quotation, like the paragraph, is for me not a sample of writing, or a taster, or a representative of the narrative; inasmuch as it's an "opening out," it's of the narrative and not of it. It has its independent existence. It can be revisited for its own sake, in a way that has little to do with the cumulative picture the book presents us with. Ideally, I'd like a book to be composed of such paragraphs only, which both belong and don't belong to the story, and, in themselves, comprise multiple instances of opening up, each, individually, with their own form and integrity. In which case, development and progression in such a narrative must be an illusion. We *think* we've moved from one point to another, while we've been actually been lingering over these entrances and exits.

•

In the early nineties, there was hardly any creative writing teaching in Oxford. I, having completed my graduate work there, became Creative Arts Fellow at Wolfson College, a job without either much of a stipend or responsibilities. An exchange student called Ted Scott from Yale—a maths student spending a year at Oxford—tracked me down through my designation and asked me if I'd read his stories and give him creative writing advice. I'd never done this before. The idea didn't appeal—but I said yes.

A year later, he said he'd read my first novel. He made a perspicacious observation: "The paragraphs don't *really* have to follow each other in the sequence you've put them, right? I mean—the paragraph that follows the earlier one could just as easily have come before it."

He was shrewd to have noticed this. Revising *A Strange and Sublime Address* had been nightmarish. I'd found that I couldn't keep much of the first half. Revision became what it often is: an act of salvaging—the sentence that works, the paragraph that works. The second phase of revision involved some writing, but I eschewed composing joins between one salvaged bit and another. I arranged paragraphs that had no innate sequentiality in order to give them an appearance of linearity. Each participated in, and ignored, the onward current. You could move from one to the other; but there was also the option of not moving if you chose.

•

Two months ago, a French philosopher and dramaturge, Jean-Frédéric Chevallier, who lives in a village outside Calcutta for much of the year, told me this about *Friend of My Youth*: "Your novel is about the present moment. But this 'present moment' doesn't just capture the process of writing, it's about reading too." It's how he saw the repetitions of phrases and sentences in the book—as the narrator not only writing again what he's already written, but reading (and possibly recounting) what he'd said a few moments ago.

Perhaps this is what the second paragraph of the novel (and of the extract in *Granta*) does. Referring to the first paragraph, the quote from Benjamin, the narrator says, "I think of Ramu when I read these lines. It's of him I think when I reread them." A journalist in Calcutta said to me that, having finished reading this second paragraph, she went back to the first one to read it in the light of what the second one had said.

•

The "friend of my youth" on whom I reflect in this novel escaped the punitive rehab in Alibag after two years. I began to see him again in Bombay. I describe a few of these post-rehab meetings in the last two sections of the book. What I don't mention is that the idea for the novel was already in my head at the time, and that I'd begun warning my friend that I was going to write about him. He told me that he expected a substantial percentage of royalties. More seriously, he asked me to ensure that his name was changed. Thus "Ramu."

Just before publication he was bristly, but, as he began to learn more about the book from newspaper reports and from friends—some of whom had a history of addiction—he relaxed. I would even say that, when I went to Bombay to launch the book in late April, he was happier than I've usually seen him. His mood was more celebratory than mine. He didn't investigate the novel by reading it himself because he didn't read books. He didn't have the patience.

But, the day after the launch, I caught him, sitting on a sofa in the club room I was staying in, reading paragraphs from *Friend of My Youth* with a faint smile on his face: now from the middle, now the end, and now the beginning. "You could read it from start to finish," I said. "It's not very long." "I know," he said. "But I've never been able to read a book that way. I get bored." Our minds may have gone back then to how he'd struggled in school, despite his intelligence and his gifts as a sportsman, and even failed twice—which is how we got to be in the same class (though he's two years older than me) when I was twelve years old. "To succeed in life, you have to be able to read from start to finish," he acknowledged. "You might be an average person, but you can be successful if you can do that. I can't."

This is one among various traits we share—a restiveness to do with narrative, a short attention span. It's why I've always preferred reading poems to novels. I remember when I first became an "avid reader." It was in school, in the fourth standard. I was miserable and alienated. During lunch break, I sometimes stayed on in class. I became curious about the library that occupied a small bookshelf on the right. I recall looking at illustrations on the pages of a book—pictures of animals—and reading from somewhere in the middle. The teacher, a young woman who'd lately grown kindly towards me, said, "Why don't you start at the beginning? You'll be able to enjoy the story." I complied, and learnt how to read books.

Notwithstanding this advice from school, which I inadvertently repeated to my friend the day after the launch, I'm still easily distracted. A sound will take me away from a book; a thought might come to me. My wife tells me that it's because I'm more interested in life than in stories—in comparison, say, to her. This may be true. I probably find life, when I become aware of it, unpredictable in a way that I don't narratives. Storylines tend to fatigue me. While watching TV, my mind will wander, making associations from the way a street looks. A scene in which nothing is ostensibly happening will absorb me; so will a paragraph that contains no vital piece of information.

When I described Ramu's manner of reading my novel to the journalist I've mentioned above, by choosing random paragraphs and admitting to his failure to start at the beginning, she said, "But is it possible that the book *can* be read in that way—that one can start at a point of one's choosing, and then move to another?" She was echoing Ted Scott, the student from Yale. I admitted that there was probably something in my writing—given how I'd been first drawn to novels, through singular, free-standing paragraphs—that was conducive to Ramu's approach.

"*I* am Ramu"

2017, *n+1*

THE IMPORTANT EUROPEAN NOVELIST makes innovations in the form; the important Indian novelist writes about India. This is a generalisation, and not one that I believe in. But it represents an attitude that may be unexpressed but governs some of the ways we think of literature today. The first half of the sentence can be changed in response to developments in the millennium to include "American"; in fact, to allow "American" to replace "European." The second half should accommodate, alongside India, Africa, and even Australia. Arguably, we go to an Australian novel primarily because it asserts Australian characteristics, and those characteristics are related to what we already know to be the newly discovered worlds and continents of the last two hundred years. If an Australian novel is formally innovative, the innovations will be related to its Australian or New World or postcolonial or vivid nonmetropolitan features. The innovations of a European novel, on the other hand, are not an assertion of European particularity, but have to do with the form of the novel itself. The sequence of deduction moves here in the opposite direction—a major European novelist effects formal innovations on the novel; pure formal innovation is a characteristic of European culture (rather than a political expression of Europeanness). If we find formal innovations in a non-European novelist, modulations on form unrelated to, say, identity, difference, or colonial history, we might say, "This novelist has a European air." We could say the same about the more formally ambitious of the recent American writers, whose innovations are unrelated to Americana: that they are, in some ways, Europeans from, say, Brooklyn. At the moment, though, because of the centrality in the Anglophone world of the USA and of New York, we don't think of innovations in fiction emerging from these locations as being primarily connected to what it means to be a New Yorker, or an American—we think of them as formal innovations in themselves. The American writer has succeeded the European writer. The rest of us write of where we come from.

What does formal innovation mean at this moment? Firstly, it probably has something to do with a reclamation of modernism, and a slightly uncomfortable cluster of symptoms and signifiers: the slowing down of narrative; Proust's madeleine; involuntary memory. Proust's return felt subversive at first, a shorthand for introducing a discussion of the subconscious in a fictional landscape that, over the eighties to the early 2000s, had little overtly to do with the randomness of memory, and saw the global or postcolonial novel as a receptacle of the world's exuberant multiculturalism. By now, however, Proust risks being industrialised; the madeleine today is probably as much a part of a literary history of memory and sensation as it is of a contemporary lived history of artisanal gentrification. On some levels, you feel, Proust has been loosed from modernism's difficult history.

The other mark of innovation that preoccupies us now involves a questioning, and extension, of generic boundaries. It reshapes the novel in the light of the essay, and, in doing so, not only challenges those obvious antinomies, "fiction and nonfiction," "the creative and the critical," but asks us to rethink what the novel might *be*. This innovation is related to the first one. Both ask a set of related questions. Does the novel have to contain an event, or series of events? Is novel-writing a way of organising and fictionalising such events? What exactly does "fictionalising" mean? Does the novel have to be a "made up story"

(Naipaul's term for what had begun to bore him in fiction)? If it doesn't, then what replaces the "made up story" in fiction? It's important to note that those who are making a break here with the conventional novel aren't offering something "natural" in opposition to the novel's artifice. If anything, the kind of novel I'm trying to describe is marked by a certain self-consciousness. Again, one must make further distinctions here. I'm not referring to the ironical self-consciousness of postmodernism. I'm thinking, instead, of the self-consciousness of the essay—its simultaneous uncovering of its subject (which might be food, art, childhood, social class, or something else) and its awareness of itself, at every moment, as a piece of writing. The "self" in the essay's self-consciousness might also include autobiography: that is, personal detail or reminiscence. But autobiography in the essay is only one element in its pervasive formal self-consciousness.

•

I feel connected to these relatively recent preoccupations and departures. Finally, I feel, the delineation of the kind of novel I embarked on in the late eighties (my first novel was published in 1991) is becoming clearer to others; is actually finding a place in the discussion. When I started out, there was the legacy of the nineteenth-century novel to contend with, and the presence of the Latin American novel. Both made the novel identical with compendiousness.

The moment I completed *A Strange and Sublime Address* in 1988, I became aware of its brevity. In fact, brevity was the shape it had assumed after revision; it was not what I'd aimed for. But, among other things, I was aiming for beauty—not just beauty of description, but beauty of form and its inner progression—and it seemed that brevity accentuated both form and beauty. I mean that the novel is not generally thought of in abstract, formal terms (form, after all, is a kind of abstraction, and has no extraneous meaning), but in relation to its content, to the life of the society, time, and human beings it represents. With the short novel, though, you are as aware of its finitude as of the life narrated within it. You can't be completely immersed in the story, as you can in a long conventional novel whose end is nowhere in sight, because you're partly conscious, from the sheer lack of pages and the negligible physical weight of what you hold in your hand, that this story is also a piece of writing, and the pages are finite. In other words, you're aware of form, in the way that, as you start reading a poem, you're already conscious that there are only a limited number of stanzas after the first one. This determines not only how you read the first stanza, but each line. One can never forget, in the more formal genres, that writing, like a musical composition, is a finite creation, and not to be confused with life and its sprawl and unendingness. Finitude is a feature of beauty and of form.

Having typed out my novel in 1988, I realised at once that, in the Anglophone world at least, I was, if not alone, a member of a very tiny minority. I had to deal with publishers—who had earlier been enthusiastic about seeing the finished work after reading a chapter in the *London Review of Books*—suddenly having second thoughts. The lack of a conventional story contributed to their nervousness, certainly; but size did too. The novel was around thirty-five thousand words. In the period of waiting (two and a half years) between finishing the book and the month of its publication, I would walk into Blackwell's bookshop in Oxford to spot the brief, attenuated volumes in the Fiction section and identify their authors. I discovered that only two writers—both women—had pursued this form as an ongoing project, and distanced themselves from the long novel: Muriel Spark and Jean Rhys. I check the shelves even today (but only occasionally, as bookshops have become abhorrent in a way I couldn't have foreseen in the eighties) to see if anything has changed, and because, after twenty six years, it turns out that most of my fiction is still the size of my first book: as is my new novel, *Friend of My Youth*. Glancing at the shelves for short books is one approach to excavating a tradition. It's largely absent from Anglophone writing, while in every other modern culture—German, French, Urdu, Bengali—this beautiful form appears "normal," and practitioners whose existence one knew nothing of keep appearing on the horizon, like Clarice Lispector.

•

When a cousin's Belgian wife read my first novel, her response wasn't, as it might have been: "I know these people, literally." She might well have said so: the characters in the novel were people she'd come to know in Calcutta on her visits from America, then Denmark, in the first decades of her marriage. Her relatives through marriage were my relatives on my mother's side. They were *in* the small novel. Instead, she said to my cousin, "It reminds me of Proust." This was in 1991. I don't recall Proust being commonly mentioned then in reference to the contemporary novel.

She may have meant that Proust too wrote of people he knew without little conventional fictional adornment. In fact, for certain readers, like Roland Barthes, who believed that the character Baron de Charlus in *À la recherche du temps perdu* was not based on Robert de Montesquiou but that Montesquiou modelled himself on Charlus, Proust had reversed the sequence by which we understand life's relation to art: that the novel is a fictionalised version of the life we know. That this may not be necessarily so became evident to me even before I'd encountered Barthes's observation, with the publication of *A Strange and Sublime Address*, when I noticed that my maternal uncle, who had his counterpart in the narrative as "Chhotomama," was studying my work meticulously to find out what he would do next.

But I think my cousin's wife had in mind, when she made that remark, a slowing down of time as a consequence of the confluence of sensation and memory. I hadn't read Proust except in fragments, mainly because of my reluctance to read long books. But the name came up again, when the Indian writer Khushwant Singh described my second novel, *Afternoon Raag*. Then again, in the citation for the *Los Angeles Times* Book Prize; then, in a review by Hilary Mantel in the *New York Review of Books*. And I remember being surprised and moved when the philosopher Charles Taylor introduced himself to me at the Wissenschafstkolleg in Berlin in 2005 and said: "Your writing gives me the kind of pleasure Proust does." This was at a juncture when I was beginning to wonder if the sort of novels I wrote were at all publishable—a question I have to reconsider periodically.

I speak of this background not to aggrandise myself (though the charge of self-aggrandisement may be inescapable), but to put on record the fact that the mention of Proust was unusual once, and to address, today, what it means to the literary history of a writer like myself. The name "Proust" began really to gain renewed currency in Anglo-American publishing circles around 2012–13, with the English translation of Karl Ove Knausgaard's *My Struggle* series of novels—though there was some undecidedness about whether the books were fiction or memoir. I heard that Knausgaard's work demonstrated an exaggerated preoccupation with how language engages with the mundane. Unlike me, who'd resisted Proust, Knausgaard, in the first volume of *My Struggle*, makes a direct and eloquent claim on his antecedents: "I not only read Marcel Proust's novel *À la recherche du temps perdu* but virtually imbibed it." There was reportedly more than a hint of the scandalous in the novels, mainly to do with how Knausgaard had portrayed his family members, but I suspected this account of the work had less to do with Knausgaard's emphases than an interpretation imposed on it by contemporary culture. I pricked up my ears. It seemed to me that Knausgaard might be a member of my species: that is, one who found deeply boring what others found fundamentally interesting (story) and deeply interesting what others found fundamentally boring (the everyday and its poetics).

It's one thing when Proust is retrieved from the cupboard in relation to a relatively young Norwegian novelist, and another when he's alluded to in conjunction with an Indian writer. In the first case, the comparison extends a lineage to do with the European novel's formal characteristics. It's a fresh turn, or a re-turn. In the second, it comprises an anomaly in the terms in which the Indian novel in English is usually discussed. In what sense could Proust and the sort of narrative we call "Proustian" constitute my inheritance? This question can only be investigated to a point. The markers of Knausgaard's writing are part of the unfolding of the form. In my case, the fact that I'm working within the history of the form is necessarily secondary to the fact that I'm writing about India.

•

In the nineties, there was an opening up in the form of the novel, not unrelated to the Proustian refusal to make a distinction between the imagined, the remembered, and the real. This involved a breaking down of the demarcation between the invented narrative of fiction and the ruminative tone and content of the essay. It made obsolete the speculation about how "autobiographical" a work might be. This new kind of novel didn't tap into the author's life for the purposes of fiction; it rephrased this relationship by making the novel essayistic—that is, by turning it into a form that was not primarily meant to tell stories, but express a writerly self-consciousness. Again, even in terms of this word, "self-consciousness," it represented a departure from the postmodernism of the 1980s. There are many differences between the former and the latter, but maybe the chief among them is the relative lack of interest in narrative in this new form; its courtship, often, of a poetic arrest, in contrast to postmodernism's ironic investment in the tricks of storytelling.

The awareness of such a development in the form—a development away from postmodernism, but not toward a renewed faith in realism (such as, say, Vikram Seth's *A Suitable Boy*, published in 1993, seemed to exemplify), nor a wholesale recuperation of modernism—came into being around 1996, with the English publication of W. G. Sebald's *The Emigrants*. It had been published in Germany in 1992. A very well-known English critic asked me to read this book: "I think you'll like it." Maybe he'd spotted a commonality of purpose. Sebald's practice appeared to look back to Walter Benjamin, and perhaps further back, to Baudelaire the essayist, and bring to the domain of fiction in the newly-globalised world an eclectic critical mind whose perceptions were determined by desultory physical exploration: by *flânerie*. Sebald's brief but productive six-year-old career in the Anglophone world (he died in 2001) and its aftermath inaugurated, in the new millennium, a way of placing the novel on the cusp of the essay and of fiction. Much of the discussion of this positioning began to take place in this century in America, especially in Brooklyn and Manhattan. I never finished *The Emigrants* myself, or read any of the other work, though I wish to: there's a time for everything. In New York, Sebald's putative descendants (according to commentators) included Teju Cole, whose *Open City* was published in 2011, and David Shield, whose highly-publicised "manifesto," *Reality Hungers*, came out a year earlier. More recent writers in this line might include Ben Lerner. Susan Sontag's championing of Sebald pointed to the essential Europeanness of this practice and temperament. Sebald's retrospective interest in the German writer Robert Walser (also brilliantly endorsed by Sontag, and reassessed absorbingly in 2013 in the *New Yorker* by Lerner) confirmed that the radical preoccupation with this particular formal and generic shift had originated in Europe and migrated to Brooklyn. A British variation in this line was provided by Geoff Dyer's hilarious extended essay with novelistic first-person narrator features, *Out of Sheer Rage* (1997).

It took me a while to comprehend the trajectory and nature of this development, from 1996 to roughly 2013, when people began to become conscious of it as a category, and publishers employ complacent terms like "genre-bending." It pleased me that my unease with both the nineteenth-century and the postmodern, postcolonial novel, my attempts, from 1991, to make a place for the kind of writing that I was doing, should be echoed and recognised, at long last, by this shift. Because it had felt like I was working in isolation. But it remained to be seen if the isolation had ceased. To be an Indian writer means, after all, that you're writing about India. What you're doing to and with the form won't determine the terms of critique where you're concerned; least of all from Indian commentators.

My own feeling is that the break was made well before Sebald appeared on the Anglophone's horizon, with the publication of V. S. Naipaul's novel *The Enigma of Arrival* in 1987. It was well received, but puzzled many. The puzzlement was related to the recognisability, or lack of it, of the genre. I think it was Bernard Bergonzi who wondered why Naipaul had called it a novel, and not an autobiography. This missed the fact that the book was not only about the narrator's life in Wiltshire, but about *wanting* to write a novel about the life of a Trinidadian writer in Wiltshire. Writerly self-consciousness had, in a very different way from postmodernism, placed autobiography at one remove. Naipaul didn't look into a mirror to get a sense of his own story, but at a painting by a European, Giorgio de Chirico, of a ship sailing into the harbour of a city. This painting became both mirror and the image, the crystallisation, of a moment. From the painting Naipaul borrowed the title, *The Enigma of Arrival*, again putting the theme of the personal arrival into Wiltshire at a slight distance.

It's taken time to for us to see Naipaul's book as a significant innovation in form. Instead, it's taken to be a document that attests to the postcolonial's life in the heart of the former imperial centre. It's difficult for the postcolonial, or Indian, artist's contribution to be discussed in formalist terms, because everything they do—the life they describe, the language they use—becomes the testimony of postcolonial history. Teju Cole's *Open City* has been saved from this; maybe enough time has passed for a certain kind of novel to be read not just as a Nigerian's effort to negotiate a Western metropolis—in this case, New York. Or maybe New York's position as a postglobalisation Paris allows us to situate one history—that of the Nigerian immigrant—within another—that of *flânerie* and the essay.

The other artist, besides Naipaul, who opened things up in generic terms was the filmmaker Abbas Kiarostami. In 1987, Kiarostami made a feature film called *Where is the Friend's Home?* set in the Iranian village of Koker. Nothing ostensibly happens in the film except a schoolboy attempting to return a notebook to a friend in a neighbouring village. In 1990, there was an earthquake in Iran. In 1992, the year that *The Emigrants* was published in Germany, Kiarostami released a film called *And Life Goes On*, in which a director sets out in a car with his son to look for the child actors who'd worked in his previous film and been displaced by the earthquake. The film isn't about the impact of the earthquake; it records how the process of filmmaking, impinged upon unexpectedly by an event, might constitute its own story. *And Life Goes On* explores what it is to make a film on an earthquake's impact on filmmaking, on both the auteur's vocation and that of the side-players, just as *The Enigma of Arrival* explores the desire to write *The Enigma of Arrival*. Wikipedia's filmography for Kiarostami lists it as both "documentary" and "fiction" (this reminded me of a sentence in James Wood's generous essay on my work in the New Yorker: "The effect is closer to documentary than to fiction; gentle artifice—selection, pacing, occasional dialogue—hides overt artifice"). The confusion is a productive one. Kiarostami's self-awareness (the film was made at a time when our understanding of "self-awareness" was still mediated by postmodernism) embraces references to the exigencies of filmmaking as well as random significances, during the journey to Koker, reminiscent of neorealism. The difference is this: neorealism employed nonprofessional actors to play characters in the story, giving cinema a register at once ramshackle and lyrical. In Kiarostami's films, actors and ordinary people often play themselves. We are in the realm of a productive confusion without abjuring neorealism's evanescence and lyricism.

•

When *A Strange and Sublime Address* was published in 1991, critics noted that "nothing happens" in it, strictly speaking. Whether a novel was the proper vehicle for conveying "nothing happening" was open to question. I personally thought that a great deal was happening in the book, things that people may or may not usually notice. When it won a prize in the UK, I was told confidentially by a judge that another judge, a literary journalist, had disagreed with the decision on the grounds that my book wasn't a "proper novel." This began to be said about my early fiction in different ways even by those who were generous to me and liked what I was doing. *Afternoon Raag* (1993), my second novel, was called a "prose poem" by Karl Miller in a British newspaper. In an interview to an Indian paper, the novelist and critic Paul Bailey said he admired the book, and added, "But it isn't a proper novel, is it?"

In retrospect, these remarks seem prescient. They gesture toward a vocabulary that was still unavailable and would come into existence only after 1996 and Sebald. The gradual creation of such a vocabulary was, and is, something of a reassurance for me. But it's a limited reassurance, as I remain an onlooker in relation to the history of the form. I'm an Indian, so of course I write about India. But then, again, I don't write about India. I'm not interested in writing about India. This means I'm not entirely, or comfortably, a part of the history of the Indian novel in English either. Nor can I be part of a history that's now been appropriated by literary journalism and publishing houses: of the form of the novel. It's not that I'm resistant to appropriation. I'm unfit for appropriation. This may be a good place to be in.

•

It's while writing this essay that I remembered that Naipaul's book, like my new novel, had a borrowed title. I knew this, but it had never sunk in. Naipaul was clearly obsessed with de Chirico's painting; it meant something to him. But the shape and sound of the title must have meant something too. In relation to my novel, "Friend of My Youth" is actually the title of an Alice Munro story I never read. Titles point to two things. The first is the book that it faintly conjures up. The second is the reader, to whom the title suggests what the book might possibly be. In imagining this possibility, the reader partly becomes a writer: he or she has started to create the book for themselves. In Naipaul's book and mine, I realise a bit belatedly, the act of reusing a title covers the duality in us of reader and writer. Both books are also—again, I spot this coincidence now—about *wanting* to write a novel, and then becoming caught up, implicitly, in writing about wanting to write the book that's being written. *Out of Sheer Rage* is at once a parody and a poetic embodiment of such a project. Dyer wants to write a book on Lawrence; he can't write the book; he writes a book about being unable to write that book. The narrative is Sisyphean, a version of Beckett's "I can't go on, I'll go on." And yet it's infected with Lawrentian exuberance. Maybe there's a name to such a pursuit.

Long ago—perhaps when I was in the midst of my third novel—I noticed that "writing" doesn't begin when one puts pen or ballpoint to paper. (I wrote longhand and still do.) Writing a novel simultaneously happens in the midst of lived life, expresses a relationship with lived life, and is a departure from, a hiatus in, lived life. It may or may not be synonymous with the time spent putting words on paper. The time of writing really begins before one has written anything. This time is not really one of gathering material or preparation. You haven't picked up a pen or notebook but are in a slightly altered state; you are writing. It isn't absolutely certain either when the writing ends. When I set out to discuss my book, I meant not the story or the hardbound or paperback copy, but a dilation in time in relation to writing and rereading it.

In this context, let me tell a story that may belong inside the novel as much as it exists outside it. The book is about a writer called Amit Chaudhuri who visits Bombay in early 2011 to read at an event from his last novel, *The Immortals*. He grew up in Bombay, but no longer has a home there. He's staying in a room in a club in Malabar Hill, opposite, as it happens, the building in which he spent most of his childhood. The other unsettling thing about this visit, besides the knowledge that he no longer has a home in this city, is the encounter with a Bombay that was attacked on 26 November 2008, a Bombay still fresh in the narrator's mind from reports and TV footage, but which has been restored to normalcy. Bombay *looks* more or less the same, but it's changed completely. The third source of unsettlement is the absence of the narrator's school friend, Ramu. Ramu, the "friend of my youth," is a recovering drug addict. He is now in Alibag in a punitive rehab that's closed off his access to the world. The narrator is surprised at the effect Ramu's absence has on him. Most of the novel covers the two-day visit in 2011. Two short sections follow, in which the narrator revisits the city of his childhood twice. Ramu is back in Bombay in these sections.

None of this is different from things that have happened in my life. "My life" became, at one point, the book I was writing. Since then the life and the writing have been compelled to diverge, as if pulled by separate destinies. But, again, the two from time to time meet. Some of this has to do with my ongoing interactions with the friend who is Ramu's prototype, who lives, like him, in Bombay, and, like him, was an addict. Even when I was beginning the novel, I was nervous of his response, as one would be of the response of a famous and abrasive critic, or, alternatively, of one's most trusted reader. Of course, Ramu hardly read. He'd told me many times that he lacked the patience. Yet he had informers. I'd referred to him in a piece of writing in the past, and not changed his name, because, frankly, I thought I was paying tribute to him. (I see my writing as a tribute, rather than portrayal or analysis.) His informer had told him that I should have given him a cut from my royalties. My friend mentioned this half in jest; but he was a bit aggrieved too. "You could have changed my name," he admonished me. I had no defence. I wasn't sure he cared for immortality.

After starting work on this book, I'd tell him from time to time that I was writing about him. He said: "Just change my name" (which I had); "And don't forget my share of the royalties." A few months before the novel came out in India, a long extract appeared in a British magazine, and I went to Bombay in February to read from it at a literary festival. The evening before, walking through the dark arcades in Kala Ghoda, not far from the college he'd been educated at and where I'd studied for a year, we had a long conversation, sometimes standing on the pavement in the intensity of our exchanges, about *why* he was in the book. Of course, he wasn't going to read it. The idea of reading the book—any book—was more repellent to him than figuring in it.

At the actual event the following evening, he sat at the back with another friend of mine, a scientist. He was complaining to him about various things, when I started to read. My other friend the scientist alerted him with, "This is about you." But I'd chosen paragraphs in which he hardly made an appearance. I'm told he grumbled later: "What—I'm mentioned only once?"

I returned to Bombay in a few months for the publication of the novel. My friend called me soon after I'd got out of the airport. The book launch event was to take place that afternoon, at a venue not far from where he lived. He was in good spirits. It emerged quickly that his informants had read reports about *Friend of My Youth* in the press. They'd said good things about it. "He's your truest friend," one of them had told him—about me. Inebriated with these exaggerations, he was now happy and at ease. He was looking forward to the evening's launch as an actor might to a lifetime achievement award ceremony.

At the event, crowded with literary readers and well-known people, he sat with a man, a recovered addict, three-quarters into the back rows. By temperament, he hated social occasions and "pretentiousness." He also shied away from running into people because of his history. But he enjoyed the launch. When, afterwards, the organiser asked me to join him for a drink at a club nearby, I told them I'd be with him shortly. I hung out with my two guests, and then persuaded them to accompany me to the club.

I found the organiser's party of three on the far side of the bar on the first floor. My two companions said they'd rather sit at a separate table and not intrude. But the organiser went across to them and invited them to join the others. The two ex-addicts said no to the offer of a drink; alcohol can lead back to drugs. I hardly drink. We focussed on snacking. I'd introduced my friend as an old friend from school. The conversation turned to my novel—its inception; how *true* it was. And then it turned to my friend: how long he'd known me; what he did. Suddenly, he said expansively, "*I* am Ramu." He wasn't looking at me. I was irrelevant. Everybody was silent. Then the organiser said, as you would to one who's made a large claim at a party: "Really?" I marvelled at my friend: at the loss of reticence and subterfuge about his social identity. It was as if he'd finally decided to endorse the relationship between writing and life. The others looked at him with scepticism, and with some of the disbelieving awe characters in Woody Allen films display when they run into fictional characters.

I felt moved by my friend's statement that night. Partly it had to do with the fact that its shape reminded me of something. It came to me later. It was the words attributed to Flaubert: "*Madame Bovary, c'est moi.*"

What, if indeed he'd said such a thing, did Flaubert mean? In what way could you be a character you'd created; especially a character you knew was doomed? However difficult Ramu's life might seem to me or, particularly, to himself, I wanted to firmly separate him in my mind from Madame Bovary. Yet Flaubert's words don't seem to me fundamentally hopeless, but shrewdly obdurate: an affirmation of something, and as much a confirmation as my friend's statement was. The author produces a work; but the work too produces the author's life. The author is a reader, and vice-versa. The writing isn't finished as long as we continue to believe, rightly or wrongly, that it is about *us*.

Storytelling and Forgetfulness

2018, delivered as a talk at the "Against Storytelling" symposium in the Literary Activism series. This revised version appeared in the *Los Angeles Review of Books*, 2019

YEARS AGO, I began to run into the claim that we are all storytellers. Storytelling was evidently a primal communal function for humanity. I was assured that we've been telling each other stories since the beginning of time. I felt a churlish resistance to these proclamations, possibly because one might decide that being human doesn't mean one should subscribe, without discomfiture, to everything the human race is collectively doing at any given point. Storytelling shouldn't be guaranteed an aura simply because humans have been at it from the beginning of history. Of course, part of my unease emanated from the fact that the "beginning of history" is even more of a wishful invention than the "end of history" is. It occurs to me that we probably began to hear "we are all storytellers," as an utterance, from the late 1980s and early 90s onwards. From the moment one first heard this utterance, one was told it had been made from the beginning of time. As with various things that happened in the age of globalisation, radical shifts in our understanding (of value, for instance) quickly acquired an immemorial air. So, for example, it became increasingly difficult to conceive of a period in history that valued things differently from the way the free market does. Middle-class ideology may have concerned itself with appropriating the universal; the "now" of the free market appears to have been more preoccupied with recruiting eternity. As a result, the popular-culture term "all time" gained a new meaning with globalisation; like the assertion "We have always been storytellers," "all-time" lists and "all-time greats" often go back over periods, and are applied to categories (like rock guitarists), that are actually thirty years old.

The disciplinary shifts in the humanities privileging "storytelling" are too numerous to go into here: I'll only give one example. A historian recently told me that she asks her students to liberate themselves from the constraints of their pedagogy by thinking of the novel and behaving like "storytellers." As I said to her, this interpretation of the novel of course inadvertently makes imaginative writing, especially fiction, synonymous with storytelling: it's as if looking outside the bounds of scholarly work towards fiction or imaginative prose as a model for loosening constraints must privilege narrative, rather than other aspects of fiction, as being constitutive of the liberations of imaginative writing.

A surfeit of "We are all storytellers" made me realise that this was not really a primary utterance at all. The primary utterance, if there must be one, is praise or acknowledgement of what makes stories and other things possible: existence; life. By "life" I mean not what narrative is "about," but what lies on narrative's periphery. What the earliest texts seem to do is to attempt to find a language with which to both come to terms with and acknowledge—even celebrate—the contingency of the fact of existence. The story, with the human or anthropomorphised animal at the centre, emerges in the aftermath of existence, but, paradoxically, has an air of being recounted and a priori, of already having happened. Existence is neither a priori nor originary; it's a moment of possibility.

In the spirit of investigating whether we were always storytellers, I went back to a canonical text. It's from the first millennium BCE: the *Kena Upanishad*. It felt important to go back to it because storytelling has been almost dutifully conflated with non-Western cultures, which themselves are often conflated with orality. Writing and inscription are, on the other hand, an Enlightenment project. Outside the West, in the lap of orality, our mothers and grandmothers have been telling us stories from when we were in the womb. Story, for us, has been an autochthonic method of nutrition. While not denying any of this, it was important to check out a primary text from an incorrigibly storytelling culture. *"Kena"* in the *Kena Upanishad* means "why," connected to the whys and wherefores of the universe. This poetic statement is from the brief opening section of this *Upanishad* (note that Brahman is not to be confused with Brahma, Brahmin, or other similar-sounding words):

> Who sends the mind to wander afar, who first drives life to start on its journey, who impels us to utter these words, who is the spirit* behind the eye and the ear... What cannot be spoken with words, but that whereby words are spoken, know that alone to be Brahman.
>
> What cannot be thought with the mind, but that whereby the mind can think, know that alone to be Brahman the spirit and not what people here adore. What cannot be seen with the eye, but that whereby the eye can see—know that alone to be Brahman. What cannot be heard with the ear, but that whereby the ear can hear; what cannot be withdrawn with breath, but that whereby breath is withdrawn, know that alone to be Brahman.

This comes across not so much as a narrative of creation as an instance of self-reflexivity that's at once curiously tortured and liberating. Its meaning can't be paraphrased, but it *can* be rephrased as a series of questions and replies. "What can't be thought with the mind? Whatever it is that makes the mind think." "What can't be seen with the eye? Whatever it is that makes the eye see." It's an account that abjures progression on behalf of the self-reflexive, of the assertion that turns upon itself.

*"Spirit," as the Sanskritist Heeraman Tiwari pointed out to me, is a Judeo-Christian translation of what he calls, in his translation, an all-pervasive "element."

Here's an excerpt from the third section:

> The Brahman once won a victory for the Devas. Through that victory of the Brahman, the Devas became elated. They thought, "This victory is ours. This glory is ours." The Brahman perceived this and appeared before them. They did not know what mysterious form it was.
>
> They said to Fire: "O Jataveda (All-knowing)! Find out what mysterious spirit this is." He said: "Yes."
>
> He ran towards it and He (Brahman) said to him: "Who art thou?" "I am Agni, I am Jataveda," he (the Fire-god) replied.
>
> Brahman asked: "What power resides in thee?" Agni replied: "I can burn up all whatsoever exists on earth."
>
> Brahman placed a straw before him and said: "Burn this." He (Agni) rushed towards it with all speed, but was not able to burn it. So he returned from there and said (to the Devas): "I was not able to find out what this great mystery is."
>
> Then they said to Vayu (the Air-god): "Vayu! Find out what mystery this is." He said: "Yes."
>
> He ran towards it and He (Brahman) said to him: "Who art thou?" "I am Vayu, I am Matarisva (traveller of Heaven)," he (Vayu) said.
>
> Then the Brahman said: "What power is in thee?" Vayu replied: "I can blow away all whatsoever exists on earth."
>
> Brahman placed a straw before him and said: "Blow this away." He (Vayu) rushed towards it with all speed, but was not able to blow it away. So he returned from there and said (to the Devas): "I was not able to find out what this great mystery is.'

Although similar in shape and tone to Judeo-Christian parables about miraculous strength, like the one about Samson bringing down the columns, this is really a parable about delicacy. After all, what's at issue here is not moving mountains, but a straw. You don't need strength to move a straw: what is it that you need, then? Delicacy is nonnarrative;

as with writing a poem, you can't coerce its workings. Narrative and story by themselves are neither the same thing as, nor a guarantee of, movement; this is what writers, like the mystified Devas, need to learn quickly. Otherwise the straw stays inert.

•

I never liked reading novels. My growing up was spent consuming comic books and poems. I was eventually drawn to novels through exceptional paragraphs cited in essays: by my late teens, I was probably more likely to read a piece of criticism about a work rather than the work itself. One such paragraph occurs in *A House for Mr. Biswas* by V. S. Naipaul, where Biswas in his early life takes a new job as a sign painter after having been a bus conductor; I encountered it in my early twenties in a critical piece about the book in an anthology on "commonwealth literature." Biswas must reproduce the edict, "IDLERS KEEP OUT BY ORDER."

> ... his hand became surer, his strokes bolder, his feeling for letters finer. He thought R and S the most beautiful of Roman letters; no letter could express so many moods as R, without losing its beauty; and what could compare with the swing and rhythm of S? With a brush, large letters were easier than small ...

I was transfixed by this paragraph, and felt it was a shame that I'd have to read the novel. I was content, instead, to reread the paragraph endlessly. This is because the paragraph presented me with a possibility. The possibility was the novel. The novel I was presented with was not the telling, the recounting, that I would purportedly have to read. That act of reading the narrative, the recounting, would, in a sense, diminish the possibility generated by this encounter with the paragraph. Where, then, are we likely to find this moment of possibility in a piece of writing;

in, say (since we are talking about storytelling), a work of narrative fiction? To me it seems it resides in the sort of standalone paragraph such as the one I've quoted, which belongs to a story but is also independent of it, in that it seems equally located in an irreducible life and textuality outside that novel as it is in the life narrated and contained within it.

The moment of possibility resides especially in the opening paragraphs of a work of fiction, or any paragraph that has the irresolution, the air of open-endedness and lifelikeness, the lack of recountedness, that opening paragraphs have. The paragraphs in the first page of a novel (sometimes in the second and third pages too) have not been bound yet by the telling, but are opening out on to something. My ambition, always, was to write novels composed entirely of opening paragraphs and then to put them in some kind of order. The order would be a sequence that was partly illusory. Of course, we are experts at creating an illusion of continuity, both as readers and writers, and I believe that if you give somebody a text without any narrative they will impose continuity on it. My subterranean aim—so subterranean that it's taken me two decades to see what I was up to—was to create an assemblage of opening paragraphs, to expand as much as possible, without introducing a sense of development, the vivid lack of resolution of the first three or four pages.

What kind of text is produced by an artist who doesn't want the moment of possibility to be closed down by the compulsion or the need to tell? Once you commit to telling, the moment in the opening paragraph is over. We know for a fact that many writers have wonderful opening pages whose magic is sacrificed to higher causes, such as observances to do with the syntax of realism, and the responsibility of portraying the arc of the existence of certain human beings or "characters": the novelist "must become the whole of boredom itself," says W. H. Auden, who was in awe of, and slightly bewildered by, this voluntary taking on of the depiction of social milieu almost as a form of social responsibility. This loss of the abandon of the opening pages is characteristic of the human compromise, the deep maturity, that the novel represents, when the writer knowingly assents to being shackled by the need for narrative and telling. Naipaul himself is a fundamental example of a writer who sometimes begins with astonishing passages of lifelikeness, but then not so much loses the plot, or loses himself to a plot, but takes on upon himself fetters that are clearly unwanted. Joan Didion recognises this, and expands on the peculiar sensory excitement of the first three pages of Naipaul's *Guerrillas*, which she confesses to compulsively rereading, almost as if the rest of the novel didn't really matter. In the novella *In a Free State*, Naipaul translates, with extraordinary vitality in the opening section, an intuition of possibility into a story about a European man and woman who must journey urgently and impulsively out of an African country in the time of a coup. Then, like his two characters, he seems not to know what to do except see the journey through. As the syntax of narrative takes over, not only does the representation of the journey feel increasingly entrapping, but—as is often the case with Naipaul when he feels unhappy—by most standards morally and politically peculiar, turgid, and alienating.

Something similar happens in his travelogue *An Area of Darkness*. Towards the beginning, a period of waiting is described: the ship, on its way to India, has stopped at the port in Alexandria. Nothing happens; horse-drawn cabs are awaiting fares. Few arrive, and melancholy settles in. This melancholy is a form of excitement, just as the waiting-for-something-to-happen is a kind of energy unmatched by the events later narrated in the book, the actual encounter with India, which is the book's legitimate subject. For Naipaul, as possibility recedes (and possibility, for him, as the chapter on Alexandria shows, has little do with optimism), questionable moral judgement begins to dominate: this is *his* response to the cost of succumbing to narrative propriety—not so much "becoming the whole of boredom itself," but an alienated chafing.

A House for Mr. Biswas opens with a short prologue, where everything is indeterminate and proleptic. It begins, "Ten weeks before he died, Mr. Mohun Biswas, a journalist of Sikkim Street, St. James, Port of Spain, was sacked," and then goes on to dwell, for five pages, on Biswas's house, a house that's "flawed" and "irretrievably mortgaged": "during these months of illness and despair he was struck again and again by the wonder of being in his own house, the audacity of it." We are suspended here, in the prologue, with Mr. Biswas, between arrival and departure. Naipaul manages to stay throughout with this sense of the possible, and he does this by constantly returning to Biswas's disbelieving conviction, even at the end of the novel, that the house on Sikkim Street is a house he's just begun to live in: "In the extra space Mr. Biswas planted a laburnum tree." In my edition, 583 of 590 pages have gone by when this sentence appears; and yet, despite all that has ensued and is now finished, we're still absorbing the prologue's "wonder" and "audacity" of arrival.

Arrival, like existence, and unlike story, lacks the air of the a priori and the narrated. In *The Enigma of Arrival*, the ship that paused at harbour in *An Area of Darkness* appears again, but this time in a de Chirico painting that gives both its title and its atmosphere of lapsed expectancy to the book. Midway through the novel, the narrator reflects that the painting is about a ship that sailed into a city, and a man who got off at the port and intended to go back, but forgot to: "The antique ship has gone. The traveller has lived out his life.' The inadvertent forgetting of the matter of going back, rather than the creation of a new existence, becomes this person's story, as it does the narrator's. Forgetting and possibility become, then, interchangeable; the life is never really recounted. It—the novel; the painting—doesn't contain the tale of an immigrant; it represents an attempt at immersion in a beginning, what Naipaul calls "arrival," involving an action endlessly postponed, which the narrator encapsulates with the words, "The traveller has lived out his life."

•

How do we construct a page composed of opening paragraphs? One is reminded, of course, of Walter Benjamin's ambition to write a book composed entirely of quotations. A quotation for him, as in his essays on Kafka, is also a paragraph; for my younger self, for reasons I mentioned earlier, and maybe for my present self too, a paragraph is a quotation. A novel is an assemblage of paragraphs or quotations, which both belong to the narrative and outside it. A quotation in an imaginative work—say, an essay—causes unsettlement. It's there not as evidence, to legitimise a claim, as it might in a scholarly work, but to remind us that the narrator is distracted, that they've made an association, and have been momentarily led from the text to another text outside it. The quote is not wholly present in the narrative; it's partly elsewhere. So the quote doesn't just further an argument; it leads to an opening up. The paragraph, as I understand it, must have the same sense of not being wholly present that the quotation, in Benjamin's sense, does. When Benjamin speaks of his ambition to write a book composed entirely of quotations, he's speaking of a method of building that brings together units that belong, but also don't wholly belong, to the argument or narrative. A quoted paragraph for him is a standalone paragraph, because it comprises a possibility that makes recounting—that is, the rest of the narrative—redundant. If the paragraph is at least doubly located in fiction, then one location lies in fiction's purported task, the recounting of a life; the other lies outside it, in acknowledging what's more powerful than "story"—the present's contingency.

•

I've not forgotten that this piece has to do with "forgetfulness and storytelling," for which reason I wish to look at the opening section of Kafka's *Metamorphosis* in Michael Hofmann's translation:

When Gregor Samsa awoke one morning from troubled dreams, he found himself changed into a monstrous cockroach in his bed. He lay on his tough, armoured back, and, raising his head a little, managed to see—sectioned off by little crescent-shaped ridges into segments—the expanse of his arched, brown belly, atop which the coverlet perched, forever on the point of slipping off entirely.

"What's the matter with me?" he thought. It was no dream. There, quietly between the four familiar walls, was his room, a normal human room, if always a little on the small side. Over the table, on which an array of cloth samples was spread out—Samsa was a travelling salesman—hung the picture he had only recently clipped from a magazine, and set in an attractive gilt frame. It was a picture of a lady in a fur hat and stole, sitting bolt upright, holding in the direction of the onlooker a heavy muff into which she had thrust the whole of her forearm.

From there, Gregor's gaze directed itself towards the window, and the drab weather outside—raindrops could be heard plinking against the tin window ledges—made him quite melancholy. "What if I went back to sleep for a while, and forgot about all this nonsense?" he thought, but that proved quite impossible, because he was accustomed to sleeping on his right side, and in his present state he was unable to find that position...

"Oh, my Lord!" he thought. "If only I didn't have to follow such an exhausting profession! On the road, day in, day out. The work is so much more strenuous than it would be in the head office, and then there's the additional ordeal of travelling, worries about train connections, the irregular, bad meals, new people all the time, no continuity, no affection. Devil take it!" He felt a light itch at the top of his belly...

He slid back to his previous position. "All this getting up early," he thought, "is bound to take its effect. There are some other travelling salesmen I could mention who live like harem women... If I didn't have to exercise restraint for the sake of my parents, then I would have quit a long time ago; I would have gone up to the director and told him exactly what I thought of him. He would have fallen off his desk in surprise! That's a

> peculiar way he has of sitting anyway, up on his desk, and talking down to his staff from on high, making them step up to him very close because he's so hard of hearing.'

What's striking is how both Gregor and the narrator have forgotten what the central predicament and theme are, or are incapable of grasping their centrality. Gregor is more concerned with the difficulty of turning on his side in his present state, a difficulty that impedes his plan to sleep a bit longer; he is made melancholy by the sound of rain; he will soon become aware of the unfairness of train schedules; in the meantime, he's incensed by the memory of his boss's posture. Another writer, a lesser writer, wouldn't have permitted this losing sight, so early on, of the immensity of what's happened. But the liberation of the opening pages of *Metamorphosis* comes from their inability to be absolutely present, their vacillation between being in the story of a man who has become a giant insect and their forgetting of this story and their leakage into something outside it: the matter of living, with its timetables and trains, which is supposed to feed its experiences into the story but also competes with and is unconscious of it.

There's another kind of forgetfulness here: that of objects, or what in literary works we call "detail." The picture of the woman "sitting bolt upright"; the gilt frame; the coverlet; the tin window ledges; the rain—these seem not to be fully conscious of being part, as background, of a story of a man who finds he's a giant insect. Their role is not even ironical, as, according to Auden, the role of the animals and humans in Breughel's painting of Icarus's fall into the ocean is: "how everything turns away / Quite leisurely from the disaster." In "Metamorphosis," detail is not so much indifferent to the disaster as it to being in a story about a disaster; its location is both in the story and independent of it. So a narrative with an easily paraphrasable centrality of focus becomes, instead, an example of multiple and dispersed openings out. Its details have their counterpart not in Breughel's *Icarus*, or in realist fiction, or in period or genre cinema, but in Abbas Kiarostami's movies, where nonprofessionals are often not playing characters but themselves, and aren't fully mindful that they're in a larger story. They're in the film and outside it. The same can be said of animals, air, water, and trees in a Tarkovsky film, or in a film like *The New World* by Terrence Malick: that all these are nonprofessional actors unaware of playing the role of the characters "animal," "air," "water," and "trees" respectively, but are, inadvertently, themselves. They emanate, if you notice them, an innate forgetfulness of the story they're in, as do the paragraphs I've mentioned. In this regard, the details I'm discussing are quite unlike those in period or sci-fi films, where objects, horses, elephants, and things exude, like the protagonist, an awareness at every point of being either in history or in the future, two easily recognisable categories that embody further modulations on the recounted air of storytelling.

•

Jean Paul Sartre was intrigued by the idea of the adventure. An adventure, of course, is another name for story: for children, "adventure story" is a tautology. Here's Sartre's narrator in *Nausea*:

> For the most banal event to become an adventure you must, and this is enough, begin to recount it. This is what fools people. A man is always a teller of tales. He sees everything that happens to him through them and he tries to live his own life as if you were telling a story, but you have to choose, live or tell.

In other words, we don't, can't, know we're in an adventure or in a story. The same can be said of history: no one is really aware of living in a historical epoch. Conversations with people who have participated in historic situations, whether it's a performance by John Coltrane or the partition of a country, confirm this unknowingness: all they recall is what it was like to be present at that time. But forgetfulness is absent from historical novels or films, as it is in films about the future; both the past and future are assembled by bringing together markers of history—turbans, togas, or forelocks—or the future: spaceships and space. Even space lacks forgetfulness in films like *2001: A Space Odyssey*, whose story is already, a priori, being narrated as the "future." Space, in Kubrick's film, becomes a metaphor for the "homogeneous, empty time" of history that Benjamin says makes the idea of man's progress possible: the historicism that imbues our notions of the futuristic and historical is enacted succinctly in the film's opening: an ape from a prehistoric epoch flings a bone into the air which, ascending in "homogeneous, empty time," becomes a spaceship.

Yet both Kubrick in *Barry Lyndon*, and certainly Tarkovsky in historical films like *Andrei Rublev*, or in his science fiction-based cinema, *Stalker* and *Solaris*, reject the notion of the "adventure." The "background" in these movies adheres, on one level, to what Sartre calls "the most banal event"; for instance, one of the first signals we receive in *Solaris* of dissonance doesn't have to do with science fiction appurtenances, but a horse wandering outside a block of sixties houses; the second signal, which also comes early, occurs when a tunnel a man is driving through takes inordinately long to end: the tunnel, a very recognisable urban feature (this bit, set in Russia, was apparently shot in Japan, testimony to a certain kind of mid-century urbanisation available in various cultures), seems to loop in upon itself without in any other way being remarkable. The horses, spaceships, horsemen, and stretches of grass or space in Tarkovsky's films, and in *Barry Lyndon*, possess not identifiable characteristics that mark them out as futuristic or historical, but a disorganised banality, a forgetfulness of the role they're playing in the setting. As a result, both the past and the future are, in these movies, undifferentiated from the nonhomogeneous present in which we live.

•

What's the relation between living and telling on the one hand, and between living and writing on the other? The prevalent model for life's relationship to telling is that we live, gather material, and then pour or transform that material experience of living into something that comes out of it: the story we consequently tell.

In my understanding, however, the moment of writing converges with living randomly. There is no decision about transforming into a story material that's been previously experienced or collected; instead, one arrives at a juncture at which there is an unexpected sense of possibility for the writer: I include all of us when I use the word "writer." This sense of possibility comprises what I'm calling "writing," which need not involve putting pen to paper or sitting down to write an inaugural sentence—as the act is portrayed in Hollywood films, where the "writer" might be a fictional character or Hemingway or Fitzgerald, poised significantly at the typewriter to start a novel. The physical act of writing, or making that break from life when one sits down to commit oneself to embarking on a work is a reification, a reduction of the actual intimation of a beginning, a possibility that writing actually continually constitutes.

Let me give you an example of what I mean. You're looking at the cover of a book and want to own it, to buy it. You study the cover, transfixed by it, and then you don't read the book. You are transfixed not only because you want to read what's contained within, but because you have begun in a sense to compose or write what's within. The story that's given to you by the book has become secondary to the story you've begun to write. This is the moment of writing. But you have not written anything; you're arrested by what you see on the cover. You buy the book; in fact, you buy many such books, transfixed by them for one reason or another—it could be the jacket or title; it could be your reading, in the bookshop, of the first page—and then you put them on the shelf, as a covert gesture towards the perpetual imminence, the possibility, of writing. Your sense of ownership has to do with owning the story, but the story is not to be reduced by recounting, by telling: the story is always to be a possibility, which is why the books on our bookshelves that we don't read outnumber the books that we do. Our bookshelves are largely made up of books that we do not read. These are our ongoing moments of writing—a self-generated accumulation of writing as possibility.

Why I Write Novels

2020, online talk for Balliol College, Oxford, then published in *n+1*

THE TITLE OF THIS TALK seems to suggest that I know the answer to the "why," and that I'm about to share it with you. I began writing my first novel in 1986, in what I elected to be my gap year: so, if I've been trying my hand at fiction for about thirty-four years now, I should definitely have some idea why I write novels. The truth is that the title has a misleading sound. It should have been, "Why *Do* I Write Novels?," with the emphasis on the "do": because I've grown increasingly, rather than less, puzzled by this part of my existence—a part that, to those who know my work from afar, may even seem definitive of my existence.

Of course, in order for me to be confident of that title, "Why I Write Novels," I have to assume that the reader knows enough of my fiction to want to learn of its backstory and provenance. I'm not making such an assumption. What I'm hoping is that the spectacle of a person who's published seven novels over three decades without knowing exactly why he's chosen that genre to write in will be a matter of curiosity to others.

People have pointed out to me from the start that I have been writing about my life. I have been at pains to point out to them that I'm interested in "life," not "my life," and that there's a subtle difference between my understanding of the first and the second. Still, when Karl Miller read a chapter from my first novel, *A Strange and Sublime Address*, which he published as a standalone story in 1988 in the *London Review of Books*, he said, "It's your bloody memoir!" I've had this said to me since from time to time, if with less passion. I have sometimes asked myself in what way a novel I've written *isn't* a memoir, especially when I definitely know it isn't. Take my sixth novel, *Odysseus Abroad*, which came to me from my urge to cast a maternal uncle I had in London, a bachelor, as Odysseus, and myself—from my memories of my student days in the early eighties—as Telemachus.

This conceit came from nowhere, as conceits do, after I'd bought a large charcoal sketch in 2002 by the artist F. N. Souza. I'd purchased the work exceptionally cheap, for fifty-five thousand rupees, and hung it up in the drawing room in Calcutta. The charcoal sketch was a portrait; a jumble of frenetic lines that had come together to create a man. My uncle, the bachelor from London, was in Calcutta. He still rented the Belsize Park bedsit he'd lived in for roughly thirty years, but, from 1991—after I convinced him to visit Calcutta to attend my wedding—spent most of his time in Bhowanipore in South Calcutta with his younger brother. Though he'd been a senior manager in one of the biggest shipping companies in Britain, he owned no property. In Calcutta, he spent his time visiting relatives. He came to our flat and asked to see the painting. He studied it and said: "You may as well have paid me fifty-five thousand rupees for farting." When I protested, he said: "I suppose the art produced by a genius and the art done by an idiot are identical."

I kept looking at the magnificent likeness, thinking how it was like my uncle, and was reminded that Souza had named it "Ulysses." The portrait resembled my uncle because it was actually a self-portrait, and there's a marked similarity between my uncle's features and Souza's, even a pronounced overlap in temperament, except that Souza hated Tagore and my uncle loved him: so, if they'd met, they'd have soon been at each other's throats. Staring at the drawing as my uncle went off,

I thought, "He *is* a bit like Odysseus." This was the surfacing of the conceit, that at first felt liberatingly absurd, then increasingly tenable. He had lived in the bedsit in Belsize Park for thirty years; he had worked in shipping; he had only lately, relatively speaking, returned home. When I was in London as an undergraduate, he was my one point of contact outside of my frugal interaction with college life. I now began to see the journey I made at least once weekly from Warren Street to his bedsit, walking past him, as he stood in the doorway, to the kitchenette inside to open the tap and pour myself water, as Telemachus's journey. I returned to the image from time to time over the next ten years.

When I committed myself to writing the story in 2012, I wondered how to approach the conceit. I considered the essayistic memoir: this would allow me to discuss the conceit while laying out the lives of Odysseus and Telemachus and their time in London. I wrote two paragraphs in this mode. I put a line through them in my notebook.

Then I wondered what to do. Joyce's behemoth was on my mind, of course. What if I, taking a cue, set my story over a day? But at which point to begin? I used to wake up and practise music in Warren Street, but with trepidation: my neighbours slept late, and the English woman below would come to my door and knock at 10 a.m. to complain. All of them, including the Gujaratis from Tanzania who lived above me, went to bed at about 3 a.m.; the Gujaratis played rap music every night; so it was always moot whether I'd have enough sleep to get up and sing and then get through the day. My neighbours were the suitors. This came to me as I considered how to proceed. After that, other details of the epic began to fall into place: my landlord, who owned a restaurant called Diwaan-i-Khaas (after the Mughal court's "upper chamber"), would be Menelaus; an episode that my uncle had related to me, of the sixteen-year-old janitress in his office making a lewd gesture at him as she cleaned the floors, would comprise the section on Odysseus spying on Nausicaa; my uncle's Pakistani neighbour, who both protected and exploited him and whose own bedsit was filthy, would be the swineherd Eumaeus with whom Odysseus had taken refuge. I implied this last through a thought that Ananda—that is, Telemachus—has when he glimpses the inside of the neighbour's bedsit on his way to the shared toilet: "It was a pigsty." And so on. It became clear that I didn't need to invent, but remember: everything in the epic had already happened to me. But this remembering was not the sort of remembering that the memoir is supposed to involve. I say "supposed to" because I have no idea what kind of memory goes into a memoir. Here, three narratives encountered or lived through in one way or another in a past life—the *Odyssey*, which I had to consult again; *Ulysses*; and my own miserable years as an undergraduate in London—came back to me over the period of writing in a steady confluence. They bore upon each other in an act of regeneration. All the elements had been waiting for this moment; this is not the way we conceive of memory, which we think of as a conduit to the past that we access at will. I had, in fact, tried to write a memoir on that assumption, and failed.

•

The questions, "Is it from your life? Did this really happen?," along with the self-contradicting observation, "Nothing happens in your novels," have greeted my fiction from 1991. How you can ask "Did this really happen?" while at the same time claiming nothing has happened in unclear to me. The first two questions I've just mentioned returned with a new acuteness with the publication of my seventh novel, *Friend of My Youth*. I was partly responsible. I had written a work of fiction in which the first-person narrator was called "Amit Chaudhuri." He was born in Calcutta and had grown up in Bombay, very much as I had, and the novel has him returning to Bombay in March 2011 to read from his fifth novel, *The Immortals*. By coincidence, *The Immortals* was my fifth novel too. He stays in a club in Malabar Hill, overlooking the building in which he'd grown up. I'd grown up in that building myself, and I knew the club. Amit Chaudhuri registers the absence of his school friend, Ramu, an on-and-off drug addict who, after recovering from an overdose, has gone off into rehab outside Bombay, and is inaccessible to the world. Amit is puzzled by the disorienting effect his friend's absence has on him. He hadn't expected it. He's also perplexed that the Taj Mahal hotel, which he visits in the evening to exchange two pairs of shoes that his mother and wife have sent with him, looks exactly as it used to, bearing no signs of the way it had been gutted in 2008. He knows the present Taj Mahal hotel is partly an illusion. The next morning he's interviewed by a newspaper journalist who turns up late; then has a Parsi lunch with his publishing rep at Britannia Restaurant; after which he goes with him to Strand Book Stall for a book signing. He's still missing Ramu. The first, and the largest section, of this short book ends before the reading happens. The second, very short, section has him return to Bombay a year and a half later for a literary festival. Ramu has managed to get himself extricated from rehab, and is back in Bombay. In the last, also very short, section, Amit returns to Bombay in the summer with his wife and daughter, and they stay at the Taj. This is a holiday, but Amit also designates it as "research": by now, he knows he's writing *Friend of My Youth*.

When the book came out, an interlocutor asked me, in the course of one of those events that newly published books can't do without, if everything I'd described in it had happened. "More or less, I suppose. Almost all of it," I said. "Then why call it a novel?" he asked, smiling pityingly, as if at a man who has a chronic problem he's not aware of. "Why not say it's a memoir?" I, by now, had an answer to this: how could a book that covers a day and a half in 2011, leading up to a reading that isn't described, followed by two short sections about separate visits, be called a "memoir"? What kind of memoir was this? A memoir must recount part or all of what has happened to oneself; here, the bits that formed the subject of the book—"bits" is not an inappropriate word, as Amit Chaudhuri's excursions are sporadic—are where nothing, in strict narrative terms, is taking place. No respectable memoir should take such a form.

A year or two later, it occurred to me that I'd been making a distinction that was important to me, but that it wasn't entirely accurate. When I'd said that most of what happened in *Friend of My Youth* was taken from life, this was true in one sense and untrue in another. For instance, that trip to Bombay in 2011; that reading from *The Immortals*; that stay at the club; the visit to the Taj with my mother's shoes—none of them had ever taken place. Each one of these events has occurred at different times, independently of each other: that is, I have indeed read in Bombay from *The Immortals*; I have undertaken shoe-exchanging missions to the Taj; I have stayed in the club overlooking the building in which I grew up (though never, perhaps, on a "book tour"); I have been interviewed by newspapers; I have eaten Parsi / Irani food at Britannia Restaurant. On visits to Bombay, I had also strangely, powerfully, missed my absent friend when he'd vanished for more than a year to rehab. This, in fact, was the prompt: the weighing of the idea of whether a novel could be written about missing a childhood friend upon revisiting the city in which one had grown up. The moment when such an idea surfaces is the moment when living's demarcation from, its anteriority to, writing fades, and the latter no longer remains a reporting of the former.

For all that, the episode I'd described in some detail over the first two thirds of the novel has no prior existence. It is an invention. Why invent such an episode? If I'm to be accused of writing from life, and if I also begin to blithely admit to doing so, I may as well earn the accusation. Why invent a situation unless to pursue a narrative goal, a denouement or dramatic event? Why construct in order to persuade a reader of something that doesn't require a suspension of disbelief: the fact that nothing, on the level of plot, is taking place? One of my dissatisfactions with the novel as a form has to do with it comprising what

Naipaul called "made up stories." But why "make up" something that isn't a story in the novelistic sense? In *The Prelude*, probably the first modern work, at least in English, to explore the intersection between memoir and poetic language, we note the convergence between artifice (that is, poetic form) with the re-addressing and re-formation of memory; that is, a performance not of memory being written about, but becoming what it is in the act of composition. But one can at least expect that the incidents Wordsworth dwells on *did* take place just as he relates them to us—"One evening (surely I was led by her) / I went alone into a Shepherd's Boat, / A Skiff that to a Willow tree was tied / Within a rocky Cave, its usual home"—and rely, too, on the fact that the point of these lines isn't some form of extraneous story-making. When Robert Lowell tells us of spotting, during his time in jail as a conscientious objector during the Second World War, the killer Lepke "piling towels on a rack," we feel that the image has poetic veracity, but also that it has a reasonable fidelity to fact. Lowell did glimpse Lepke with the towels. However, when I write, in *Friend of My Youth*—

> I have crossed the road. Opposite me is the building that came out of nowhere in the late seventies and partially blocked our view. Before then, we had an unbroken view of the Arabian Sea. The building is irrelevant to me now, but still causes a pinprick of irritation. It was an interloper—a tenant on the landscape—and continues to be one.
>
> In front of the building, upon the road—there's no pavement here—sits a woman on her haunches, displaying a basket of fruit. What she offers that the grocers' opposite don't, I can't say. In another area, there'd be a gaggle of squatting women. Here, she is one. One is enough for Little Gibbs Road.

—when I write these sentences, I have to think of each one carefully: not only to be true to my sense of what's significant, but also because I'm giving shape to what's never existed. Although I have crossed Little Gibbs Road many times, I never crossed it in March 2011 in the early evening, mainly because I wasn't in Bombay in March 2011. I never saw that woman sitting on her haunches selling fruit, though I may have seen such a woman at some time. The "pinprick of irritation" Amit feels when he glances at the building I may have experienced too, but not at that precise moment. Why not say what happened rather than fictionalise a nonhappening? Is that what Lowell meant when, struggling with self-doubt about his method and the fear that his poetry was "paralyzed by fact," he countered, "Yet why not say what happened? / Pray for the grace of accuracy / Vermeer gave to the sun's illumination"? Or did he have something slightly different in mind when making those connections and distinctions between "fact," "accuracy," and "illumination"? I'd certainly responded to the lines as a credo, though I now realise that, repeatedly, I haven't said "what happened." The July day in 1985 whose arc *Odysseus Abroad* follows is nonexistent. Everything in it is from life, and nothing in it is. In July that year, personally speaking, I was in Bombay, so there was no question of me running into Menelaus on Warren Street, Nestor at a college that was closed, let alone meeting Odysseus in Belsize Park. It's possible that I fabricated that day—dated, in my head, precisely, as 19 July, six days after the Live Aid concert, which Ananda / Telemachus has watched on TV with disdain, and one day after Shahnawaz Bhutto's death, which he learns of from a newspaper headline—it's possible I fabricated it in order to map on to it the Homeric epic. But there was no such compulsion towards inventing situations as far as *Friend of My Youth* was concerned, or *A Strange and Sublime Address*. In the latter, I describe two childhood visits made from Bombay by the boy Sandeep with his mother to his uncle's house in Calcutta. I made those visits too, to an uncle's house, in the same period in the twentieth century: though there are no dates in the novel. But the difference between the real visits and the ones in the novel isn't that something clearly "fictional" takes place in the latter. There's one factual divergence that would be important if I were for some reason looking for an alibi to cover my movements at the time;

my uncle had a heart attack, and I heard about it on the phone. Sandeep's uncle has a heart attack, and Sandeep is present, then, in the house in Calcutta. Otherwise, the difference between my actual visits and Sandeep's doesn't have to do with "fictionalising" in the sense we understand that term—that is, arranging for an element of "story" to creep in. The difference is that the former occurred while the latter never took place.

•

In 2000, I tried to make a break from the novel. I had returned to India from Britain in 1999, and these two events are, for me, related. My escape from Britain, where I'd lived in one capacity or another—student; poet manqué; published novelist—since 1983, was prompted by the startling changes, the homogeneity, coming over its culture. Thatcher's legacy affected the novel too. It seemed that a certain kind of novel—state-of-the-nation; multicultural; possibly compendious; possibly employing the dramatic monologue; exploring dystopias; novels with, for the want of a better definition, an entrepreneurial vigour—would flourish in Thatcher's Britain. Poetry would go out of business. The interesting young novelists who had made their name in the eighties—Ishiguro, McEwan, Barnes—would, over time, abandon the lyricism (*An Artist of the Floating World*) and eccentricity (*The Cement Garden*) that had marked their early work. The novel would morph into a robust form which would benefit from, and contribute to, the new features of literary culture in the Blair years, and, in fact, become indispensable to them: the Best of Young British Novelists and books of the year lists, and the annual Booker Prize spectacles which have ended up comprising the sole cultural landscape of planet Britain, with McEwan, Ishiguro, and the major figures of that literary generation keeping watch over it today like retired but still-active cabinet ministers.

My plan was not to flee Britain towards the Indian novel in English.

In fact, it was essential for me to flee the Indian novel in English too. The Indian novel in English became a major entrepreneurial form in the run-up to, and aftermath of, globalisation: this is what was meant when it began to be said commonly that it "straddled several worlds." No, my plan was to move to Calcutta. I remember thinking: "Why must the variety of the creative impetus I feel be accommodated by the novel alone? Certain things I want to say might be better expressed in an essay, story, poem, or even a musical composition. Why foreclose those options?" I formulated these questions because of the pressure on writers to write novels, and on the novelist to prove that they were novelists by producing a novel every two years. I took a break for what looks like, on paper, nine years.

•

Then I went back to it again; and then again, and again.

And now I ask myself why, when I could have stayed with the essay. It was not that I made an adjustment; that, having detoxified myself of the literary over those nine years, I'd finally started writing viable novels. *The Immortals*, published in 2009, is longer than all my other novels, but it is, I suspect, resistant—to, among other things, the expectations a bookseller might have of an Indian novel in English. Perhaps it's resistant at a more basic level. I recall the Pakistani novelist Nadeem Aslam saying to me that the thought, "But what will happen to Amit Chaudhuri?" had flashed through his mind when the chair of the Booker Prize judges in 2011, author and former director general of MI5 Stella Remington, had said of that year's reading, "We want our novels to zip along."

Today, I think again of how I have devised situations in novel after novel: situations in which there's no drama, but which, for me, try to convey great, if contained, excitement. It's the potential that this paradox has that probably draws me to the novel. I'm dependent on its structure and syntax—which otherwise bore me—to lead me to this excitement. By novelistic syntax I mean a kind of sentence without which the narrative's grammar—that is, the rules by which it is comprehended—falls apart. I mean a sentence like, "He got off the car and walked to the door"; or "I looked out of the window"; or "It seemed as if she was about to say something." The novel is full of sentences like these. You barely notice them, but they comprise the tools with which the narrative progresses. These sentences separate prose from poetic language, and fiction from the essay. You needn't structure your essay around such bland declarations because the essay, as a form, isn't reliant on a situation. It is more meditation than situation: time doesn't move forward intrepidly in it. A poem is a disjointed artefact. Two lines that follow each other in a poem don't necessarily constitute a progression; even two parts of the same line might retain an independence from each other.

The novel's syntax depends on joins, however: the sort of sentences I've mentioned above. When you hear that a novelist writes terrific sentences, you can assume safely it's not the joins that are being referred to. The great sentences are the ones that could just as well occur in an essay, or take the form of a line in a poem. But "He got off the car and walked to the door" can't have a durable habitation except in the novel. In the essay, it's a domiciled émigré rather than a natural member of the community. In the novel, it's invisible but always there, at the writer's disposal, essential to what Virginia Woolf called "the appalling business of the realist: getting from lunch to dinner." I can't think that I've turned to the novel repeatedly except for this reason, because of the availability of this peculiar syntax of fiction-writing. Otherwise, my interest in language and its relationship to the world is poetic and essayistic.

I abhor this syntax and its instrumental role in creating the effects of realism. So when people say to me that my novels aren't novels but are taken verbatim from life, they don't mean, then (obviously), that my novels are too real and not fictional enough to be called "novels," but that they don't abide by the rules of realism, which proclaim that a sentence like "He got up and opened the door" must lead to a story. Yet, as I've admitted already, it's precisely a sentence like "He got up and opened the door" that leads me again and again to the practice of writing fiction, rather than only essays or poems. What is it about such a sentence that I find enabling? And why, at once, do I find it so difficult to use? It's a difficulty that separates me from "natural" writers and readers of novels, who read, and presumably write, such sentences without exertion.

The difficulty lies in my resistance to the air of recounting; the air that something is over—that what you have before you as you read a novel is an event, or life, as well as an artefact, that's already finished. Discussions of narrative in creative writing classes will occasionally fall back on the edict, "Show; don't tell"; but this is an empty edict because, for me, the crux is "How do I not recount, and access the moment?" "Showing" is as embedded in the language of recounting in the novel as "telling" is. Roland Barthes, in *Writing Degree Zero*, quotes an observation from the poet Paul Valéry while reflecting on fiction. Valéry, Barthes reminds us, noted that novels always begin with a sentence like "The Marchioness went out at five o'clock." What's the distinction between telling and showing here? They've become one. The sentence ensures that the novel and the Marchioness are plunged into an action—something is about to happen—while, simultaneously, communicating the lulling assurance that the action is over and has been turned into, and domesticated as, story. For Barthes, this domestication is achieved by the preterite or simple past tense in which the sentence is written: it immediately introduces the reader to, and places the narrative within, "the unreal time of novels, cosmogonies, and histories," an "unreal time" that, Barthes complains, suppresses the "trembling of existence."

Yet it's only in the novel that time is a significant subject; rather than, say, a thought-process, as in the essay, or image, metaphor, or language, as in the poem. And, as a form, the novel is unimaginable without the simple past tense and the "The Marchioness went out at five o' clock" kind of sentence. But, while time can be presented as a recounting, it is also coterminous with the present moment, which is where we encounter time. Resolving these two things—the first a formal matter, inextricable from the grammar of narrative; the second (to do with encountering the moment) one of the possibilities of the form I'm most interested in—has been my chief preoccupation as a novelist, voluntarily undertaken. If I had written only essays and poems, there would have been nothing to resolve in this regard. It's because I'm a novelist that I need to work this out. It might even be that I am a novelist *because* I want to work this out. If you were to take Barthes literally, then exchanging the simple past tense to present tense should fix the problem. This is not the case. "He walks into the room" is really no better than "He walked into the room" at placing the life that's being written about (I mean not just the man's life, but the room's and what's outside it) in the present moment rather than in a story.

This is something I've had to grapple with from the start. For instance: I could have written *A Strange and Sublime Address*, my first novel, as a story about my childhood, set in the late sixties and early seventies. But I didn't, because I had no impulse towards recounting. I wrote it, instead, to place the action in the present moment, rather than in the past, or inside a recounted story. I didn't set about achieving this by writing in the present tense, but by aiming to arrive, during the nightmare of revision, at a sequence of sentences and paragraphs that didn't have the air of being "made up"; by which I mean they needed to sound as if they weren't "finished." A huge number of sentences and paragraphs were taken out, or their positions changed. The latter were left homeless, without their originally assigned locations. Other sentences were added later, not as bandages or plaster would be, to cover abrasions or absences, but in response to belated promptings. Words were removed and added on the same principle. What was left behind or then came into existence—words, sentences, paragraphs—didn't really follow each other but still aimed for an illusion of continuity.

It was a demoralising process. At first I thought I would be able to keep nothing except, maybe, a chapter. Without realising it, I'd started working at some point solely on the basis of the question, "What can I keep?" I'd put to one side the matter of how these bits of writing would hold together. I recall thinking, "So editing, in this case, is closer to a film editor's job than I'd realised": because the job of editors in cinema is to know what to keep and what to destroy, to spot what will survive from among the hours of footage, snip out the rest, and deal with continuity later. I see I made a note on my phone in June this year: "My novels are not made up of the sentences I've written, but the sentences I've kept." Composition, for me, is salvage.

•

To me, a sentence that serves as a purely functional join in the syntax of the novel, like "They drove towards the building," is as much hard work, and requires as much attentiveness, as a sentence like this one from *Afternoon Raag*, my second novel, in which the narrator is describing his mother's hair: "It falls in long, black strands, but each strand has a gentle, complicated undulation travelling through it, like a mild electric shock or a thrill, that gives it a life of its own; it is visually analogous to a tremolo on a musical note." I don't consider "They drove towards the building" easier to write than that sentence from *Afternoon Raag*. If anything, it's more difficult. It has the potential to plunge the narrative into the "unreal time" of fiction. But it also presents an opportunity vis a vis situation that I wouldn't have in an essay or poem, the sort of situation in which no drama takes place, but through which the present can be encountered. This encounter involves an immersion quite different from immersion in a story. I must now determine what the join's shape, sound, and position are in relation not only to the story, but to the moment. Do I say "They drove towards the building" or "They drove to the building"? Do I want "towards," with its particular weight, or the closeness to speech that "to" has? What kind of adjustment would lead to freedom from recounting? Do I wish the building to take greater charge, as in "The building became visible" or, more strongly, "The building rose before them"? But "The building rose before them" is too dramatic. Can I get away with "The building came up," even though it sounds odd? These decisions need to be taken as one deliberately employs the grammar of recounting, but not in order to recount. This leads to my courting minor discrepancies and, occasionally, an unobtrusive element of unevenness in grammatical construction; such as, for instance, writing a sentence in the past perfect tense in its first half and changing the tense to simple past in the second. These changes will sometimes be queried by a copy editor, as will the fact that I'd referred to "houses on Marine Drive" on page thirty-two but wrote "They stopped at the Marine Drive to look at the sea" on page fifty. "Which should it be?" the copy editor will ask. 'Marine Drive' or '*the* Marine Drive'? Change to 'the Marine Drive' throughout?" I will lamely say, both about the transition from past perfect to simple past tense and from "Marine Drive" to "the Marine Drive"—"Please keep as is." Then I'll wonder why I said this: am I lazy, or in love with my own writing? But what's there in *these* sentence*s* to be in love with? I then start to reluctantly understand that my request to not do away with the discrepancies is my way of both using narrative syntax and fighting it. Recounting is dislodged by the nonobservance of house style.

•

The sentences I've quoted above were invented for the purpose of this talk. They aren't *real* sentences from a work of fiction, though that's where they belong. My novels have them too; my first novel opens with:

"He saw the lane." If I quoted only these sentences from my fiction, you'd think I write "normal" novels.

Let me turn to two sentences, selected at random, from *Friend of My Youth* to share with you specific examples of my use of the syntax of fiction. Amit has woken up in the club, had breakfast, and is killing time until the journalist arrives. Tired of waiting, he gets up. Should he return to his room? The narrator says, "I decide to walk up the stairs to my room and glimpse, through the latticed window, the building in which I grew up. It isn't as if I'd forgotten it; it's just that I see no point in looking at it directly." The opening of the first sentence, "I decide to walk up the stairs," is the sort of join that Woolf said was charged with the "appalling business of the realist: getting from lunch to dinner"—a sentence that's meant not to waste time, but kill it, as Amit is trying to do. It is only justified—that bit of time-killing—if it fulfils the expectation of a happening. The happening, in this case, would be the arrival of the journalist. But the second half of the sentence involves Amit in the kind of nonhappening that absorbs me more than the journalist's arrival: "I decide to walk up the stairs to my room and glimpse, through the latticed window, the building in which I grew up." What kind of work have I done on a sentence like this? I can't actually remember, but am extrapolating after rereading. First, I haven't put a comma after "my room," although I know I risk causing momentary confusion as to whether Amit had decided both to go up the stairs *and* glimpse the building through the latticed window: "I decide to walk up the stairs to my room and glimpse, through the latticed window, the building in which I grew up." A comma would have made clearer that "decide" pertains only to walking up, and that the glimpsing is part-accidental: but I want this experience to remain in a continuum where I'm not assigning hierarchy to one bit of the sentence over the other. If I'd placed a comma after "my room," the opening, "I decide to walk up the stairs to my room," would have been functional, and the second half of the sentence would have priority in terms of emotion and shift of perception. Which is why, presumably, I jettison the comma, risking a moment's confusion for the reader as they yoke different parts of the sentence, and Amit's experience, together.

The other modulation has to do with the word "and": "I decide to walk up the stairs to my room *and* glimpse, through the latticed window, the building in which I grew up." Another word I could perhaps use here is "but": which would, as with a comma, make a clear break, and indicate which part of the sentence is join and information, which bit emotional charge. I'm reluctant to make that distinction, and opt, instead, for "and." The conjunction is possibly the most unnoticed of words in language: "but" can have a degree of portentousness; "and" is entirely instrumental. Yet it can also help in belying expectations, as it is meant to in this case, by *denying* the emotion that "but" would have introduced. There *is* a shift in emotion in the sentence's second half: flagging it up would deaden it.

Of course, the fact that the narrator glimpses the building in which he grew up should itself constitute an event in a novel. The sentence that follows the one I've been discussing is a reiteration of what the reader already knows from what they've read so far, but may no longer have in mind: "It isn't as if I'd forgotten it; it's just that I see no point in looking at it directly." This means that glimpsing the building through the latticed window isn't accidental at all; it's related to a deliberate plan of avoidance. This is why Amit allows himself a look at this point—because of the partial view the lattice permits protects him from a frontal encounter. These dramas need to be shaped by the words which comprise the most humdrum bits of fiction, those that have to do with killing time, but which contain fluctuations between anticipation and anticlimax.

•

There's a popular TV show on British television called *Would I Lie To You?* Two teams face each other, and tell each other stories. The aim is to find out which of these stories are lies: points are giving to teams accordingly. The winning team is the one whose members have been best at sniffing out the other one's bluffs and themselves been most successful at bluffing. What makes the lies and truths—all of which constitute real or so-called episodes in each team member's life—so hard to distinguish from each other is that they're equally absurd or unbelievable. What's clear is that no claim that has the air of the commonplace or everyday could ever be anything but true. The lies pose as truths, and truths pose as lies: they can play these double parts because they all possess an element of the extraordinary. As I write about what's deemed to be "ordinary," my stories are taken to true. Why would anyone *make up* an episode that has nothing aberrant or outrageous in it, a "story" that has no "story"? But this is precisely what I do. I make up stories about my life, but, unlike the contestants on the panel, about those bits in which nothing much is happening. I turn to the syntax of fictional narrative to do this. My aim is the same as that of the bluffers on *Would I Lie To You*—to make the extraordinary seem plausible. None of my stories—according to the rules set down by the show—can be called true.

•

A few times each day, we experience moments that awaken our sleeping selves as we go about our routine. These are moments of anticipation, but they're unrelated to any actual development. Actual developments in life are rare, and, when they happen, can be confusing, disappointing, or boring. The moments of anticipation that stimulate us in the midst of our daytime sleepwalking have to do with getting up from a chair, changing position on a sofa, opening a door, or looking out through a window or from a balcony. The day would be unbearable—inconceivable—without these, to all purposes, pointless internal departures. The joins that are legitimately scattered throughout, and which structure, the novel have the unique potential to trace the journey of this excitement—for instance, "She opened the door"; or, "He looked down from the balcony." Instead, they're seen to be unimportant in themselves, admissible only in order to introduce an actual development. To me, the actual development is a bogey of realist fiction in its many varieties, including historical and science fiction. Drama is also contained in sentences that are only meant to carry us, like those small cars inside airport terminals, from one place or happening to another.

•

Part of what I've called the novel's syntax also comprises what Nabokov termed its "subliminal coordinates." One of the things he probably meant by "subliminal coordinates" was that if you, the writer of a novel, introduce an uncle with a limp on page 24, you are obliged to have him reappear at two or three other points in the narrative. I say this from memory, but, even if it isn't reliable, it defines the kind of observance that realist fiction needs to adhere to. The novel isn't a form in which you can mention the uncle with a limp and forget about him for the rest of the story. The uncle with a limp, or the coordinate, is yet another metaphor for the novel's grammar of recounting.

For me, there's an element in narrative composition that I think of as a countervailing force to the limping uncle. I'll call it the "outlier." An "outlier" is a detail that doesn't perform a structural duty in the novel; it is among its unacknowledged raisons d'être. I will provide three examples from cinema. The first is a scene from *North by Northwest*, in which Cary Grant finds himself creeping through, then hanging from an escarpment on, Mount Rushmore, adjacent to the carved faces of America's founding fathers. Hitchcock had carried the idea with him for a long time—to make the face of Mount Rushmore the scene of action somehow. The opportunity presented itself with *North by Northwest*. Another example of the outlier is the head massage scene in Guru Dutt's *Pyaasa*. When Dutt saw an itinerant barber administering a massage in Calcutta, he knew he needed to incorporate this moment in a film, and, in *Pyaasa*, his penultimate feature, found a way of doing so. My third example of an outlier is again from Hitchcock, though Hitchcock has never spoken about this scene as he did about the one in *North by Northwest*. It's from *Vertigo*. A retired private detective played by James Stewart has been recruited by his friend to investigate his wife's mysterious behaviour and movements. Stewart discovers that his friend's wife is often deluded that she is an obscure but tragic character from San Francisco's history, Carlotta Valdes. To find out more about who Carlotta was, Stewart and his ex-fiancée and partner Midge, played by Barbara Bel Geddes, go to a secondhand bookshop run by a local historian. Once they've finished listening to the historian's account, Stewart and Bel Geddes step out onto the street. The light has faded and the sun's gone down during the discussion. As Stewart and Bel Geddes stand there, talking animatedly, the light in the secondhand bookshop is turned on, illuminating the space within. You feel that Hitchcock had to wait to find a place in one of his films for this moment. It is an outlier.

By outlier I mean something inessential which waits for years for a plot to accommodate it. In the meantime, it lies out there, without a home, but also without impatience. Nabokov's subliminal coordinate is a structuring device, working in cooperation with the syntax of realist narrative. The outlier waits for the plot to structure itself around *it*. The outlier sees no inherent purpose in plot or narrative except as an excuse to give a home to its own redundancy. A great deal of the process of artistic composition has to do not with narrative using detail to inform and order as it goes about the business of recounting a story, but with detail waiting for plot to recognise what its own function truly is: a structure justified by the outlier's existence.

When I go to the notes at the back of the exercise book in which I wrote *A Strange and Sublime Address* in 1986, I find no plot directions or jottings about theme or character. Instead, there are numbered points covering possible chapters, many containing no more than a reminder for things to do on a particular day might: "Goes to the tailor's"; "Aunt buys a fish from the market"; etc. These are not subliminal coordinates, but outliers. They are redundant to my story, which, as it happens, is quite basic—a boy from Bombay visits his uncle, who is struggling to run his business. On the second visit during the winter, the uncle will have a heart attack and then recover. There isn't much about this in the plan I made in the back. Instead, I find a list of redundancies around which the plot is meant to arrange itself.

•

A year prior to my making those notes, I was intent on becoming a published poet. I had no idea I would begin writing a novel the following year, not least because I'd never been a great reader of fiction. Today, I still wonder why I write novels. It isn't to master an art that I have no desire to master, but, evidently, to create something out of my perplexity with the form.

Two Floors Above the Butcher

2023, *McSweeney's*

I STOPPED LISTENING to Neil Diamond around 1977. I was drawn to him when I was eleven or twelve, in '73 or '74, and he became part of my weekly listening routine, along with a bunch of other musicians, some of whom I became disloyal to very quickly (like the Carpenters and John Denver), and others whom I continued to flaunt till I was sixteen (like the Who, Deep Purple, the Beatles, Paul Simon). Neil Diamond inhabited a location between these extremities. I had only two records by him: *Hot August Night*, the capacious double-album recording of a live performance at the exotic Greek Theatre in Los Angeles, and his *Greatest Hits*. Of the tracks on the latter, "Cracklin' Rosie" and "Sweet Caroline" were too optimistic and upbeat for me, but there were other songs I listened to even when I no longer owned up to doing so: "Holly Holy," "Brother Love's Travelling Salvation Show," "Brooklyn Roads." I liked the way Neil Diamond could work up raucous emotion (as in "Holly Holy") with, predominantly, two chords and words that didn't mean very much ("Holly holy eyes"). The way Diamond created energy and affirmation with just a couple—or barely more than a couple—of major chords (the simplest of harmonic structures) in songs like "Cherry, Cherry" and "Holly Holy" makes me think of him, retrospectively, in relation to the African musicians who created the "happy tunes" that became important to Paul Simon. This affirmation seemed part of his makeup, but it was also vulnerable to a commercialisation that turned it into something cheerful—with songs like "Sweet Caroline," to an extent, but more so as his career progressed and the world itself, with the onset of the '80s, changed to a marketplace.

"Brother Love's Travelling Salvation Show" was so full of voices, personae, and shifting imagery that listening to it felt like watching a short film; with its portrayal of the ecstasies of evangelism one "hot August night" inside a "ragged tent" in the South, it was evidence of Diamond's gift for delving into local histories that lay well outside his Jewish childhood in Brooklyn. Sitting in my drawing room in Malabar Hill in Bombay, I had as diffuse an idea of what "gospel" and "preaching" meant as a boy in Manhattan or London would have had, but songs like Diamond's (besides comic books and movies) gave those diffuse sensations the immediacy of the local—they felt more real, sometimes, than my actual surroundings. The drawing room in Bombay seemed pallid at times. To escape it, I went to my uncle's house in Calcutta—or to the urgent realities encountered in such songs.

The song I liked best on *Greatest Hits* was "Brooklyn Roads." No one who listened to Neil Diamond ever mentioned it. I wonder now how it made it onto the *Greatest Hits*: was it an indulgence on Diamond's part? Nor have I been able to track down a live recording except a middle-aged version which I've not had the courage to listen to in its entirety. The way the song lay concealed within the album— there but not there, camouflaged as a hit and thereby doubly unnoticed, taken to be a hit but never spoken of—meant that the relationship I had with it was equally hidden, part of my pop song landscape but also outside it. Though I couldn't make out every word, I could follow most of them—enough to realise that something deep was being recovered in the song, deep and deeply ordinary, things that didn't find a place in pop songs:

When I close my eyes
I can almost hear my mother
calling, "Neil, go find your brother..."

The first shock was the word "Neil." The names of pop stars were indistinguishable to me from inventions, and, to a thirteen-year-old who still didn't know Jewish names well, "Neil Diamond" was generic, like "Ziggy Stardust" or "David Bowie." It was disorienting and affecting to register, each time I heard the song, the singer singing his own name and reliving his mother's voice and directive. Why was I affected? I had no brother myself. My mother was in the midst of life. I didn't need to "close my eyes" to see her. The act of recall in relation to her and my home would come eight years later, when I'd go to London. The "closing of my eyes" would come after 2016, when she died. But a part of me already contained who I would become, which included what I would lose, just as the person I would become would contain who I had been (which contained who I would be). That same echoing space-time was also the experience of the man who had written the song.

Dinnertime made up the song's opening scene:

Go find your brother.
Daddy's home and it's time for supper.
Hurry on.

Having closed his eyes to bring back the past, Diamond gazes upon it as if it were happening to someone else, and the lyrics shift to the third person:

Two boys
racing up two flights of staircase,
squirming into Papa's embrace
and his whiskers warm on their face.

Then there's a groaning return to the present: "Oh, where's it gone?," which would risk sentimentality were the song mourning a greater loss, but is made real by its longing for the banal. The chorus locates the childhood precisely:

> Two floors above the butcher,
> first door on the right,
> and life filled to the brim
> as I stood by my window
> and looked out on those
> Brooklyn Roads.

I took this to be a provincial location, slightly cut-off but "filled to the brim" with its own reality. The songwriter I met in "I Am . . . I Said" seemed to be a kind of universal voice laying claim to a city that existed only in the popular imagination:

> Well, I'm New York City born and raised,
> but nowadays I'm lost between two shores.
> LA's fine but it ain't home.
> New York's home, but it ain't mine no more.

This was the kind of thing any songwriter could say, irrespective of nationality. New York in pop songs (like Elton John's "Mona Lisas and Mad Hatters") was the place everyone belonged to and had been exiled from. "Brooklyn," in Diamond's song, was inalienable and nonmetropolitan; I forgot, listening to the song, that it was in New York.

The next bit of "Brooklyn Roads," still lingering on "smells of cooking in the hallways," moves closer to the kind of boy I was becoming by the time I was fourteen: "report cards I was always afraid to show." Then there were my parents' visits to school in 1976: "Teacher'd say, 'He's just not tryin'. / Got a good head if he'd apply it." In bringing back that conversation, Diamond revisits some of the upheaval it caused. The boy's way of coping was familiar:

> I built me a castle
> with dragons and kings,
> and I'd ride off with them
> as I stood by my window
> and looked out on those Brooklyn Roads.

By the song's end, the singer speculates on a form of continuance:

> Does some other young boy
> come home to my room?
> Does he dream what I did as he stands by my window
> and looks out on those
> Brooklyn Roads?

The life that Diamond describes was more like my cousins' lives in Calcutta—two brothers and a sister; flights of stairs in a three-storey house; smells of boiling rice, mustard oil, talcum powder—than my hovering, incorporeal existence in a twelfth-storey apartment in Bombay, looking out not from a window onto a street and other windows, as my cousins did, but—where California and Manhattan merged—on the expanse of the Arabian Sea, the palm-fronded Marine Drive, and the tall buildings of the '70s skyline. Desiring other worlds ("dreaming") gave me corporeality: I led a plausible, proxy childhood in Calcutta, and Diamond's Brooklyn felt close for those three minutes, as if I were racing up the staircase myself. But through the shifts between selves that poetry and fiction create, and that make ideas like point of view and identification limited in their usefulness, I was also that "other young boy" who came "home to my room." The contradictions language accommodates without blinking! How could another person come "home" to *my* room? It was possible, apparently. You become part of someone's life without knowing it.

In 1977, I began to direct my attention to Joni Mitchell. The next year I started learning North Indian classical music. I became less up front about having listened to Neil Diamond.

•

In September 2022, almost exactly three years after I'd last been there, I was in New York again, accompanied by my wife, having strategised for the dates of my visit to coincide with the publication of a novel. We stayed on Second Avenue in Manhattan, not far from the United Nations—though we never ventured in that direction, but walked only toward Third Avenue and Grand Central Terminal. I had loved New York's "terrible oxygen" of fumes and urine when I'd visited it in 1979. It had seemed incomparably novel, like Calcutta. (The words I've just put in quotation marks are from Elizabeth Bishop's "The Fish." They're meant to remind us that an environment that's life-giving for one creature [man] may be fatal for another—the fish of the title. In 1979, New York was proof that the opposite was also true: a noxious atmosphere can be vitalising.) By the time I went to New York again, in 2000, something in it had died, and what I experienced on subsequent visits was a hollowness. But on this occasion (Was it my wife's company? Had something in New York come back to life after the pandemic? Or both?), I was more grounded and felt connected to the city's everyday—like the lonesome people who ambled outside the homeless shelter on Forty-Fifth Street—in a way I hadn't before.

So, in that upbeat mood, I started making plans for expeditions: not just to the Met or MoMA or Central Park or the High Line, but to revisit with my wife half-remembered locations from my prepandemic excursions in the city—places I didn't really know but where I'd crossed a street or arrived at a junction or church and thought, There are parts of this city that are real, after all, or where I'd stored away a number, like Thirteenth Street. I did not know exactly where to go, but clung to the realisation that there was more to New York than I'd assumed. Ever since we'd passed through Chelsea in an Uber one afternoon (a September afternoon in which one neighbourhood gave way to another like cards fanning out) on the way to a venue (the City Winery) at which I was going to perform, I'd thought we should return later to look for the Chelsea Hotel. This was because of these lines, which contain something epochal and unfinished:

> I remember you well at the Chelsea Hotel.
> You were talking so brave and so sweet.
> Giving me head on the unmade bed,
> while the limousines wait in the street.

Unfinished because the act itself seems incomplete, unless it comes to some sort of fruition later; there is also that moving, clumsy shift to the present tense in the fourth line, as if the singer is distracted by the possibility that the limousines are *still* waiting. This was a song that had not been in my Leonard Cohen selection (*Songs of Love and Hate*, et cetera) as a teenager. I discovered it on YouTube seven or eight years ago. It immediately brought back the world of that time as well as the fact that much of it was unknown to me. And my wife and I did find the hotel two afternoons post–Uber ride. I have always eschewed author-related tourism. If I should come upon a poet's house, living or dead, by accident, or because someone has taken me there by the scruff of my neck, all well and good. But as an objective in itself, it never seems worthwhile. But pursuing the scent of songs! That's a different matter. It was on this trip that the fact that songs can be habitations crept up on me. I wanted to know what the Chelsea Hotel was. Expectedly, it's a tourist destination. We viewed it from outside—so recognisable, like a building on Chowringhee—and then went in for ten minutes, barely noticed by the doorman. We peered into the bar and used the bathroom, as we always do when we're at a hotel. Within and around it, the atmosphere was sexually charged, a large part of the charge emanating from a tall androgynous woman who dominated the corridor and who, when we walked out, was chatting with the doorman. This was the kind of area that took a step further the pink-rimmed spectacles and pink shoes that have multiplied in the last decade; a home for every common-or-garden exhibitionist. When your gaze fell on them, as mine did on a muscular man who had adorned his bare torso with a dinner jacket and bow tie, they looked deflated, as if I'd brought back a memory of a place they'd come from and were pretending no longer existed. My wife and I did not belong here. Still, we liked Chelsea very much.

•

Then my wife left. She was scheduled to fly back a week before me. I had to deliver a lecture in Massachusetts and perform in a concert. Then I would return to New York for a day and a half, though that drawing out of my stay served no clear purpose. I wanted to go home. But suppose something came up beyond my planned itinerary, something I hadn't foreseen when finalising my schedule? The last day and a half were added for such a possibility.

An author I hadn't seen for years and I decided to have lunch on the day of my departure. On the penultimate day, I thought I'd follow up on a long-deferred project: interviewing the poet Charles Bernstein with my phone camera at MoMA, where he'd elaborate on what he'd called, when my wife and I had visited MoMA in February 2019, "MoMA's view of modern art." Ever since that evening, I had hoped to one day record Charles's—not his *tirade*, but the part-flippant, part-interrogatory stream of thought he'd shared with us as we'd walked through the various rooms. I'd had to wait three years—and for the pandemic to recede—to record this conversation. We decided to meet at MoMA at 11:00 a.m., before the crowds entered in full force.

But for more than a week, I'd been thinking of "Brooklyn Roads." I had been thinking, on and off, of Neil Diamond. As I walked between gigantic outgrowths of buildings, snatches of lines came back to me: "Neil, go find your brother"; "it's time for supper. Hurry up." I'd already been to Brooklyn on this visit, to Greenpoint Avenue, an area that still retained accumulations of history—the everyday of another time—in its facades. But the boutiques were there, too, disguised but unmistakable. Across an empty lot, you could see the East River. Still, the area had a purity that I had missed in DUMBO, my first experience of Brooklyn, in 2013. When I'd taught at Columbia University for a term in 2002, a friend, Merv Rothstein, had urged me to go to Brooklyn, where he'd grown up, to check out the museum. The semester ended and I realised I never went. A decade had passed, but DUMBO was not what I had expected Brooklyn to be. This was because DUMBO itself, caught between gentrification and the ghosts of old neighbourhoods, didn't know what it was.

I googled "neil diamond's birthplace" and "neil diamond house brooklyn"; I googled "Brooklyn Roads." I discovered he'd lived in the Coney Island section of Brooklyn. From comic books, Coney Island had associations for me of fairground violence: bright lights, Ferris wheels, gangs. Yet Wikimapia gave exact coordinates for "Neil Diamond's childhood apartment" as Church Avenue, N 40°39'3" W 73°56'54"—or perhaps these numbers located what were classified as "related objects": Tövhid Mescidi (with the *e* facing the opposite direction) and Ram's Roti Shop. A box that said "apartment building" above it, but displayed only a grey strip running through a light grey background, had the caption, "The Apartment Neil Diamond sang about in Brooklyn Roads is on the third floor of this building. These are the windows he 'looked out on those Brooklyn Roads.'" Custom

NYC Tours had a post from 2017 whose opening sentence was promising: "I was contacted by someone today about the possibility of doing a Neil Diamond–themed tour in Brooklyn." Another post from four years ago by the same man—Jeremy Wilcox, who claimed he often walked by Diamond's old apartment—revealed that a one-off excursion had taken place but evidently had never been repeated. I began to feel frustrated, but also very close to the communities, individuals, and shadow-objects I encountered on these pages. I also found that Diamond had grown up in a house near the Oceana Theater, a movie hall by the Brighton Beach subway stop.

Post-MoMA, after I'd had lunch and said goodbye to Charles Bernstein, I realised I had nothing to do for the rest of the day. I weighed my options and decided to go to Brighton Beach. I had no idea where or what it was. I liked the name.

Google Maps said it would take me an hour to get there. This would mean two hours spent on travel and maybe an hour or more looking for Neil Diamond's house. This was a bigger commitment than any I'd made so far in New York. I had avoided parties and social calls on this visit—almost everything except promotional trips. Thinking these thoughts, I made my way to Grand Central Terminal from Fifth Avenue.

A self from another historical age wondered if I would get lost if I went that far. My present self reassured me that that wasn't possible; I had a smartphone. What I had to do was make sure I didn't lose my iPhone (which I had done in New York in 2019, in a taxi)—but I was more careful these days about the trousers I wore and the pockets they had.

At the entrance to Grand Central, a few seconds in, someone always sat next to a shop on the floor, with their feet stretched out, reading aloud to themselves from a book, ignoring passersby and being ignored. This was the last familiar thing I'd see for a while. I took the line 7 train to Times Square, not sure if it was uptown or downtown I wanted, and then I took the line Q to Coney Island, three stops before which was

Brighton Beach. There was also the line B, whose last stop in the Brooklyn direction was Brighton Beach, which I didn't take for some reason.

Once I was aimed at Coney Island, I relaxed and allowed myself to puzzle over which stop I really wanted. The previous day, I'd seen a video, posted twelve years ago, of Neil Diamond arriving on Church Avenue with the intention of walking to his erstwhile "home." In fact, the video was called "Welcome Home Neil Diamond." It was mobile phone footage; he had caught the attention of passersby because he had a camera crew with him. Maybe they were making a documentary. The first question he got was from a Black woman, clearly curious about his entourage: "What's your name?"—an ingenuous and, under the circumstances, engaged query, and Diamond sees it as one; he smiles and shrugs slightly and says, "Neil Diamond." "Ah, okay, Neil. I'm Angie," says the woman. "Hi, Angie!" says Neil, and then, in reply to another question, "I lived here when I grew up here when I was a kid." "You gotta be kidding! How many years ago?" "You want me to tell you for real?" "Yeah." "Fifty." "Fifty *years*? I've lived here since... thirty... thirty-seven years. Guess how old I am." Now comes a display of Diamond's gallantry: "You look like twenty-one to me." "Oh, thank you! I'm forty-eight." "*No*..." In that moment the video is no longer about Diamond but about Angie and how exceptional she is. It is about her life story, emerging from Diamond's life story ("I lived here when I grew up here"), which she knows nothing about. And I felt it was possibly the same for me; that I had a life outside my own on Church Avenue. Diamond himself looks middle-class, not in the English sense of being university-educated, but of being modest, unassuming, on the right side of the law, a man who did not disappoint his parents. In a sense, he's free of his tortured pop past, free to wander Church Avenue. He points to the front and says what sounds like "I grew up here, between Argo and Westminster Road." I don't know if "Argo" is right. I google it. I wonder if I should disembark at Church Avenue.

•

But I didn't. I went to Brighton Beach in the state of arrest that comprised the protracted journey. The train wasn't full. It was also not stopping at each stop on the line. People got on and off without the fixity of purpose you saw in central Manhattan. As we went farther, the commuters grew visibly desultory and more remote from whatever it is that drives Manhattan and the rest of the world. I asked a girl with vaguely punk-like attributes if I was on the right train and she nodded with the pity and understanding you show a stranger, and confirmed, when she got off, how many stops away I was. To emerge into sunlight again was a revelation: bits of the city I had not seen before and didn't know when I'd see again. I subdued my restiveness, my urge to get off at Church Avenue, for example, or Cortelyou Road, which research had told me was germane to my quest. As the train moved closer to my destination, I took photos of some stations because of their vacancy and width and pastoral names (Sheepshead Bay), but the pictures couldn't capture what I saw. As we pulled into the Brighton Beach station, the tracks seemed to narrow, shielded by platform, and from the window I saw rooftops, flat and white, platform-level, ripple back, a counter to the infinitely high buildings I'd been with on my visit and the memory of which had started receding.

Everything here was narrow, staircases and escalators included. I didn't know in which direction to exit, and, as is often the case in the United States, but was especially true here, a porter and I spoke to each other in English without understanding each other, as if each were speaking a foreign language. When I descended and walked under the frozen filigree of steel girders and then crossed the road in the sunlight, I obeyed Google Maps and turned left. Out of the corner of my eye, or with eyes I had in the back of my head, I spotted a shop called Tashkent Supermarket under the bridge. From the journey so far, and the view from the platform, I knew—as if I had already lived here for a month or more—that this was a predominantly Russian area. But the war with Ukraine seemed as removed from what I was entering (as I walked farther in) as Manhattan did: this was a Russia of groceries and retired people. At the end of the brief stretch I saw two street signs, CONEY ISLAND AVENUE and VALERIY "LARRY" SAVINKIN STREET, the first reiterating that I was deliciously close to the edge of nowhere, the second reminding me how street signs are at once local and universal; they make you intimate with a history even if you have no idea where you are, something you forget when you're surrounded by names that perform their own meaning, like Columbus Circle, and tell you, literally, that you've "arrived." Discovery stops there.

I crossed the road after those signs. My destination was at hand, Google said. A woman was rearranging things in her shopping bag and, next to her, on a bench on the pavement, a man who could have been from anywhere was speaking and swearing into his mobile phone in a severely Punjabi-inflected Urdu. SHOE REPAIR, read a shop sign, with presumably the same words below in Russian. An elderly lady in a red cardigan was reviewing her display of porcelain dolls and crockery on a table. Behind her was the New Brighton Jewish Center. I realised I was on the wrong side of the road. I asked a woman (almost everyone had shopping bags with them; maybe not being at home meant holding shopping bags) if she knew where Neil Diamond's house was, and she said, "Who?" Guarded by scaffolding were a couple of optimistic figures: a small man with a rucksack, and a woman who was wearing what appeared to be a combination of a Rajasthani ghaghra and a costume for a Bollywood dance number, complete with head covering, goldwork, and border. They seemed like neither migrants nor tourists, but something out of Picasso. I didn't bother to ask them about Neil Diamond. Instead, I said: "Where are you from?" The woman said, "Russia," and I asked if I could take a picture.

A taxi company came up. By now I knew that the Oceana Theater, the continuous warehouse-like block next to me, had been converted into a supermarket. "Did Neil Diamond live here?" I asked the operator behind the glass. I spelled the name and asked him to look it up on the internet. "Ah, a singer!" He assessed me, not without empathy. He said the Oceana Theater was where we were. We were both talking about a man and a location that one of us thought he knew and the other thought he didn't, but neither could be sure that what he knew was, in fact, true. Having wasted each other's time, we parted cordially. I stepped into the sunlight, turned at the end of the road, went up the steps, and peered inside at stacks of fruit. I confirmed that the supermarket also occupied the second floor. I had in mind some corroboration of the precise directions: "Two floors above the butcher, first door on the right." Whatever might have corresponded to this had been replaced by something that wasn't simply a usurper but had its own ongoing heaviness and presence. Or it was likely that I hadn't got my bearings right.

•

Crossing the road, I entered a park that had curving art deco steps going up to areas where retired men and women sat on benches, waiting for a moment when, as at the end of a film, they'd reach the end of what they'd come for. As is always the case, the men looked indifferent and at ease and the women subtly unhappy. I felt the urge to sit on a bench and become part of the park's life, but something in me, a posthumousness, resisted and drew back. One is so often at a threshold of another life but chooses to retain, in a moment of wakefulness, what one takes to be one's identity. So I turned back toward the metro station, thinking, But where is Brighton Beach? Is there such a place? A Sikh appeared, white-bearded, in a purple salwar kameez, and I followed him, as you do a person who reminds you of home, in case they *take* you home. But he did not, and instead stopped at a shop on the boulevard, going in and, with equal efficiency, coming out in a few seconds because they didn't have what he wanted. I took a photo of him against the light—a diffuse, blinding radiance surrounding him, as if there had been an explosion. He noted me without caring, as ghosts or beings not bound by gravity hardly care for the living, among whom he counted me. I would always remember seeing him, as you do a being from another world, but I would have no place in his memory. The light behind him indicated (I didn't think this then; I feel it now) that the sea was *that* way, which is probably why I kept walking, turning at Brighton Sixth Street, stopping to peruse the Soviet delicacies on the menu of Café Euroasia, going farther, ostensibly to embrace the buildings, but also because I had glimpsed the ocean. I finally came to the boardwalk. Frozen largesse: gold—the sea, sand, and sunlight. It made me feel Brighton Beach was a fiefdom unto itself. A young woman in a bikini, every part of her body reflecting the sun, was complaining to an old man, her companion: "It's hard, you know? It's not easy." He was like the aging hunger that sought nourishment; she like the prize that telltale marks say is not as young as it seems. Next moment, after I'd veered off and returned, they were like brother and sister reunited, he a prematurely aging boy, she shrinking into childhood, curled up against each other on the deck chair.

I went back to the stairs going up to the metro station and had to decide how to proceed. The Oceana Theater location might have been wishful thinking. I could go back to Manhattan; that would be a relief. I mustn't tire myself out before a long journey—although the journey back to India the next day felt long only academically, in light of my present outing. I could check out Church Avenue, where Diamond had been when he'd said he was heading for the place he'd grown up in. What was the name? Westminster Road. To get there, I'd need to get off at Church Avenue, or at Cortelyou Road and take a bus. Where on Westminster Road, though, was this apartment, "two floors above the butcher"? I got onto a line Q train headed toward Manhattan, putting in abeyance the stop where I'd eventually get off. I disembarked at Newkirk Plaza. Its platform tapered to a point where only two human beings could stand comfortably. (Consulting my photo, I see this is not strictly true. The entire platform is narrow and tapered, and the end feels like a jetty, like an idea that's fading, because you can see the tracks vanish from there.) There was an object on the platform that was neither palanquin nor cage. It was latticed on top and had a gazebo-type covering. It was locked. At first, I thought there was an animal inside. It could be that metro employees traditionally kept their belongings in it. I waited for the train to Church Avenue.

•

Church Avenue underlined what the video had suggested: it was in a Black (and, as I'd see, Jamaican) district. Even to cross at a traffic light was a tropical event. I asked a couple of people about Westminster Road, and they complied with a wishful "over there," as if saying so might make it true. So I decided to go down East Eighteenth Street instead.

Turning left into Albemarle Road, I found a group of women, between fifty and sixty years old, chatting in front of an old residential building. They were so absorbed and happy and oblivious that I wanted to introduce myself. "I have a question," I said. They blinked, as at an incursion by a fly or a ball from across the street. "Any idea where I might find Neil Diamond's house? I've heard it's in these parts." "Neil who?" In a moment, this changed. One of them said, "Oh, the singer! I know who you mean!" They looked a bit put out. "Oh, he's in Manhattan!" This threw me. "In Manhattan?" "Yes, Manhattan!" It came to me that she was conjecturing that anyone successful must live on that side of the city. "No, no, the house in which he grew up! Haven't you heard it's in Brooklyn? Have you heard "Brooklyn Roads"?" This put them into a semi-embarrassed state of recouping. "Where you from? India?" I was impressed by how I embodied my nationality so transparently. "Yes!" "You just got here, fresh off the boat?" Boat? I reached for a word with which I have never described myself, except at an airport immigration desk: "No, no, I'm a tourist! I'm going back tomorrow!" "Oh, a *tourist*." Those were rare here.

I thought I'd proceed toward Ocean Avenue—the light, which I assumed was from the ocean, made hazy what felt like a terminal bit of the city: pure surface, one-dimensional, inscribed with letters and graffiti. A young man on a motorcycle was coming up the pavement, moving, in a double infraction, in the opposite direction from the cars on the street. Then he swerved gently into a building entrance. This momentary turbulence hinted at something topsy-turvy—a contrary flow. What I saw farther off, where Albemarle Road ended, wasn't Ocean Avenue, in fact; Ocean Avenue was yet another crossing. What I was approaching—a city wall—was beyond it, the closeness an optical illusion. Then I grew distracted by the Salem Missionary Baptist Church, the structure itself futuristic, as someone might have once conceived of the future. Having read up a bit more on the building, I find it was built in 1958 as a synagogue, and then merged with the Baptist Mission in the '70s. The truth is that things are ever-changing; that's what I must have felt, passing, already prepared for this departure from fixity by the counter-directional motorcycle on the pavement, and the end (Ocean Avenue) which gave way. The real border turned out to be Flatbush Avenue, the wall the (scaffolding-veiled) facade and sign of the Assembly Hall of Jehovah's Witnesses.

There was a lot of God about. On the way back to Church Avenue, I took a small detour off Albemarle Road to investigate the Flatbush Seventh-day Adventist Church. Back again on the capacious avenue, I overheard a group of loiterers, men and women, murmuring in French. West Africans. I had a feeling that these people—who viewed questions to do with street directions or Neil Diamond with suspicion—would open up more readily about God if asked. This is just an inkling, but I've noticed that working-class people, including those I've overheard in Calcutta, have a special investment, a greater sense of excitement in discussing God, or gods, or even life and destiny, than they do loans, property, or sports, but not because of a desire for paradise or salvation: it's as if the discourse liberates them for a while from the terms they've been presented with to measure themselves: livelihood, small attainments, expectations, duties. Having paid nothing for it at all, they want to inhabit the overarching long term, of life itself, but also, in India, of birth and rebirth, and not just the time of deadlines and the finite day.

On my way back, too, a motorcycle boarded the pavement, disregarding the boundary between route, thoroughfare, and home.

On the other side of Albemarle Road, I noticed a "white person." She was walking a dog. A "white person" is a euphemism for an outsider. The word *white*, in its associations with "outsideness" (outside communities, outside culpability), represents a reversal of terminology. In this reversal, the outsider controls the world.

I'm not an outsider, despite claiming a tourist identity (over and above my Indian one) to the women I was talking to. I find the places I recognise are my own, intimately.

•

From evening, bridge, and sky, we entered a tunnel at some point, and remained ensconced going to Times Square. I understand this now: that to resist gentrification, Brooklyn must move away from the East River. Any glimpse of the East River allows, at that point, global markets a way in.

Also, home. It's a cliché to say so, but one must choose between home and elsewhere. We have chosen elsewhere. This journey back to Manhattan is also a journey away from home; not Neil Diamond's home, but something, some world, we repeatedly leave behind.

There are no easy solutions to knowing where to go. Tomorrow, when I fly back to India, I'll be choosing elsewhere again. I'll have the vaguest memory of where I started.

Acknowledgements

I AM INDEBTED to a great number of people, including editors of periodicals, for making these essays and this book possible. In the interests of simplicity, I will keep this list short and mention:

Edwin Frank, for proposing the idea of this book and helping make the selection.

Sarah Chalfant and her team, for standing by, and believing in, the various kinds of writing I do.

A close and indispensable circle of friends who have read and responded to these essays over decades.

My wife, Rosinka, for sharing with me her sense of nineteenth-century Bengali history, and for being the first reader of what are sometimes quite long expositions.

AMIT CHAUDHURI is a novelist, essayist, poet, and musician. A fellow of the Royal Society of Literature, he lives in Calcutta and the United Kingdom. He has written eight novels, the latest of which is *Sojourn*. Among his other works are three books of essays, including *The Origins of Dislike*; a study of D. H. Lawrence's poetry; a book of short stories, *Real Time*; two works of nonfiction, including *Finding the Raga*; and four volumes of poetry. Formerly a professor of contemporary literature at the University of East Anglia, Chaudhuri is now a professor of creative writing and the director of the Centre for the Creative and the Critical at Ashoka University, as well as the editor of literaryactivism.com. He has made several recordings of Indian classical and experimental music, and has been awarded the Commonwealth Writers' Prize, the Los Angeles Times Book Prize for Fiction, the Indian government's Sahitya Akademi Award, and the James Tait Black Prize.